As Bees
in Honey Drown

The author (right) with Elbert Hubbard II in the latter's study. In Mr. Hubbard's Foreword, he tells of their long association leading to the writing of this biography of his famous father.

Photo by Rile Prosser

As Bees
in Honey Drown

Elbert Hubbard and the Roycrofters

Charles F. Hamilton

South Brunswick and New York: A. S. Barnes and Co.
London: Thomas Yoseloff Ltd

A. S. Barnes and Co., Inc.
Cranbury, New Jersey 08512

Thomas Yoseloff Ltd
108 New Bond Street
London W1Y OQX, England

Library of Congress Cataloging in Publication Data

Hamilton, Charles Franklin, 1915–
   As bees in honey drown.

   1. Hubbard, Elbert, 1856–1915. 2. Roycroft Shop, East Aurora,
N. Y. I. Title.
Z232.R8H35   808'.00924 [B]   77-37811
ISBN 0-498-01052-X

Printed in the United States of America

Affectionately dedicated to the late Elbert Hubbard II, friend and mentor, without whose encouragement and counsel this book could not have been written.

Contents

Foreword

My father, Elbert Hubbard, was 45 years old in 1901 when Albert Lane of Concord, Massachusetts, published the first biography of the man, who, in six action-packed years, had become internationally known as "Fra Elbertus—The Sage of East Aurora."

At the time, my father stood back, took an objective look at the "Fra," and wrote a letter to the woman of his heart:

> Elbertus is a product of the Devil knows what and how much. Not of soap, but of passion, hope, aspiration, ambition and love. I don't care just yet to analyze the mixture and it will be time enough in 50 years to tackle the job. . . .

With all due respect to my father, he underestimated the task. Full blown biographies were tackled by sincere and capable persons in 1926, 1929, 1940 and 1968 and they came to realize the enormity of the challenge. And though each brought out varied facets of this many-sided man, the "mixture" of what and how, of "passion, hope, aspiration, ambition and love" has not yet been thoroughly analyzed.

Instead, too often the focus has been on the one thing he said was *not* part of the mixture—soap. And love, a part of the formula he confessed, has been either unfairly characterized as love of self and money or as a base tendency toward promiscuity.

In the process, the man and his role and influence on the American scene have been blurred though he still stands there as a constant challenge and a temptation to biographers.

I have spent a lifetime trying to analyze the mixture and have had the privilege of seeing the mixers of the ingredients up close—the man, his parents, his two wives, his children, his relatives, his associates and admirers as well as his detractors; his works, his actions, his emotions, his love, his personal words, his personal letters, his charisma, the legend he was and the legend he has become.

Sixty-eight years have passed since Elbertus said, "it will be time enough in 50 years to tackle the job" of analyzing him and here I am in my eighty-seventh year, goodness me! The task of now putting down my analysis in the form of a biography of my father would weigh too heavily —particularly in view of a certain handicap in my locomotion I acquired three years ago—but it must be done and there is a way. Collaboration— of course, that's it!

I have spent part time of most every week of the past decade or so with my close and long-time neighbor, Charles F. Hamilton, helping to prepare him for the writing task. There are no intimate facts about my father's life that I have kept from him, knowing full well that his interpretations will always be fair. He is a wise and discreet man.

My father's papers and letters have been available to him and will continue to be though they will not be otherwise unlocked before 1980.

Charlie is steeped in Hubbard lore and tradition. He has read everything my father ever wrote, as well as writings about him by others.

He has traveled where my father traveled, where he worked and played in East Aurora and elsewhere. He has talked for hours with every living East Auroran who knew him and worked with him. He has talked with persons never known to me, or long since forgotten, who have shed light we both sought.

I have read several finished chapters and am delighted. They are his words with occasional reflections of my thoughts and words. But to him goes the credit for finishing a task he so much wanted to do. His heart is in it. It will be done more completely than ever before.

As Bees in Honey Drown will be a labor of love but at the same time a work of objectivity, sans soap. Without Charlie, I never could have done it alone.

I am satisfied that together we will have done justice to my father and others.

Elbert Hubbard II

Acknowledgments

A debt of gratitude for valuable assistance in this work is due several persons other than the late Elbert Hubbard II to whom it is dedicated.

My sincere appreciation to my wife Virginia L. Hamilton for devoted assistance in many ways, to Mrs. Brent L. Smith for typing the manuscript and particularly to the late Alta Fattey Hubbard and her daughter Nancy Hubbard Brady who shared husband and father, respectively, with me in their home over the years so that he might devote endless hours to reminiscing and steering me to the truest possible picture of his famous father in the light of the letters that we together perused and selected for inclusion in this work.

As Bees
in Honey Drown

Prologue

1

The serenity is heaven-like at Hingham in the autumn. For Alice LuAnn Moore, in the autumn of 1894, the quiet Massachusetts seacoast village was heaven itself.

It was September and only recently had she taken the keys to the "Crosby Cottage" at 32 Lincoln Street, having rented it for $35 a month from the owner Samuel T. Crosby. Through Mrs. Miriam Crosby Tyler of Boston Alice had learned of the home, set back from Lincoln Street on a slight knoll at the end of a long, tree-lined lane. Really too spacious and well insulated to be called a cottage, it was so dubbed only to distinguish it from the principal Crosby home on the same property. But it suited Alice in every respect.

Her husband, back in East Aurora, New York, had written saying it sounded fine. He told her to rent it and that he would send the money promptly. Alice was a school teacher and had once been preceptress at East Aurora Union School. More recently she had been teaching at Potsdam (N. Y.) Normal School and had come from there to Hingham via a short stay in a Maine convalescent home.

Old Hingham, aside from the peace she sought, provided Alice with history to delve into, teacher like; and, ideally, her new home was just diagonally across the street from "Old Ordinary," a landmark house dating back to 1650.

Tall and slender, poised and reserved, Alice Moore could easily have been mistaken for a native New Englander. She fitted the dignified surroundings and got along well with her Massachusetts "old family" neighbors, including Mrs. Millet C. Stringer whose stately home was next door to Old Ordinary and along the way to the Hingham postoffice where Alice daily posted a letter to her husband and generally at the same time picked up one from him.

She was not alone in the big cottage nor on her walks to the postoffice. In her ninth month of pregnancy, she was carrying the child of her beloved Elbert Hubbard. He was a businessman turned novelist with whom she had secretly collaborated on his first work, *The Man,* three years previously.

More recently, within the year ,in fact, he had been briefly associated with the Arena Publishing Company of nearby Boston. But he was temporarily back in East Aurora now and she felt certain he was headed for bigger things in the literary world.

In the waiting weeks ahead, "Mrs. Elbert Hubbard," presently of Hingham, would think of her past and future with the man she loved. She knew that, at the moment, her title to the married name was quite premature; that there was a much more attractive woman in East Aurora who had legal title to it. But in staid Hingham a pregnant 33-year-old spinster would not long enjoy the hospitality and serenity she sought.

Anyway, the important thing right then was the new life she could feel stirring inside of her and somehow that made everything seem right —even to a person as intelligent and otherwise sensitive as she was to fine degrees of right and wrong.

There was a freshness to the gentle ocean breezes swinging in from the coast, and all around the cottage half-tinted leaves were now and then dropping and nestling beside still-bright flowers, like advance samplers for tree-top colors in the making.

There would be brighter days ahead, Alice mused, and so thoughts of hurt to others or of any possible course now but blissful togetherness for her, Elbert, and their soon to be born child were totally incompatible with the whole unreality of Hingham in the autumn.

Yet hurt was to come, and surges of conscience were to leave scars on a togetherness that did eventually arrive, did stay, and did provide a bliss with a poignancy that rarely comes to brilliant persons who err against the very conventions they normally champion.

In East Aurora, a man who was fast becoming known and admired as one who said what he thought in a way that made others want to emulate him (or at least quote his views as a safer way to express their own) found himself suddenly bound to a state of secrecy not imposed upon his admirers. Elbert Hubbard had a wife in that little Western New York village, charming and attractive enough to make other men envious, and three fine children by her that would make any man abundantly proud. But at Hingham there was Alice, whose beauty was intellectual and whose child by him was yet unborn.

Elbert was, by all standards, a straightforward man in his thinking, words and dealings. Yet now his love was divided and his life's course changed by a chain of circumstances that his admirers would never comprehend, even if they were privileged to know and study those circumstances. It is doubtful that, even to the very end, Hubbard himself would know how it all happened.

That his love for Alice was real and consuming there can be no doubt, any more than could there be doubt of the love he had for Bertha Crawford when he proposed to her at the village of Normal in his native Illinois and brought her back to Buffalo, and eventually East Aurora, to live and raise a family.

Elbert Hubbard knew, as did Alice Moore, that a man of his growing reputation couldn't be posting letters daily from East Aurora to a Miss Moore in Hingham any more than an obviously pregnant spinster could be receiving them there without suspicion—even if they were addressed to a postoffice box number. And letters addressed to "Mrs. Elbert Hubbard" at Hingham would cause equal suspicion among East Aurora post-office personnel when Mrs. Hubbard was to be seen almost daily on the streets of that Hingham-like New York village or at social functions where she was well known. It was necessary, therefore, for Hubbard to make a daily horseback ride to a neighboring village to mail his love letters to Alice, addressing her at Hingham as Mrs. Elbert Hubbard.

When he had business in Buffalo he would find borrowed hotel or bank envelopes a convenient subterfuge.

And it all seemed right because he, too, was deeply in love and the leaves were taking on bright colors in East Aurora as well as in Hingham. The air was fresh and good there too and he had tried and was still trying to be a good husband and father there.

He, like Alice, would think that autumn about the past and the future, but his thinking would of necessity include obligations beyond the ken of a pregnant, unwed school teacher in Hingham or that of a dutiful wife in East Aurora—really, beyond the reasoning of two women deeply in love with the same man.

Time never seems to stand so still as in the final waiting days of pregnancy. There is an impatience then, in the midst of tender waiting, that is akin to the same man–woman relationship that sets it all in motion.

With Alice and Elbert it had its beginning in 1887 when she moved from Cedar Falls, Iowa—where she had been teaching primary school— to East Aurora Union High School. This change in positions brought her back to her native part of the country. She had been raised on a farm in nearby Wales Hollow, had gone to local schools and to Buffalo State Normal School, from which she graduated in 1883. Now—just three years after Elbert G. Hubbard, his wife and first child had moved there from Buffalo—Alice was back in East Aurora and living with her spinster teacher friend, Allie Long.

Bertha was three years Hubbard's junior and nearly fetching enough to be a Gibson girl. Elbert, always a fashion plate as a young soap salesman in Illinois, had met Bertha in his door-to-door selling days, and after he had moved to Buffalo as a partner in the Larkin Soap Co. he had gone back to make her his bride and bring her East. He had a flair for advertising, had originated the "club plan" of selling soap with

Soap company executive Elbert G. Hubbard looked much older than his 26 years because of the mustache. Two years after this 1882 photo, Elbert, Bertha and their first-born, "Bertie," moved from Buffalo to East Aurora.

premium offers to housewives, and was fast moving up the ladder to financial success.

In all of this Elbert wasn't hurt a bit by his athletic build on a 5′ 9″ frame. To top it all off was a noble head with noble features. He had a strong chin, a nose like that which later generations were to identify with the "John Barrymore profile," and brown eyes that compelled attention from beneath thick, gracefully arched eyebrows.

His high forehead and his whole countenance was framed by curly dark brown hair which he allowed to grow thick and long in a theatrical manner. There was an almost wicked saintliness to his appearance and it brought out both the goodness and temptations in others.

To meet him face-to-face and engage his magnetic eyes was no ordinary experience for anyone, and Hubbard, whether by design or accident, took advantage of this.

An inquisitive and creative person by nature, Hubbard found both relaxation and mental stimulation in attending the meetings of the fifteen-member East Aurora Chautauqua Literary & Scientific Circle, known familiarly as the "CLSC." Alice Moore reacted the same way to the circle metings. There, in quite proper circumstances, they would see each other, and from the outset were strangely attracted to each other, intellectually.

In later years, Hubbard described their first meeting at a gathering of the circle:

> . . . my eyes looked straight into those of a personage . . . it was all in an instance but we had met, this fine strong woman and I, in a soul-embrace, and there was a perfect understanding between us.

But this was when he better understood what had happened. At the time it was not so neatly fathomable though the magnetism was undeniably there. They both felt it then, and it was present ever after.

Alice couldn't help but notice Mr. Hubbard's growing willingness to take the floor to read papers to the Chautauqua Circle meetings, even though he had earlier remarked to a friend how he envied the poise of lumberman Harris Peek, one of the more articulate male members of the group. And his eloquence grew and seemed to reach unusual heights when he knew that Alice was observing him.

They would discuss each other's readings and literary interests while partaking of the host member's refreshments, which were always served at the conclusion of the formal parlor meetings.

With children to put to bed, Bertha could not attend the circle meetings as frequently as her husband; when she did, she too saw Alice as a friendly, intelligent person but hardly as a beauty who might boldly attempt to woo her husband away from her.

In this she was right, at the time, if indeed the thought of appraising the relationship ever entered her mind. But why should it have? Alice couldn't match her beauty and an interest in things literary was common to every person at the CLSC meetings.

It was therefore unsurprising that when Alice's roommate, Allie Long, married Dr. Arthur Mitchell (Elbert's best friend and next door neighbor on Grove Street), Alice sought a new boarding place and was welcomed into the spacious home of Mr. & Mrs. Elbert G. Hubbard.

Allie soon gave up her job as preceptress at the East Aurora Union School and Alice succeeded her in that post. And she got it partly through the intercession of Bertha Hubbard, then a member of the school board, and, logically, with the added recommendation of prominent businessman Elbert Hubbard.

It was not unusual for teachers to board at the homes of civic- and culturally-minded local families—and how nice it was in this instance that the new preceptress could be a next door neighbor to her friend and predecessor!

At first it was a nice situation within the Hubbard home too. The young Hubbard children liked Alice and she liked them. She and Bertha got along well and certainly Elbert was a delight as they all chatted in the living room after supper. Sometimes the newlywed Mitchells would drop in for a visit and, of course, Alice would be helping to play hostess to her old friend Allie Long Mitchell. And Alice would often go along when the Hubbards would go next door for an evening with the Mitchells. Yes, all went well—for a time.

2

By the end of the 1889 school term, as a result of the natural intimacy of sharing the Hubbard family life, danger signs were evident of an Alice–Elbert friendship. These signs struck fear in the heart of Bertha for she deeply loved her husband. And that same deep love that made her so sure no harm could come to it by the presence in her home of a sedate school teacher, who was only two years younger than she, caused her to at first ask, and then demand, of her husband that he tell Alice to leave.

There were strong insinuations—aided by Bertha's mother, Mrs. Crawford, and sister, Myrtilla Crawford—and harsh words that awakened the children on several occasions. Bertha finally won. Alice not only left the Hubbard home but proceeded to find herself a teaching job in far off Springfield, Massachusetts.

In her insistence that Alice move out, Bertha unfortunately fanned a flame that might otherwise have eventually smouldered and died. As she was to learn years later, to her great heartbreak and sorrow, she had fanned an incipient fire into a blaze of near holocaust proportions.

Like Bertha, Alice and Elbert couldn't have imagined what was really happening or where it would all end. More likely, the end seemed to have wisely already come—to the *flirtation*. These two resolved, however, that their *friendship* would continue on the high plane it had started—though now, necessarily, by mail.

Eighteen years later, in his book *White Hyacinths,* Elbert Hubbard was to declare his *love* for Alice to the world and confess, "I have known this woman for twenty years. I have written her over three thousand letters and she has written many to me. Every worthy theme and sentiment I have expressed to the public has first been expressed to her, or more likely, borrowed from her. I have seen her in most every possible exigency of life: in health, success and high hope; in poverty, and what the world calls disgrace and defeat. But here I should explain that disgrace is for those who accept disgrace, and defeat consists in acknowledging it."

Elbert and Alice saved most of their letters and, as the carefully tied little bundles are now dusted off and untied, those letters—reopened and read in the mood that set the lovers' pens aflowing—reveal a consuming and creating love.

Through their love and these letters, Alice's Elbert—and the Elbert Hubbard the world heard of—is finally more fully revealed and understood. He emerges as an independently creative man who was almost mystically influenced—for better or worse at times in his literary career—by a gentle woman of fierce and tractile tenacity.

Hubbard came to understand her grip. In his *White Hyacinths* eulogy of Alice he told of it.

In my wife's mind I see my thoughts enlarged and reflected, just as in a telescope we hold to the stars. She is the magic mirror in which I see the Divine. Her mind acts on mine and mine on hers. Most certainly I am aware that no one else can see the same in her which I behold, because no one else can call forth her qualities any more than any other woman can call forth mine. Our minds, separate and apart, act together as one, forming a complete binocular, making plain that which to one alone is invisible.

1

"As My Good Friend"

If to the relationship of Elbert and Alice there had been more than the familiarity that comes naturally to people under the same roof for several years in an atmosphere of complete family acceptance, it wasn't especially evident in the several letters the two exchanged in 1890 after Alice got settled in a Springfield boarding house, owned by Louise B. Emerson, at 175 State Street.

There was warm admiration, yes, but none of the deep protestations of undying love that might be expected of a man and woman suspected of romancing when a wife's back was turned.

On May 8, 1890, Alice wrote to Elbert:

> 175 State Street
> Springfield, Mass.
> May 8, 1890
>
> My Dear Friend:
> Your letter received this P.M. I cannot tell you how glad I am to get your letters, nor how much good they do me. I again call your attention to the reply Charles Kingsley made when asked wherein his success in life lay. If I am successful in my life's work it will be because "I have a friend"—an Emersonian friend—. There are times in life when we *feel* the need more than at others—April, May, June 1890 is one of the needy periods. I could easily take a pessimistic view of things and say there are people and people, but their souls are so covered up that they can't get out.
> Not only "ten men love what I hate" but ten hundred thousand. Well, perhaps they ought. Now my dear friend, I want to make a little confession to you—it is as good as dark so I can—I get so disgusted and provoked at myself for being so put out and disturbed at little

things. Petty things are forced upon one which ought to be recognized and stamped as *petty* but perhaps someone whom you cannot stamp *petty* insists upon your noticing them and discusses them to you, at you, and before you—and the first thing you know—there you are—not in the seventh heaven at least.

This afternoon I have recalled George Eliot's definition of a privileged person—one who is so disagreeable when crossed that everyone prefers to give up to enduring the disagreeable. This is an example of small things simply. One ought to be so strong that . . . well, what?

I want to tell you of my visit to the U. S. Armory here—but I haven't time now. This is just a note—too personal perhaps too, and better be made up into boraxine.

The custodian[1] has not written me this week and only a wee little one last so if she doesn't write so I get it before Sunday—I give *you* warning—*you* are going to be the afflicted one. I am working this week on Civil Government. I was way down on that subject and I have sentenced myself to hard labor until Sunday. My head is becoming wise and full of the constitution, laws and courts. I hope to be the next Chief Justice. I am thoroughly glad to have been put into this line of work for I needed it. Helps to round out—and also to understand Nationalism.

The article on women which you sent is fine. There is one in the last Arena that it reminded me of. Have you seen it? "The Cosmic Sphere of Women."

Have just read and folded that paper on Words. 'Tis poorly copied and I fear you will not be able to read it easily. I offer no apology for the poor child. 'Tis mine—and like its author consists of the joining of sayings of others. I know my style is broken (choppy). This written when my heart was full of fears and hands empty. 'Twas employment. Now, if you consider it not what the circle wants—as my good friend—don't read it to them. If you do, I prefer to have you read it.

Am sorry the "girls" don't "work in" well. I fear I should have been very stupid as I have never done any work of that kind; but do you know, I want a taste of that life sometime to see another side of life. Goodnight—

> Very truly,
> *Alice Luanne Moore*

Alice's apologetic sending along of a paper she had authored, asking Elbert, "as my good friend," to appraise it for its likely interest to the Chautauqua circle was bound to be food for the ego of a man who secretly aspired to be a writer. Her plaintive plea to *him* to read it, rather than to have someone else do so, was an undisguised reminder of her special feeling of admiration. He rose to the occasion—and the bait.

He went beyond the call of duty and not only did he read Alice's paper to the next meeting of the CLSC, he added these laudatory words of his

---

1. Alice's older sister, Mrs. Wayland W. Woodworth of Buffalo, N. Y.

own about Miss Moore, recently of East Aurora:

> We will ask for quotations on the Misuse of Words, and the paper will be by Alice Moore. Unfortunately Miss Moore will not be here to read it so it will have to be read by another member. A message from so excellent a young woman to the circle will be listened to, I know, with pleasure and satisfaction. I am inclined to think that Alice Moore has exerted a greater influence for good on the young people who are attending our public schools than anyone who has recently lived in our midst, and perhaps it might be worthwhile to stop just a moment and enquire how it is possible for an obscure farmer's daughter from Strykersville to exert such an influence. We are told in physics that action and reaction are equal—the pendulum swings as far in this direction as in that. And people influence or rule others in the exact proportion as they rule themselves. Greatness consists in this very thing and this alone. Ability to rule over one's spine. Seems to me Solomon said something about this very subject some years ago.
>
> Now if women are to inaugurate the millenium by rule of intellectual might and ethical right, it certainly behooves the Chautauqua Circle of East Aurora, which is certainly a feminine institution, to choose well their course of study.
>
> (You observe I take it for granted the circle is to continue for strong women of Aurora must keep step with their intellectual sisters of the world if we are ever to bring about the Sisterhood of Woman . . . a thing we certainly believe in and are working for.)

Elbert Hubbard served as Clerk Pro Tem that night at the circle meeting, in addition to reading Alice's paper on the misuse of words. The Rev. Mr. Brown was chairman. It was obvious from Hubbard's remarks that Alice's departure had shaken the circle and that he was trying to make her leaving seem more like an academic loss than a tongue-wagging incident.

A few days later he mailed his scribbled notes to Alice at Springfield and thereafter the exchange of polite letters would increase in frequency and warmth. Her "good friend" had proved his friendship!

Alice's letter had not only served its purpose with respect to their Chautauqua Circle association—a thing now of the past for them—but showed welcome sympathy for Elbert's complaints about his problems with the office girls at the soap company. Moreover, the letter stimulated him to think about the possibility of her working with him at some time in the future. Alice had said: "I want a taste of that life sometime."

Although, as her letter modestly stated, Alice would have been "very stupid" as an office worker at Larkin's Soap Company, the remark nevertheless set Elbert to thinking how they might work together most effectively—though the miles separated them—on an intellectual project.

He was creative, as his advertising and selling spiels for Larkin products amply indicated. He was submitting little essays to various newspapers and magazines and had enjoyed seeing some of them published in the

Morris (Ill.) *Herald* a while back and subsequently in the *Buffalo Sunday Times*. Collaborating with Alice in writing a book was a possibility that he weighed as they continued a correspondence that was drawing them closer than they had really been when they lived under one roof in a landlord–tenant relationship.

Intellectual Alice was missing Elbert but couldn't yet bring herself to express it in the direct, appealing fashion of an impatient, warm, young heart. The mixture of affection and literacy made her letters all the more intriguing to him. What *was* she saying?

In a letter dated May 23, 1890, from Springfield, Alice gave him some clues neatly woven into some scholarly observations:

Springfield, Mass.
May 23, 1890

My Dear Friend:

Should one friend ever apologize to another? I mean of course about little matters of custom, etc. Explanations are sometimes due I know on account of this poor way we so much of the time have of communicating. But I write you tonight because my heart is so full of good things that I can't keep still. My pen *will* go—or try to.

First let me say that your letter was so good that it lifted me quite out of the slum of discouragement. What a slum that is, and how it does take a strong, good hand to help us out! I liked every word you wrote and it put new strength into my heart—and I rose and shook off the despair and put on a fresh armor or strengthened my old one and went on. Surely, all things *are* good to us. "God's in His Heaven. All's right with the world."

What you said of *Friendship* impressed me much. The greatness of it never came to me with so much force and meaning and you gave me additional thoughts too, precious ones. You speak of the perfect Friend—surely One whom we can strive to be like. But what a thing it is to say to one, and mean it in the great sense . . . I am your Friend. Let us think well before we say it. Is there a difference between Friend and friend?

I have been having a most *delicious* (?) time all by myself reading the first volume of Correspondence of Carlyle and Emerson. I would get so filled with the good things that I would break out with a rare gem of thought to Miss Oliver. Poor girl! I have bored her I know with Browning and Carlyle and Emerson for she doesn't read any of them now and of course can't understand my great heat sometimes. Why, in reading those letters I can't keep still and if I didn't talk to her I would shout to the very walls I suppose.

Those letters let you right into the very heart and soul of those men. Weren't they Friends? Listen a moment—Emerson to Carlyle—"I have few pleasures like that of receiving your kind and eloquent letters. I should be most impatient of the long intervals between one and another, but that they savor always of Eternity, and promise me a friendship and friendly inspiration not reckoned or ended by days or years."

And Carlyle—

"A man has *such* a baptism to be baptized withal; no easy baptism; and it is straightened till it be accomplished. As for me I honor peace before all things; the silence of a great thing is to me greater than anything it will ever say, it ever *can* say."

Perhaps you know these books but to me they are a new vein of gold. I must make them my own one day. Do you know, I think Ruskin is nearly right about library books. If a book is *good* and I *read* it, I feel as though it not only ought to belong to me but was a part of me. I have carried some books back to the library and felt as though I *couldn't* let them go.

Now what I started to write you about was this day. Have been to the Hampden Teachers' Association all day, held at the High School. No school. Program I will send, but I can't send the day. Note please. Dr. C. W. Emerson.[2] The name was a good deal—and the man was more. He is 5 feet 9—240 lbs.—reminds me of Dr. Bashford. Past sixty and acted thirty or less. Every motion was expressive and graceful. He is a near relative of R. W. Emerson's and it must be a nephew is it not? Is it Edward Emerson's son? He spoke of R. W. E. as near and also of the tendency in their family to consumption. Said he was dyspeptic for twelve years and both lungs badly affected—tubercles, etc.

All this to show "before rising and after rising." He spoke of the four systems—Muscular—bone—vital—and nerve and then of the physical culture that would reach them all.

His wife and four young women who have been pupils of his school went through a series of movements which he said were *all* the voluntary motions possible for the human body. All the apparatus they used was the human body. It was to me the most beautiful sight I have seen. They were fifteen minutes about, in doing this. Every motion meant so much and the expression changes with the motion so that *every* feeling could be expressed by the motions they made it seemed to me.

These points he made as to that—the methods by which the system can be educated—first considered as a *whole*. Next as to *parts*. Parts in relation to parts.

Bring parts of the body into symmetry. Symmetry *first*. Get the crown of the head in position and the other parts of the body will fall into place. Educate the *dominant* center (the crown of the head) and it dominates the rest of the body. He said many teachers of Boston came to him Saturdays to learn his methods so as to teach the children in their schools this development—and the past winter he had taken great pains to find what effect it had had in the schools where it had been used. And he said this had been the universal report that the *physical* influence had been less than the *moral* influence upon them—and that both were very marked.

Mrs. Emerson was as nearly a physical beauty as I ever saw. Naturally not pretty but her every motion grace. They could put the whole strength of the body into one part—for example, standing on one foot reaching up with the same hand—lift all the weight or strength of the

---

2. Charles Wesley Emerson, President of Emerson College of Oratory, Boston, Mass.

whole body into that hand. Dr. E. said if we cultivated our physical bodies so that they were "rounded out," each part in harmony with the others, the drug stores would be no more and doctors would only be necessary in case of accident. A well-rounded life—think of it.

There is a bee in my bonnet and if it keeps buzzing until Monday P.M. as it is now I shall do what the bee suggests.

Tonight the bee says that in this city there is a woman who is a disciple of Dr. Emerson who has given the necessary instructions to classes here. She has a niece in one of my classes at school. The bee remarks that perhaps this a golden opportunity for Alice Luanne to help herself way up to strong physical heights where she is far from now and that in that way she may be of help to others.

Sometimes a bee cannot be relied upon—so I will let this one buzz awhile and in the meantime what do you say of all this? Mental culture—physical culture—spiritual culture. How related—how joined. Do they grow out of each other to the same extent? Dr. E. made it seem very clearly so.

Did I warn you first that this letter would savor strongly of ego? I mean't to. Pardon if I did not.

Many things compass me about and I seem to need to be so very strong and *watchful*—and brave. Are we made to feel *very* weak that we may find the source of all strength? To me it is so. My work is hard—very hard and perplexing. The school is difficult to control and all this year has run wild. I am the fourth teacher this year.

All the teachers are *very* kind to me and flatteringly attentive which I am wholly unworthy of and feel that it is not right as I am not what they think but so weak. I suppose they know too, I shall not be here next year.

There is a very good book on Browning's life. Have you seen it? I have had the number on my library ticket ever since I had one but it is always out. You may have it before this, but it is new to me. Some letters I think—. I get little time to read since hard work began and it seems a rare treat and tastes all the better when I have opportunity.

What may the Lady H. be doing that keeps her so silent? Or does she think June 27 is very near?

Very truly,
Alice Luanne Moore

Alice was building up the tease with rare expertise and her helper was Cupid—whether or not she knew it! Hinting of the difference between "Friend (with a capital letter) and friend," protesting all sorts of weaknesses and general unworthiness, dwelling at exciting length on expression through body motions, and wrapping up the whole enticing message by saying she was planning to come back to East Aurora for the summer— these things weren't designed to create calm in a handsome, virile man of thirty-four!

And for good measure, in reply to a remark in one of Elbert's letters about an apparent new moodiness in Bertha, she speculates that "Lady H" might just be dreading the end of the school term in Springfield and Alice's return to East Aurora for the summer vacation. It was another way of saying, "Do you suppose she still jealously thinks we might have a deeper interest in each other than as just Friends?"

Not long afterwards Elbert found he had to make a business trip to Springfield. He stayed at the popular Evans House on Main Street, a short distance from where Alice was boarding. She joined him for dinner and they talked all evening about her work, Browning, Ralph Waldo Emerson and people back in East Aurora.

It was a delightful reunion and, inevitably, the conversation drifted toward their happier days in the Hubbard home when they read from the same book of Browning's works in the Hubbard library and attended the Chautauqua Circle meetings.

They unhappily recalled how Bertha's suspicions grew beyond all reason causing Alice's abrupt departure the previous summer. And they recalled, too, how Alice's equally suspicious sister Emma, and her lawyer husband, Wayland Woodworth, practically dragged her with them that summer to Connecticut for a "vacation" at Sachem's Head.

"Your infatuation with that married man can only lead to trouble," puritanical Emma warned, "and you had best get away with us and forget him before it is too late!"

Alice chuckled as she recalled that the only bright moments in that dull summer were when an occasional note would arrive for her from Elbert, care of the postoffice at the resort.

But all that was behind them and here they were, together again, in far away Springfield with no suspicious relatives around to spoil their perfectly proper and platonic conversation.

"Why is it that people always think the worst?", Alice asked.

"They will say what they will say!", Elbert mused, and reminded her that, if she returned to East Aurora for a summer visit, an innocent meeting could easily set "tongues awagging" all over again. They joked about maybe having to meet secretly or, worse, the Woodworths might drag her off again to Sachem's Head. They would have to weigh the various alternatives.

After dinner they strolled arm-in-arm down to the river front and then Elbert walked Alice to her rooming house. The "goodbyes" were awkward and hesitant as though suddenly Bertha or Emma had happened by. A warm and meaningful—and Friendly—handclasp would have to do for now. The next morning Elbert took the early train back to Buffalo.

The *Chautauquan Magazine,* a "must" for all of the circles, was making much of the rising importance of women as writers, inventors and—daringly—as emerging rulers of the home. Back in the April 1887 issue of the magazine, Mary A. Livermore had written at some length on "Homes Built By Women." She had quoted Frances Power Cobb as saying, "The making of a true home is really the peculiar and inalienable right of women—a right no man can take from them." But she overlooked another aspect of domestic tranquility. What can another woman do to that "peculiar and inalienable right"?

Bertha Hubbard had already pondered that question and had exercised a right that Frances Cobb had not discussed. The spinster teacher was no longer in her home.

Alice Moore was equally familiar with that Chautauquan article and was now exploring, more with her heart than with her head, her own personal and inalienable "rights" as a woman. And Elbert would figure in her enlarging explorations.

2

"Winter Boarder"

When Elbert finished reading Alice's last letter from Springfield before school closed there for the summer he *knew* they would be seeing each other again and be exchanging, briefly at least, the glances that were beginning to say more than words.

June 23, 1890
Springfield, Mass.

My dear Friend,

The spirit moves more fluently than the pen. It usually does. The pen may be mightier than the sword but it isn't so mighty as the spirit. Many and many times have I thought things which I wanted to communicate and when I tried words failed and so did the pen.

Today I want to say unutterable things but no—it is so different when I am in Mass. from when I am in some places in N.Y. East Aurora, for example. Sometimes there you don't need to say a word and yet you are satisfied. Eyes can do so much in this perplexing case— you see and feel and words are idle. But in Mass. it is very different, as to be born in Mass. (poor things, how I pity them) one must be polite and frigidly so at any cost. Please tell me the benefit of forever dwelling on the civil war. Is that the highest, noblest topic to be thought of? When I get home I'm going to get a relic of the war and worship it and tell stories about it to the young people to make them patriotic, or would you try to teach them of goodness and peace and trust and faith. There is the story of One who died—who suffered—who was Truth—who was a type—and *the* perfect one. Well, our fathers suffered and died for truth—all honor to their memory. Let us give them our thoughts for a time and do honor to their memory, but what they did is not for *us* to do—our times are not theirs—we must *on*.

Next Friday night may the R.R. Co. move me swiftly toward Buffalo.

If the weather (ha ha) is fair—not too warm nor too cold withal, nor too damp nor too dry, I think I shall be early at the W.N.L.&P. station where the train leaves for E.A. at 6:00 P.M. on all Saturdays, June 28 not excluded. (I'd like to see the weather that could hinder) Shall I go to E. A. as a summer boarder or a winter boarder? Hardly. I don't understand that class of unclassified animus. Last summer I was the summer boarder at Sachem's Head, this spring I am the winter boarder at the Evans House, Springfield, but we don't assimilate. I can be lazy enough and stupid enough—I was last year. The only times when I have been so quiet—three times in my life—I felt the Hand and knew whose it was, and many times the occasions were too sacred to desecrate with books or work. Don't you think one must be silent many times when God speaks? There are some who won't stop to listen to his voice but fling blindly and headlong and He kindly stretches forth His hand and says, "Stop, listen, I have somewhat to say to thee." And perhaps He holds you still a long, long time and He speaks many many things to you and then you are lifted up above the scenes where you were and you see that had He not done as He did you would have died miserably. But you saw this a long time after. And then when you start to go again you want to go *very* carefully and you want to be guided every step and you want to hear His voice all the time—and you may if you only listen. I truly believe that ere this beautiful week has gone I shall see you face to face and grasp that hand of friendship.

Yours,
Alice Luann

The "winter boarder" relationship, a reference to visiting with Elbert at the Evans House in Springfield was the type of reunion Alice sought—no more separations like the previous year's when she was a "summer boarder" at her sister's cottage at Sachem's Head!

Elbert could hardly wait to see Alice when she got back to Buffalo at the end of June. He wanted to tell her about a novel they could write together. Staying any place in East Aurora would certainly set tongues wagging in certain small circles; then too, Bertha, as well as Alice's sister Emma, would be promptly put on the alert. So Alice went to the Woodworths and divided her time that summer between Emma's home and the Moore farm at Wales Hollow, a few miles away from East Aurora.

Being together intellectually—they told each other—was all Alice and Elbert wanted. And those who thought of their togetherness in sexual terms were, they felt, wrong and petty but couldn't be ignored.

Nothing could have pleased Alice more than the idea of collaborating with Elbert on his novel. She was a capable researcher but the novel they decided upon didn't require research as much as the searching of each other's hearts and souls to see if what they were beginning to suspect of themselves was true. They suspected that they were in love in a clean, platonic way—a love that transcended any sexual connotation.

They met secretly and regularly all that summer. For Elbert to have lunch with a plain looking young lady at one of Buffalo's favorite dining rooms, in the Hotel Broezel, was not unlike the many other luncheon meetings that businessmen were there for; but their meetings out East Aurora way were necessarily more secretive for they were both well known there. Each would ride horseback—she from the Wales Hollow farm and he from East Aurora—and they would meet at predetermined wooded spots in the sparsely settled farm country that lay between their homes.

Here they would plan and write their novel and, indeed, they lived it into being. For it was about themselves and the people around them who, they felt, did not understand their relationship and saw it as something sinister and ugly.

Titled *The Man,* the novel was ostensibly to be written by Elbert. However, the narrator of the story, written in the first person, was a legendary 37-year-old school teacher named Aspasia· Hobbs. Even the name Aspasia had a special meaning to literary minded Elbert and Alice, for there was another Aspasia of ancient Greece who became the wife (though not legally recognized) of Pericles, the Greek statesman who 400 years before Christ brought the highest form of art and science to the ancient world. Their home became the meeting place of the most learned and distinguished persons of Athens.

The novel centered around an intellectual "Soul" relationship between the spinster school teacher and a saintly, sagacious, white haired, mysteriously preserved 300-year-old man whose life didn't really begin until he was 40, at which time he met and intellectually married a comely woman (much like Alice) with whom he still communed though distances and circumstances separated them! *The Man,* except for his white hair and his age, fit the description of Elbert, and in the story he met her on weekends at his cabin or in wooded groves, where, oblivious to their difference in sex, he expounded high thoughts and Aspasia soaked them up and prodded him for more philosophical revelations.

In the end the trysts of Aspasia and The Man were broken up by low-thinking people who got suspicious, followed Aspasia one day and had them arrested for illicit love making—a charge that could not be proven.

In *The Man* it is often difficult to separate the contributions of Elbert and Alice. For instance, "When the right man meets the right woman and they live rightly, there is an atmosphere formed where no poisonous draughts can enter. There two will say, 'Between us there must be honesty and truth forever more.' "

Thinking about what other people might be thinking of their togetherness did cause Elbert and Alice to experience those warm flushes that come when an accidental brushing of hand or body coincides with such thoughts, but it quickly passed as they both more furiously pursued the platonic plot of *The Man*. All the same, the more formal "Dear Friend" salutations were giving way to, they thought, a platonic "dear."

When they were apart they jotted down additional paragraphs and chapters for *The Man*. Sometimes they would discuss ideas through notes handed to each other when only brief meetings were possible for, though Elbert was toying more and more with the idea of becoming a full-time author, right now he was a busy businessman, an active citizen in community affairs and a dutiful husband and father.

The road to life as an author requires that your writing get published. Elbert wanted to see *The Man* published, but under the circumstances his secret collaborator could not be acknowledged. It might be well, they reasoned, to have someone know that Elbert was writing a novel for, if and when it was published, it would have to bear the copyright owner's name of Elbert Hubbard, especially if he wanted to write and publish other works and establish himself in the literary field.

Elbert elected to go over his manuscript with their good mutual friend of Chautauqua days, The Reverend Dr. Brown, Episcopal rector of East Aurora. Dr. Brown was enthusiastic and offered suggestions, little suspecting, at first, that there was another collaborator whose suggestions would, in the final writing, be the dominant ones.

The element of secrecy and the adding of the Reverend Dr. Brown as a collaborator heightened the excitement of the whole project for Elbert, whose successful business career was beginning to settle down to a dull routine of making more money and traveling in those dull circles that business success imposes.

Alas for sweet and attractive Bertha, this was the kind of uncomplicated life she had always sought, and logically assumed, had been and still was the aim of her ever-ambitious Elbert. It was a tragic oversight or a tactical error if she knew of his literary ambitions and sought to divert him from them, for she wasn't really fighting a dangerous woman: she was fighting a much more formidable foe—a man's dream.

One of the notes that Elbert wrote to Alice during that summer of collaboration was about the Reverend Dr. Brown's views after reading a finished portion of *The Man* manuscript.

Elbert told of the minister's enthusiasm:

We need not repeat his language which was pitched largely in superlatives, but suffice it to remark that he says the character of The Man is clear, clean and strong and vivid and such picturing has enough meat to endure the most [that] captious and quibbling critics can bring against it.

He also says The Man speaks truth and not a line of the middle chapters need be changed. But if I (we) will rewrite the setting of the picture, enlarging the book one third—giving, say, two more chapters to The Man on lofty themes, the book will sweep the land and live. Dr. Brown is not the most practical man on earth and what he says about sweeping the land we will take with "cum granim salis" as they say in Oshkosh. Yet the scheme he proposes interests me, Dear, 'cause why it is what you have already suggested.

He has written out a rough draft of the proposed plot as follows—

Aspasia to be let down among the Hobbs as it is. They are proud, vain, rich and ignorant. She is refined, sensitive, spiritual. Let the grossness of the Hobbs tribe stand as a foil for her sweetness and purity. Make her aspiring, lofty and draw her sweet and spiritual nature on the canvas with a strong hand, so she will stand as clean as The Man.

The Hobbs will misunderstand her—thwart her attempts to subdue her great and noble yearning for Beauty and the Goodness. She will be a mocking bird in a nest of crows. Give her a lover—a poor aspiring author whose work is started. Let the Hobbs badger both she [sic] and her noble youth because they are "infidels." The youth goes out to find his fortune and Aspasia (give her a better name, though) longs for better things and finds The Man just as she did before. Then let The Man tell his five or six chapters and Shakespeare story and have the aspiring author find an attentive audience in the west with honor and prosperity close in hand. Make Aspasia not over thirty years of age when she receives the good news from her lover with word to come to him at once. The Hobbs family withhold their blessing but The Man gives his in a most gracious manner and prophesies for her a world of happiness and let the curtain fall.

Alice's only reaction was a series of question marks scribbled in on Elbert's note just after the "let the curtain fall" suggestion.

There was a postscript to Elbert's note. He added:

Dr. Brown wrote a novel ten years ago and is going to give me the MSS to read. He tells me to finish The Man and then he wants me to rewrite his and we will publish it together. Ha ha! Of course he does not know I now have a partner.

In his observation of Dr. Brown as being "not the most practical man on earth" and his assumption that Dr. Brown did not know he now had a partner, Elbert was guilty of errors born out of the inevitable naivete that overtakes a man caught up in either flirtation or serious association that, even innocently, goes beyond the bounds of propriety. The *very* practical Dr. Brown was, by his suggested changes in the script, pretending not to recognize *The Man* as the story of his friends Alice and Elbert but, having recognized it he hoped the proposed changes would lead Elbert (alias The Man) to take the hint and bow out and Alice to begin thinking in terms of lending her literary talents to a young, established writer in another part of the country.

Dr. Brown was practical in his solution but the approach was far too subtle. For Love—even intellectual love—is far too blind to see subtleties directed at the practitioners.

The Man was not changed as Dr. Brown suggested, and by fall neither Alice nor Elbert was about to let the curtain fall on their togetherness. Though another separation was imminent their ties would simply revert to the teasing yet learned sort of letter writing—a growing, flexible, yet tenacious bond that began to fence out reason and loved ones.

In the fall of 1890 Alice went to Boston for graduate studies instead of going to Springfield to teach. She had applied to and had been accepted at Emerson School of Oratory.

Elbert polished up the manuscript of *The Man* and sent it off to J. S. Ogilvie of 57 Rose Street in New York City, a publisher of paperback novels whose "Sunny Side Series" were a popular buy at 35 cents a copy.

When word came back from Ogilvie that *The Man* would be published, Hubbard was elated and he mused about how his teacher friend had brought about a new and truly sunny side to his otherwise routine life. It had thus far been very much the prototype successful business man's life. Now, a whole new world—that of a man of letters—seemed to be opening up!

He and Alice began to talk of this new life in what soon became a steady flow of letters back and forth.

When the book came out early in 1891, it was favorably reviewed in the Buffalo papers and Hubbard enjoyed the new thrill of autographing copies for old friends and new admirers. Alice, of course, received her special copy as did Dr. Brown and Hubbard's close friend Dr. Arthur Mitchell.

It wasn't an exceptional literary work and Hubbard knew it wouldn't establish him as a writer of note but he was now "published" and it was a step in the right direction so far as he was concerned. Moreover, while some readers didn't enthuse about the plot, his portion on Shakespeare did impress them and so it provided a hint of what direction he might better consider should he decide to make a career of writing.

Bertha read the novel with cold chills because it seemed to confirm her suspicion that, while she had sent Alice out of her home she hadn't successfully sent her out of Elbert's life. There were too many similarities to Elbert and Alice in the book's main characters. And the opinions Aspasia and The Man held of their critics sounded suspiciously like what Elbert had said about people who imagined that Alice was anything more to him than a good, moral young acquaintance whose principal interest was in literature, not men. And though Bertha decided the best course was to pretend that she didn't make the connection, she began to wonder how often, and where, Elbert and Alice had been meeting after Alice moved out. But now the book was out and maybe this was the end of the affair. She reasoned, too, that if she showed a reasonable interest in Elbert's latest accomplishment, it might at least prevent similar conjecture by others and avoid nasty gossip.

If Bertha had known that Alice and Elbert had been together *after* the manuscript had been written and sent off to a publisher she would have taken a far different view of the whole matter. But she didn't know.

During the 1890 Christmas vacation Alice came home and she and Elbert met in a park in Buffalo and had dinner together a number of times at the Hotel Broezel. There was now no manuscript to keep their hands busy and their minds safely occupied. They touched each other with hands of love and their minds forgot Aspasia and The Man. Non-platonic raptures filled their thoughts but they fought it off.

Back in Boston, after vacation, Alice was troubled after she attended church one Sunday and heard a stinging sermon about sin and the holy state of matrimony.

She penned an emotional reaction in a letter that day to Elbert and, in it debated the out-moded reasoning of the minister.

The high point of her letter read:

I have been thinking very much of our last talk at the Broezel. Shall we whose souls are lighted with wisdom from on high go on living in the twentieth century and talk in tenth century language? Dare we do it? People used to say such or such priest of Isis performed a marriage ceremony. Now they say such a priest of Isis married that man and woman and I am not sure but the manner of speech is simply to keep time with the people. The two unhappy people who sat in front of you the other morning on the train were married by a man and look at the result. In their souls they loathed each other but before man (for they were made by man—married by man) they would pretend they were married but before God they knew they were not and, look you Dear, do you not think they were ashamed before God and hid way in the dark and did not dare to look into each others' eyes. Yes, you are right, M H D it would bring the most awful loathing. You and I would prefer death to such defilement—yes we would kill ourselves rather than be so defiled. And note—if there is an awful hell, just as surely is there the other extreme—a most wondrous Heaven—and we know there is. Rossetti was right and it is that which shall give the completest oneness of soul that can even think. We have had only a suggestion of this yet, but what has been the reaction? Hath eye seen or ear heard? Sex nature without soul and intellect is lower than brute. O, far lower than anything I can imagine . . .

After a discussion of Rossetti Alice again showed her distress at the minister's obsession with orthodoxy:

O, Dear Me—O My? I wish that minister had never, never come here for he preached more orthodoxy than when he is at home. I do believe he talks to me until I wish I had never seen or heard of him and almost wish I were one of those dough women who have no mind of their own and need religious instruction from the clergy.

Alice and Elbert had both been raised in home atmospheres of the strict, orthodox, hellfire and damnation type of religion. They both knew the Bible well and both were God-fearing persons. Their love could not grow within the boundaries of conventions or religious beliefs under which they were raised and which still governed the society of which they were a part.

Alice was beginning her long and successful drive to find a way, with Elbert's full blessing, to widen the boundaries so their love could grow and be free of guilt. Thus, she reasoned that a marriage for two people who were no longer in love, i.e. Bertha and Elbert, could be seen as a fraud and "defilement" before God even if it seemed absolutely proper to small thinking orthodox ministers. And, on the higher plane, there could be a marriage of lovers, pleasing in the eyes of God and not requiring the blessing of mere man.

And so another stage of their relationship was under way. The platonic friendship was a thing of the past and now love-making of a high and noble nature seemed possible. Not a low and merely sexual gratification, but gradual marriage of the bodies that housed minds which had already formed a union.

Many months would pass before the physical would catch up with the mental but catch up it would. And a force stronger than either Alice or Elbert seemed to have taken over the direction of their lives.

3

"Then Wept Again to Think the Day Was Gone"

The year 1891 was one in which men about whom Elbert would one day write emerged as persons of growing national importance. Some he would eventually come to know personally. Indiana lawyer Benjamin Harrison had been elected President of the United States in 1889, the year Alice was invited to leave the Hubbard home. John Wanamaker, the Philadelphia merchant prince, was Harrison's appointee to the office of Postmaster General and Theodore Roosevelt was appointed to the Civil Service Commission. The Sherman Anti-Trust Act was passed the year before and the "moguls" of industry and banking were beginning to see a new and sinister day dawning for them. Elbert Hubbard would become their champion and paid conscience before the end of the decade. Just now, he was wrestling with his own conscience, and in his wildest dreams could not imagine what was in store for him in either his personal life or his career.

Alice came home from Boston for the summer vacation and they resumed their secret meetings in Buffalo and in the hills between East Aurora and Wales Hollow. Their happiest moments were spent in the hills under the canopy of heaven and they sensed no guilt for they had become convinced that here they were hiding nothing but were, instead, pursuing a course set for them by the "Divine Presence." They felt it and were happy.

Sometimes Alice would be first to reach their predetermined rendezvous spot and she would pick a bouquet of wild flowers and lie back on the soft grass with her head tilted to the west from whence her lover was certain to come. Sometimes, with ear to the ground, she would pick up the thumping hoof sounds of Elbert's horse galloping up the rise to "their spot" and her heart beats would meet that galloping pace. And then he would appear through the dancing leaves and, dismounting before his horse was fully reined in, Elbert would dash to her side and smother her with kisses such as Aspasia Hobbs would never know.

Then they would walk and talk and breathe the sweet air of freedom, togetherness, and the countryside they loved.

Each parting became a separate torture, for their careful caresses always left, ever stronger, something more to be desired. Each return to the reality of their separate lives brought an involuntary sense of guilt to each. But they had become better acquainted with their natures and this part of their being was reaching out for the same understanding their minds had long since found.

There was a day in June of 1891 when that physical union nearly came to fruition. They met in the hills and frolicked together 'till sundown. They fell exhausted to the ground and lay quietly side by side as the moon and stars in the sky arranged themselves for inspection. Darkness moved in to close out the rest of the world, and they loved, not completely, but so nearly so that it was as though they had. Then their minds—already wedded—seemed to say, "Enough for now, there will be other nights like this."

Parting, as dawn approached, was strangely free of torture, and the love glow lingered to erase all of the homeward bound guilt they had felt at other times. And it lingered long after that!

In mid-August Elbert sat at his desk at the office and penned a poem dedicated to Alice:

To A.M.   *The Day*

From out the dull and listless gray
Of times gone by there gleams A Day.

And Nature sighed—did her tears outpour
Then wept again to think The Day was o'er,

Clear and pure as marble white,
It stands all hallowed in my sight.

The Moon across the hilltops gleamed
And sank to rest while lovers dreamed.

The Darkness fell, with *Stillness* sweet
Time lingered long, with leaden feet.

Seeming afraid to break the spell,
Not fearing that they'd love too well.

And gentle zephyrs from afar
Played back and forth thro' doors ajar

Open the doors—'Tis said [sic] but true
For love and life flow'd thro' and thro'

Then full across the eastern sky
Great beams of light burst forth on high.

Heralds they were of the coming King
Who rules the day—his praise we sing.

Too generous he, to rush pell mell
Where lovers sleep—their secrets tell.

So up he peeped behind the wood
And asked permission if he could

Send his bright beams in gentle guise
To show the light in lovers eyes.

Permission granted—forth from his home
He gilds trees, fields, flowers and dome

The Day—what can I say of all such bliss—
'Twas worth the while to live for this.

Oh! Heavenly Joy, Oh, Day of bliss
Back from the past I call thy kiss.

We laughed and lived and lov'd did we
Careless and thoughtless, happy—free.

The Day—what! *Tell* of those sacred hours
Avaunt, vain man! Canst paint the flowers?

Picture that perfect happy time
Of loving hearts in lisping rhyme?

Away thou pen—give back The Day,
Softly let me live it o'er I pray.

With closed lids and bated breath
If in an hour should come grim Death,

This only would I ask—"Oh! Stay
And let me keep, yes keep My Day.

'Take all my wealth, power, knowledge, skill
Place round my heart oblivion—Kill

'Each memory of this worthless clay
But let me keep, O keep My Day

'I'll clasp it firm and hide it deep
Down in my soul where sorrows sleep!

'In another life I need not weep
This much I crave, this *must* I keep,'

I'll hold it up, this will I say
"See My Beloved—I have Our Day."

Then will *She* know at once 'tis me
Arms will reach out—in Heav'n we'll be

Take all—I'm done, but leave, I pray,
'Tis all I ask—*The Day! The Day!!*

Aug. 14, 1891

He read it over, made one correction, placed it in a Larkin "Sweet Home" soap advertising envelope and daringly mailed it to Alice care of the Strykersville post office where Wales Hollow farmers received their mail. Many such envelopes were in the mails those days but still it was the dangerous sort of thing that only a man madly in love would do.

When Alice received the envelope she knew it wasn't an ordinary advertising piece inside. When she read the poem she knew a new day had dawned from a day and night they would never forget.

"What was it Rossetti said? Wasn't it something about complete oneness? Oh Elbert!" And she pressed the poem to her breast, for oneness was nearing and she knew it couldn't be any other way.

A glorious summer was drawing to a close and *The Day* remained the high point of that season's intimacy. Subsequent trysts did not lend themselves to the same reckless abandon of that day.

Elbert and Alice would have had it otherwise but she had to start thinking about her return to Boston, just a few weeks hence, and Elbert was finding that his work at the office was piling up, due in part to his time away to meet Alice and in part to his inability to think about his duties, his love for Alice, and his strained relationship with Bertha all at the same time.

He loved Bertha, though in a different way now. He loved the children she bore him but their last-born was now four years old and the still beautiful mother of his three boys had been too preoccupied with home making to pursue or desire love making. Moreover, the scenes she had rightly or wrongly created over Alice when she lived in their home had built an icy wall between Bertha and Elbert. Thereafter, both had been too proud to try to melt it. She busied herself with club work in any idle moment she had and Elbert spent his free time with his friends, Dr. Mitchell, Reverend Dr. Brown and other interesting professional men in the community. Later he was to spend much time with Alice when she reentered his life and thoughts in a consuming manner.

Now he was at a crossroads and a choice toward one of the two women was one he could not bring himself to make. Alice had the advantage in pressing for a decision because she knew while Bertha did not that the crossroads—the alternate choice—was there.

Alice returned to Emerson College of Oratory that fall with a kiss on her lips and a dream in her heart—and a poem that told her something its lines and stanzas did not spell out. She knew that Elbert would remember "The Day" and forget *The Man* and that in search of many more days like it, Elbert would take further steps toward her as he pondered at the crossroads.

Settled down again in Boston for the 1891 fall term at "E C O," Alice was not long in bridging the gap with letters, nor was Elbert.

He was hardly surprised, but much moved, one day when an envelope arrived from Alice and in it was a copy in her handwriting of the love poem he had sent her in August. The fire was rekindled and he knew that he would take the road to Alice though it could not be a permanent one just yet. A visit when another business trip would take him to Boston would have to do for now. There were too many scrambled thoughts. Too many obligations. Too many business ties that would have to be broken and that would not be easy because his sister Frances was married to his partner, John D. Larkin, and there would be much explaining and probably family pressure to stay on and keep the status quo.

Not infrequently when Elbert traveled to distant cities on behalf of his company he would put up at boarding houses. Theirs was a factory-to-home soap business and residential sections of the cities, not the downtown hotel section, was where the market for Sweet Home soap was. In Boston he had most frequently stayed in the boarding house of Mrs. Miriam Crosby Tyler at 149 West Canton Street. A genial woman, Mrs. Tyler had come to know and like Elbert more than others who would lodge there on business trips. He knew she would see no harm in his bringing a family friend over to meet her some time when he would be in Boston and decided that on his next trip he would do just that—and the friend would be Alice Moore who was staying at nearby Emerson College.

When it happened it was just as Elbert had imagined. Mrs. Tyler liked Alice, and so on subsequent trips they would get together again; but Mrs. Tyler would find she had chores to do and leave the parlor to her friends. There was nothing in these meetings that could come close to the abandonment of "The Day" in June, and the frustration was disconcerting to both of them.

Elbert knew that to continue to enjoy the mental stimulation and broadening that Alice had brought him from the very beginning, he would now have to run the risk of still deeper physical involvement. The temptation to do so wasn't lessened any by the situation at home. A husband distracted by a sense of guilt and a wife cool with lingering suspicion rarely get a mutual hold on the fan that fires passion. Instead, they hold back, each hoping the other will make the first move. By now, four frigid years of distraction and doubt had passed since Elbert and

Bertha's last child had been born. The three sons, born in 1882, 1886 and 1887, were now, respectively, in their ninth, fifth and fourth years.

Neither Bertha nor Elbert was unmindful of the fact that it was in 1887 that Alice entered and changed their lives. Elbert *knew* that Alice was still there and effecting more changes; Bertha merely *suspected* that Alice was still a factor and was frustrated by her inability to change the course of events. She could have done so with her superior physical charm which, naturally, wasn't responding, but even so to turn the tide she would have had to display a greater interest in things intellectual and an interest in seeing her husband give up sound business pursuits in favor of a shaky new career as a writer. Not in the wildest stretch of her imagination could she see Elbert in any other role than as the successful businessman that he was. She reckoned wrongly, and, as she put aside love making for chiding Elbert's literary ambitions, she gave Alice two weapons where before she had only one. And one that might have been forever dulled with just a little boning up on literature and a little deeper probing of Elbert's real ambition in life.

Alice knew her man. She sensed and pursued her advantage. It would be no more honest to say that she was a scheming woman than it would be to say that Bertha was beautiful but dumb or that Elbert was a born philanderer. All three, to varying degrees, sensed the direction in which Hubbard's career seemed to be headed, but it was Alice alone who now correctly sensed that the pivotal point would turn on a sexual relationship —an area in which she was less naturally endowed than Bertha. Alice was prepared to encourage Elbert to the utmost sexually as well as intellectually. Bertha was dead set against silly intellectual encouragement and was by this rigid approach automatically withdrawing sexually.

Alice was capably filling the void in both aspects of Elbert's confused existence . . . and largely with letters! In the now dull atmosphere of his Buffalo business office Elbert read many letter like this from Alice in Boston:

Thursday P.M.
3:30

My E.A.—

Buckle—Yes Dear, I have read a few pages and it is magnificent— He lived far in advance of his time and it is a great mystery to me how he was appreciated as he was. Do you note what he says about *consciousness* not being a faculty of the mind because it changes—varies. Does it, except to grow greater—acquire—add, as do will, affection, etc.? But he has a wonderful insight. You own the books? So we can read them without haste. I have only tasted.

Your A.M. is a poor sort of an inheritance, Dear. She has accomplished nothing for two days except to write to her Beloved and lie on the lounge thinking, thinking of him. Have you felt me lean over your shoulder Dear as you sat at your desk, and put my hands upon you and you put your left hand up and took mine and worked away so fast all conscious that I was there. I felt it Dear and I could see your face change as you worked and I too gathered strength.

And I saw you open your package and I kissed away the tears that started in your eyes and I saw you put your face in your hands once and then you felt my breath on your forehead and your face was radiant with the D.P.

And, Dear, you were here with me when I opened my box and I felt your hands, your kiss, your embrace.

And now I want to quote to you from Phillips Brooks and I wish you might give it to those people you speak to tonight—yet the same Voice will speak to your soul that spoke to his—

"And now, once more comes Christmas—Lift up yourselves to the meaning of the great Day and dare to think of your Humanity as something so sublimely precious that it is worthy of being made an offering to God.

Count it a privilege to make that offering as complete as possible, keeping nothing back, and then go out to the pleasures and duties of your life having been born anew into His Divinity as He was born into our Humanity on Christmas Day."

Surely it is a magnificent thought stated majestically by a king of Humanity. Note the *Use* of capital letters.

Yet, I note the paradox of thought here. He says, "*Lift* up yourselves and count it a privilege to *make* the offering etc." So poor is our language—in reality we do not lift ourselves any more than the man lifts himself with his boot straps. Can we *make* a *real* offering? When I say I give myself into your keeping, do I do it? No, No, it is not I but the Divine within me that goes to meet its own. All we *do* is to take ourselves out of the way, cease to hinder the Divine Influence. June 2 was simply saying each to the other what we know of the working of this Divinity. The saying, the sensible presence of the Infinite at that moment made the union what it had never been before—just ourselves farther out of the way—joined the hearts "and our *spirits* rushed together at the meeting of the lips" — . So when we say these words we open the way more fully for the Divine to enter and claim its own, just as at each time we meet, each time you enfold me to your breast does the spirit enfold and make me thine, and it is Reaction.

Yes, Dear your letter of Wed. is here in my hand—I have read and reread. I will not write of this great subject tonight because of its intensity. You show me most beautiful truth. What I wrote you was not mine until you read it back to me and a hundred fold more. The facts you tell me I did not know before yet it seems already digested. Not like the last stroke that Frank Beard puts to his pictures. It is lines and curves and lines until that last touch and behold, there it is— plain as life.

But I won't write more tonight for this longing heart wants only you, you my Beloved—my Darling, and I reach out my arms to you. Take me, press me to your breast and I shall be nourished and assured. O, the greatness of love.

The D.P. the High Estate, and few there be that find it. To the minds (I might add *hearts*) of most of the refined people you will find to live without quarreling—to hear and forbear is genteel and refined. Not to let an unkind or hasty word pass the lips (except in their own room) is all that can be expected of mortals. Well, Dear—I do try your patience *badly,* do you have to bite your lips hard? Why Darling, what a Hades it would be to have a suggestion of anything but love cross our paths—what a blot on our Day of Light. I can't imagine it can you? Do I want you to do aught you do not wish to do? Do you want me to do what my heart does not rush forth to do? No, No, there is a Higher Law to those of High Estate. Do you not think, Dear, that sometime we shall look back at these years now almost with dizzy brain, at the haste we seem in now. Yet it seems necessary now and for sometime to come—

But there *will* be no hurry sometime.

After reading letters like this Elbert was stimulated in mind and body and began thinking ever more constantly about how both could be brought to the fullest gratification. It had almost happened on June 2, The Day! Somehow Alice made it all clear—mind and body work together; love and literature were inseparable. And how well both were interwoven in her letters! He mused as he sat at his desk, "Yes, there could well be a 'Divine Presence' in the combination, for hadn't mere written words just brought Alice to his side where she touched his face and warmed his spirit which was already flowing back to her in Boston? And nobody there in the office could see her or suspect that this wondrous thing had happened in their presence!"

More and more now, Alice and Elbert were talking in their letters and during their rendezvous in Buffalo and Boston about a life together some day. She was free and was ready. He was ready but far from free in terms of conscience, business ties, family responsibilities and legal marital ties, the latter breakable only through the committing of adultery. Alice would always emphasize that Elbert could sweep away the barriers if he could only see that their love was created on such a high plane that it could be consumated in a marriage that transcended "man-made" marriages. More and more she urged him, even using Biblical passages, to make the choice between her and Bertha, cut the bonds and begin a new life with her.

4

"How Many Times Do We Need to Be Born Again?"

The year 1892 was to mark the deaths of an unusually large number of prominent men of literature. American poets Walt Whitman and John Greenleaf Whittier were among them as was French historian-philosopher Joseph Ernest Renan. In the same year businessman Elbert Hubbard was to make a decision that would, within seven years, give him national prominence in American literature.

Always an avid reader, Elbert was spending far more time with books than with Bertha during the winter of 1891–1892. And, as he read the works of a wide variety of authors, past and contemporary, he shared his thoughts about them with Alice in their now constant exchange of letters.

It made no difference whether Elbert wrote to her about Henry Thomas Buckle, the English historian who died in 1862, or about Renan, Robert G. Ingersoll or other prominent figures on the current scene—Alice could always add to what Elbert had learned about them. They were loving literature—and each other—with greater warmth and understanding.

Each love was an avenue of understanding to the other. Both set the stage for things to come in the public writings of Elbert Hubbard. He sensed this as he read letters like this that winter:

Wed. Night

MHD—

I will send chapters on mythology as you wish and you may keep the typewritten copies but please return to me the original manuscript —it is good enough for me. I rather have a "violent tip in your direction" than in any direction at all—in fact rather than to stand still.

Renan—yes. I will send that too and it is very full of fresh love from my heart for I read it Sunday and turned the leaves very, very tenderly and with moist eyes. Renan was a rare soul and I cannot separate him from his sister. All the week I have thought of them, the perfume of sweet violets and the picture of the anemone nemarosa—the delicate wind flower made only for heaven's smiles, the sun's kisses, the gentle whispers of the angels—And tonight I went over to the branch library and read RGI's[1] article on Renan and lo—he had used the comparison of flowers—and too, Dear—don't you think he was inspired by his subject to write more tenderly, lovingly and sweetly than usual? It seemed to me so. I did not get any of the sneer in it—It seemed *honest* to me. He seemed to follow Renan's mind as it was led up and out of the depth of superstition and did not cry out because he went no farther in his research or, rather, his embracing reason's disclosures.

Then note what RGI says at the close about—"If a man die shall he live again?" "The brain says—perhaps—the heart hopes for the Dawn".

I could not find anywhere in Renan anything but the tenderest love and respect for Jesus. More perhaps than any superstitious believer about Him could. He writes of Him as tenderly and lovingly and with as great regard as you could write of your Wife—and yet he is free from nearly all superstition about Him. I did not read all the book Sunday but I did not find about the natural conception and birth of Jesus. Did you tell me that Renan gave the same view of it that you told me at Ill? Is it not strange—Dear—that so many years of super-stition cling to us for so long a time and we meet these rational views of facts with something of a trembling of heart and wonder almost "What is true?"

If the superstition that what you believe is going to save or condemn you were true it were well to cover one's head with a blanket, stop the ears with cotton and sing ones' [sic] self away to a senseless heaven as soon as possible. No investigation—and the Catholic rules are none too narrow. Are we afraid—Dear—to look things in the face? You have proven that you are not.

I can see how when Jesus recognized his parentage, then claimed God as his Father—felt all this as a separating from his fellows—a conse-cration greater even than that of Cannon Farrar's—In his birth, God had put a mark upon his forehead and He was His for His Special Work—*called*—.

Your sister boasts of her ancestors—you have none—God is our Father. When I was 8 or 10 Mother's daughter[2] tried to build herself up by trying to make me believe my father and mother were of ignoble birth—I dared not ask my father and so it rankled in my bosom—such pain—until it was so firmly fixed in my mind that I would make it *noble*—I would make the star of glory yet set above our honor by claiming the highest birthright of education and high spiritual attain-

---

1. Robert G. Ingersoll
2. Alice's older sister, Emma.

ments. It firmly implanted and ingrained this desire within me. It does make one look up and find The Power when every earthly prop is removed.

We have Faith that we shall Live eternally—("Faith is a filament fastened at one end"—*Good*) Does not the brain as well as heart look to the Dawn?

Thank you—Dear One—for the order of the waterproof. I forget what I write you and what I whisper to you on the street—in my room—in the night. I'll write you some things five times and others not at all—but you don't mind Dear, do you? There is everything to tell you and only pen and paper to give verbal communications—but there is [sic] Soul Messages that laugh at space or any difficulties. Don't you hear it all the time whisper—I Love You Dear?

In the not too distant years ahead Elbert would put his Renan studies—and Alice's contributions to his Renan thinking—to work for him in his own literary works, *The Song of Songs, The Book of Job* and *The Man of Sorrows,* the latter a Renan-Alice-Elbert slanted story of Jesus. Renan, too, had doubts about orthodox religious teachings and about the Virgin birth of Jesus and his doubts caused him, as it later did Elbert and Alice, to delve ever deeper into the texts that orthodoxy had provided. Renan was famous (and condemned by the church) for his *Life of Jesus,* published in 1863, and was also well known for his studies of the Book of Job and the Song of Solomon.

Ironically, the strict religious teachings of their childhood were now both a source of despair and solace to these lovers. They were God-fearing all the way but they cried out for an understanding from God of a complete man–woman relationship which the Bible, the Church and society would not permit of people in their circumstance. As they sought and waited for that miracle of understanding, they together elevated their literary thoughts and knowledge and together lowered society's bars to their physical communion with each other. In the latter action, they told themselves that each such lowering was that only in terms of man-made interpretations of God's laws. To them, each breach of man's interpretations was really a step closer toward fruition of a love born in the "Divine Presence."

No matter how sweet the ultimate togetherness of physical love, even Alice and Elbert had to resort to the not-too-unique, man-made, methodology of arousing the physical senses. The mixture of the lofty and the trite may differ in letters of love but rarely, if ever will one be present without the other. The following letter, one of a series of letters from Alice while at Emerson College of Oratory illustrates the point:

Our Evening

MHD. I watched the stars come out one by one tonight. I felt the great curtain of Night being drawn down—"Softer than silence, stiller than still air"—and as the feeling of the majesty and grandeur of the scene increased—like trained soldiers the stars—Night's sentinels—took their places. First came Mercury—our star of the East—as tho to make sure you would know where to find me Dear. He came out—twinkled so blithely and I almost heard him say—"Right here she is—come— come—this way, this way—I see you both and watch over you until you are united again and then I shall smile and smile upon you and send the glad tidings throughout the great Universe, and if you will listen you will hear grander music, then one mere chord of harmony will swell the great chorus of love." Wasn't that what he said, My Love? And didn't all the stars shout a glad "Amen"? And then, Dear, did you see the Western sky? Why it inspired me with such life. It said, "Peace beginning to be—deep as the blue of the sea. Don't you see that this glow is a promise of the joy that cometh in the Morning— even the West gives promise of the East." And, My Heart, all the sky above whispered "Amen"—and the waters of the river stood so still and placid and flushed with the thoughts and mirrored on its face the promise made so sure by that Western sky. And I came home Dear and put the red shade on the Little Love Lamp and shall keep it until the promise is verified. It will be the red shade until you come Dear—to keep me *sure* and then it will be the beautiful yellow one. Wasn't it a pretty story the ancients had about the rainbow Dear? Everytime the bow came in the cloud I imagine they uncovered their heads and bowed low and whispered a prayer of thanksgiving for having this sign in verification of the promise. And so Dear will you and I when we see the red sky. Yes Dear, red should be a symbol of promise. Wherever we see a bit of red we will be sure Dear it is to remind us that the Promise is sure and we will whisper a glad note of joy and praise and go on our way rejoicing. And how fitting it is Dear that my Love Dress is red. It is the one I made for you Dear and I will not wear it until you come Dear. The first night I will put it on and we will rejoice as they who saw the bow in the cloud. Only Dear ours is positive joy and theirs was negative. Theirs was because He would not come again—ours is because He *will* give to you your own.

Oh yes of course I did Dear. Dr. Mitchell (which is to say Maud Husted)[3] and I went to Mt. Auburn. We rode out there from Boylston Street and sauntered for an hour in the cemetery—climbed to the top of the tower where we could look for miles and miles every way. A grand sight—fills one's soul with the sense of grandeur and freedom. We do go where our thoughts do, don't we Dear? And we are free in a great sense when we can mount with wings as of eagles. Not a cloud in the sky—nothing to hinder *progress*—think *limitlessness*. Then we walked home—six miles at least and neither of us tired—both said again and again we were so glad to be alive. Maud respects one's holy sanctuary and does not try to enter. Lets you think and enjoy because she has thoughts and enjoyment of her own. Four hours out in the oxygen today and think I am born again. How many times do we need to be born again? Did not the Eunuch marvel because Philip told him

---

3. Maud was Alice's classmate at Buffalo State Teachers. A dear friend and confidant to her as Dr. Mitchell was to Elbert.

a man must be born again? I should say again and again and again—
why, in fact, as many times as he needs it—and how many times is that?
I think I need it every day at least. Does not nature suggest that? Is
it not a symbol of this each time we waken in the morning—are we
not born again? Do we not waken to the newness of life? And a better,
more glorious life?

Dear One I have been thinking very much about you lately. Now
Dear don't smile that way else your little girl will be coming over there
very close to you and will have a severe attack of smoothing your face
and your hair and touching, touching, touching every part of your face
with her lips. Won't smile any more? Well she'll come just the same
Dear so you may smile on if you wish. It is alright My Love. Yes
Dear—thinking of you as an individual—of your *power*—your intellect.
After thinking in this way if I try to find where I am inside you, I
can't. I am so so small and I have not yet found a microscope large
lensed enough to discover me—*but* I never feel this when I am with
you. You lead me on and on, arm in arm with you Dear. Your grasp
of Life and truth is greater than of anyone's I know for you see from
so many sides. And most of all Dear do I remember your purity of
soul—your high and noble purpose. My little vision has seen so short
a way into our future and Love has filled my eyes so that I saw little
else. Yes, Dear One, I want to confess it all to you Dear. See me just
as I am Dear—it is miserable enough I know but you must see. Take
love out and it is a blank to me—put love in and it is all I see.

There has ever been a vague vision of our doing something and
doing that earnestly but nothing clear but the Love Life. To be with
you every moment is all the heaven I can imagine—for being with you
means going on and on and up and up. Nothing would seem suffering
or sacrifice to me but to be separated from you and that I could not
brook. I feel my unworthiness more than I can ever express to you. I
cannot be to you what you are to me. Unworthy, unworthy I cry and
I pray that the purifier may come and make me white and pure as the
flames we love so dearly. All I can say to you my Beloved One is that
I love you with all my soul. My whole being poises toward you as its
Life and its salvation. And since you love me Dear and make me to
partake of your life in every way, make me a very part of your self, I
feel the mark is set upon my forehead. I am separated and dare do no
unclean thing. And the most intense prayer of my life is this now which
rises many times in the day and night—"oh may this waiting purify me
—enlarge and enrich me—ennoble and glorify and when I am worthy—
not before—may He take me in soul truth unto Himself, never from
one moment after to be separated from Him, My Love, My Heart.

On one of his now regular "business" trips to Boston Elbert added a
new dimension to his relationship with Alice. He became financially involved by lending her $200 for tuition and other expenses. Alice insisted
on signing a promissory note, pledging repayment, without interest, two
years from March 28, 1892. For obvious reasons, Elbert wrote "Allis"
over the name Alice in her Alice Moore signature.

The summer of 1892 found Alice and Elbert following the pattern they had set for themselves the previous summer. More frequent meetings in Buffalo and in the hills back of East Aurora and, at each, an accepted greater intimacy that was always just short of complete abandonment. More walks in the park near Elbert's office and more dinners together at the Iroquois and Broezel Hotels. All of this, while it meant more frequent periods of togetherness, just didn't have the same security from discovery that they had enjoyed each time that Elbert had found business reasons to visit far away Boston.

It was time, they resolved, to do something about it. If Elbert were to sell out his interest in the Larkin Company and enroll in college at Boston too, they could be together all the time and soon he would have the formal educational background that would insure his success as an author. She would do his research and be his good right arm. Then, too, the money he would realize from selling out his interest would make it possible for him to do the right thing in the way of taking care of Bertha and the boys. He would be "born again" just as Alice had carefully suggested in her letters. To Elbert it was a possibility to be considered. To Alice it was the only solution. And, once more, Bertha was not a party to the deliberations; she didn't know they were taking place. In a way, though, she helped shape the course of events to Alice's conception of how they should evolve because she failed to recognize and gratify her husband's intellectual and physical needs. Alice was doing both to the limit that the mails and the male would allow.

Alice went back to Emerson School of Oratory that fall with the feeling that Elbert would soon follow. The seed had been planted and his now consuming desire to become a man of letters would speed the germination. All of his other desires—and hers—could from then on be met in freedom and abundance.

With Alice away at college—but as close as the next mail delivery— Elbert decided to get ready for the first step, at least. Certainly his share of the soap business would bring enough money to support Bertha and the boys and still permit him the luxury of higher education—something that his parents hadn't been able to afford for him. He had earned that luxury, he told himself, and then, too, he and Alice would be together enough to find out, once and for all, if they were really meant for each other in the "never separated" way that Alice knew and he suspected. Something had to change. Leading a dual life seemed all right when it was a purely intellectual arrangement but now it was much more than that and was unfair to both Bertha and Alice. They couldn't go on this way.

The born salesman faced the biggest selling task yet to confront him. Bertha would think he was out of his mind if he just announced some night that he was going to sell out his share of the soap business and go to college. His sister Frances, who was married to Hubbard's partner, John D. Larkin, was a proud woman and would share Bertha's view of his insanity. His parents, Dr. Silas Hubbard and Juliana, would take it in their stride. His mother liked to write and could dash out good little essays. The old doctor had been helped through college financially by an older brother and was grateful for his own higher education though sorry that his income as a country doctor hadn't been enough to provide Elbert with one when he reached college age. Both were proud of what Elbert had accomplished and had complete confidence that, whatever he might undertake, he would succeed. Dr. Hubbard wrote rather well himself and, as a frequent contributor to the Buffalo Medical Journal in the 1880s, liked to see his articles and byline in print there.

Elbert thought it through. In the final analysis, Bertha would have to see it his way, especially if he could prove that there would be ample funds to keep her and the boys well provided for and still permit him to improve himself. Morever, he would point out to her that he wasn't intending to go to just *any* college, it would be Harvard or nothing. This latter approach should also take some of the sting out of the "silly" decision insofar as proud Frances was concerned. There would be no real problem with the remainder of his family.

First he told Alice that he had made up his mind but he didn't tell her that Harvard was his choice.

A letter from Alice in the early fall of 1892 made it clear that he could rule if only he'd come to Boston:

Friday Night

MH. I cannot go to lie down and call upon the spirit of Night to take me to you until my heart expresses to you somewhat of the gratitude and Love for all this you have sent me!

Last night after writing came the beautiful Browning book fresh from the hands of Love. And how gently and lovingly I touched it, opened and read and reread what was marked. I knew what you had marked then and what you marked years before when we first knew Browning. The book became fairly radiant as I read and all spoke of Love, Love, Love.

This afternoon The Letter came. My Heart have you any idea— Dear—of the sublime grandeur of that Letter? It is magnificent. For several days I have been thinking of Boston University for us for a course in Literature but your letter told me that we do not want it. What we want is time and the library here and we can study for ourselves. I want no other teacher but you Dear. Gladly would I give up my work here in college to roam the Elysian fields hand in hand with you. Dr. D was very fine. You brought me more of the reality of Art-Life than he has in his three lectures.

Night and Morning you have filled it full to the brim of meaning— more than I can comprehend now. The Spirit of the Morning carries Love—and Love needs nothing not even clothing—sufficient unto itself. Ah, yes—we know, we *know*. Come Dear—take me as your pupil— Dear—let me learn from you and with you. Take me to the art galleries —to the fine arts and there teach me, show me and then shall I know. You are the real teacher—Dear—yes Teacher. I will tell you why when you come, Dear.

There are so many who are so loaded down with knowledge that as they talk they seem to cast their burden upon you and you are bowed down to earth with the load. You put your loving arms around me Dear and waft me on and on thru fields whose flowers are truth, whose perfume is truth—mountains of truth—all beauty, splendor, grandeur, tenderness, and Love. I grow lighter and lighter as we go, freer and freer until I am not and all there is is Truth and Love.

These Letters are sublime Dear and lift me up and away from the old self into the True Self.

> "Teach me, only teach, Love!
> As I ought
> I will speak thy speech, Love,
>
> Think thy thoughts
> Be a God, and hold me
> With a charm!
>
> Be a Man and fold me
> With thine Arm!
> Teach me, only teach, Love!"

Elbert usually penned a full letter to Alice but he sometimes just sent back answers, penned in darker ink and bold handwriting diagonally across Alice's letters. In this instance he felt it was wise to cool her down until he could make his plans, announcements, etc., back home. He sent Alice's letter back with just this hastily scribbled pencil notation on the back: "Have been kept from writing a letter all the PM. Will make up tomorrow." Nevertheless the die was cast and it was now only a matter of time.

Bertha accepted his decision, after his carefully told explanation of how he had worked hard and now wanted at least to try to get a college education. They could afford it, she knew that, and she loved him too much to stand in his way. With a resigned smile—one that took all the courage she could muster—Bertha gave him a pat on the cheek and a nod of approval. "If that is what you want," she added. But she wasn't happy about it and wondered to herself if sometime, somehow, Alice had brought him to this decision.

Indeed Alice, using Biblical references, was relentlessly pushing him to another decision beyond the choice of occupations—a choice between her and Bertha. In that fateful fall of 1892 she wrote to Elbert, indirectly likening him to Jacob's indecision about Rachel and Leah. She told him that she considered Jacob "an idiot" for not being able to distinguish between the woman he loved and the woman he hated. She pointed out that she had little respect for either Leah or Rachel, saying, "The only way I am like them is in hating swine and in getting my money's worth (of love)."

Late that October, after telling Bertha of his plans, Elbert spent an evening with partner John Larkin and sister Frances. He told them that he wanted to sell out his interest and, after a four-year stay at Harvard, followed by some study abroad, he wanted to become a full-time journalist. They reacted as he had expected, wondering if he had taken leave of his senses. But they knew he was dead serious and soon saw the futility of trying to dissuade him.

Having thus "made his peace" with Bertha and the Larkins, Elbert penned a long letter to his mother at Hudson, Illinois, where Dr. Silas Hubbard had practiced medicine since giving up his practice at Buffalo in 1855, a year before Elbert was born:

My dear Mother:
    Next to the selection of my parents I have completed the most important move of my life, in fact my death would not be a matter of such importance—or fraught with greater moment, so to you above all others should I write it first.

I have sloughed my commercial skin.

    That is to say I have sold out my entire financial interest in the Soap business, my last share was transferred today and the money is in the bank to my credit. It has taken me just a year to complete the matter and I have carried out the arrangement exactly as I planned in the start. Why have I done gone and done this thing? Because my Dear Mother I have all the money I want and there is a better use I can make of my time. That excellent man Hubbard MD and myself are probably the only men in the whole United States who have all the money they desire. Ten years ago I would not have thought this possible my desire was to be rich and if I still had the same ambition I believe yet I could be a millionaire. Possibly, however I might "bust" in the attempt like balloons filled too full, or the frog that set his heart on swelling to the size of an Ox. But Dear Mother, I can't "bust" now even if I should try. I have placed my funds even beyond the reach of my own indiscretion on long time mortgages on real estate in different localities (so the eggs are not in one basket) and only the interest will be paid to me. This will yield about $3,000.00 a year. My expenses of household, etc., are 2,000.00, so you see I will still have a thousand a year for whoever needs it most. In addition to this I have our little farm at E. Aurora, a thousand acres in Kansas and Colorado and 80 acres in Orange trees in Florida.

    The next question is what do I propose to do; I am going to Harvard College probably shortly after Jan. 1st and it is my intention to put in full four years there in study and I hope to spend a year in some German University as well. My old friend the Rev. Dr. Brown of E. Aurora, of whom you may have heard me speak, that has been of so much help to me and he will be in the future. He is a genuine patriarch in learning and righteousness and Heaven be praised is never a theologian excepting in the pulpit. Bertha and the boys will remain at E. Aurora, but of course I will be with them much of the time.

Bertha is much pleased over my plans but John and Frank look upon it as a wild form of insanity but I am glad to say I am at peace with them both and all the world beside. I have not paddled away from a sinking ship either, for the business here was never as prosperous and flourishing as at present. This year will show the biggest profits of any year we have ever had, and I have trained a force here that I think is able to continue the work with success. But he who would excel in the realm of thought must not tarry in the domain of dollars. Another thing I believe that he who would live long and well, must live like a poor man, no matter what his income is. We must be washed and fed of course but we must die the death. Many men here tell me they want to lay up enough to give their children a start. This is John's ambition. Money will give them a "start" but it is down grade. If my boys cannot get along without my financial help they can't with it. Of course, I can boost them but it will only be into a position where they will likely tumble out and the concussion might jar their spinal columns.

Daisy wrote me a short time ago, asking about investing in Soap stock. I did not reply—You now know why. Shares in stock Companies are speculation and no security is given. It all depends on the management and the many changes from time to time. I own no shares in stock Companies, neither do I wish to unless I manage the Co.

I enclose you a cheerful letter referring to one we know and love. I wish you and Pa would both write me giving me your blessing in my new arrangements. I will remain here in the factory until Jan. 1st to break in new men.

With much love, as ever E.G.H.

P.S. In this move I do not even have the excuse "on the advice of my physician," for I never was stronger and in more sturdy health.

5

"The Life Which Mortals
Seldom Know"

Alice graduated at mid-term and, since her Elbert would soon be coming
to Boston to stay, she decided to take post-graduate work at least until
the spring of 1893. They would talk it over when he arrived in early
January.

She wrote and told him, "Mrs. Tyler jumped from the lounge when
I told her tonight I was going to stay until January 1 and clapped her
hands. She kissed me on the cheek and seems so happy to have your little
girl here."

Back in Buffalo Elbert was impatiently winding up his affairs at the
Larkin Company. He had hoped to be in Boston by January 1 to start off
the new year of 1893 with a new career. Alice was counting on it too, in
terms of a new life and, eventually, a new wife for Elbert. But there
were details that caused delays and so, by January 5, Elbert was still
at the factory. His revised plans called for finishing the phase-out by the
weekend and head for Boston on Monday, January 9.

He wrote his last letter on Larkin stationery to his mother on January 5:

Buffalo, N.Y.

My Dear Mother:

I have just two more days here at the factory, and then I step down
and out. On Monday I leave for Cambridge, and as soon as I get
settled there I will write you.

Some time ago, I began writing a sociological history of the United

By 1893 the new Elbert Hubbard was emerging. He dropped his middle
initial "G," shaved off the mustache, and let his hair grow long in
theatrical fashion. He looked much younger at 37 than he had at 26.

States, and this plan has taken hold of me to a degree I cannot describe. You hear of men taking up a plan, but in this case the plan has taken up me, and you need not fear I will sigh for the soap factory and the days of yore. When the chicken is ready to leave the shell it has to go or *die,* and that is the kind of Plymouth Rock I am.

As to the History, you may have pondered the fact that what we call History, is a record of fighters, warriors, and politicians. It concerns itself with the nobility who manage the affairs of state, not the common people—when the real fact is the people are state, not the nobles; so I am writing a record of events that have influenced the popular mind. In our day, Vincent has moved the people more than Cleveland— Edison more than Blaine—Frances Willard more than Harrison. So you see, it is the *thinkers,* not the politicians, who change mankind.

I am following the advice given in Revelations I,19: ("Write the things which thou has seen, and the things which are, and the things which shall be hereafter")

With great love for you, dear Father and Mother.

I am ever your son,

EGH

As the Boston-bound train carried Elbert Hubbard ever closer to a new life on January 9, the landscape seemed to be sweeping by rather than to be approaching as something new to behold. The moving panorama would at times remind him of his trips West to woo and wed Bertha and, at other times, of his secret trips of later years to rendezvous with Alice.

A hill here would remind him of his horseback rides with his boys. Another, there, of his trysts with Alice in the hills back of East Aurora. But as the moving scenery seemed to suggest, the old life was sweeping aside and things from here on would be better for him, Bertha, the boys and, yes, even for Alice. At least now there would be an extended together- ness that would surely bring everything into better focus. He and Alice would have weeks, even months, to meet daily and see if they were meant to work together. And, if that should mean eventually live together —well—Worry about that later! Right now he had better consider how he, a grade school dropout, could enter Harvard. He had announced his plans to about everyone but the college officials! Well that, too, would have to wait until he got on the scene. There would be a way. There *had* to be a way!

Alice met the train as it arrived in Boston and as they embraced the old feeling of The Day raced through them. Their "work," their futures, could wait a bit. A *new* day had arrived and had to be celebrated. But it was late, and tomorrow would soon be at hand as would countless to- morrows together.

Elbert had a room waiting for him at Mrs. Tyler's and, of course, Alice was already staying there in a room of her own. The genial landlady was delighted, as always, to see Elbert back and thrilled to learn that he would be making Boston his home for a while. However, even though she felt a special warmth for both of them, Elbert felt he should not arouse any unnecessary suspicions and announced that he would not be staying there but would look for a rooming house where some of the college men were staying.

The next day he rented a room at 24 Mt. Auburn Street, in nearby Cambridge. Alice announced that she would be away for a few days and they registered as man and wife in a Boston hotel on January 10. They settled down to four days of togetherness in room #79.

Late at night on the 10th, after they had taken as much license as two unlicensed lovers dared, Alice wrote what her heart felt:

My Lover—
1,2,3,4   1,2,3,4

79

I had a dream which was not at all a dream.
I drank, I bathed complete in Life's Eternal stream,
Where he who drinks and bathes can't fear nor faint
Again, and Life is full and free without restraint.

I lived, I moved, I breathed. O, Life! Such bliss!
Could angels in the skies know Life like this?
My heart was joy, my body light as air,
Methinks my face and fever grew wondrous fair.

The air was filled with fragrance of sweet flowers,
No time we knew; how could *we* count the hours
Of perfect Love when cares were all forgot?
We count the hours when Allah counts them not!

There is no speech nor language, no, nor voice—
Had we ideals from which to make our choice—
That could express this world of Love, of bliss,
This Passion so Divine, this perfect, complete, kiss.
This waking but to feel Love's holy touch,
God ne'er intended we should feel but such—
This waking but to see the Loved One's face,
And form, and knowing only Love's embrace.

This breathing naught but Love's Life atmosphere,
This gentle whispering into Love's quick ear,
This highest Heaven of knowing naught but Love,
To live the Higher Life and this to prove.

This, this is the Life which mortals seldom know,
'Tis Life complete where Love has perfect flow—
'Tis Life on earth with all its dross withdrawn—
The Heaven of our Rest, the joyous Calm.

Then every place and thing seemed full of God.
All sights and sounds were but hosannah's laud.
We smiled with joy at everything we saw,
As they in Heaven, without a law.

"The time has passed and gone" did someone say?
'Tis gone we know, and yet we say them nay—
'Tis *here* in truth in heart and soul and Life,
'Tis ours forever more from life to Life.

"I had a dream which was not a dream at all a dream"—
Within my immortal soul there is a gleam
So bright of this True Life of Passion so Divine,
all else bars law
And worships at the shrine of this pure dream
Which was not at all a dream
But purest truth and Love which human heart can know
When kindled with Love Divine by Passion given by God.

To My Beloved One   Jan. 10.—

1,2,3,4   1,2,3,4

79

The ecstasy was repeated for three days more . . . 1, 2, 3, 4 . . . and
that symbol henceforth appeared on their love letters for years to come.
There was to be a step #5, the complete abandonment, and Alice would
explain it one day in the future . . . and it *would* come to pass.

The sweet and reckless togetherness of "79" had to give way to the
realities of life. Alice had to get back to her classes at Emerson College
of Oratory and Elbert had to see about enrolling at Harvard. They left
their dream world but they took with them, as a love souvenir, the quartz
room plate from the door of 79. They had been each other's there, and
it belonged to them.

Upon inquiring at the Harvard registrar's office, Elbert found that he
could enroll only as a special student, and then only if he could obtain
satisfactory letters of recommendation from back home. Discouraged but
not dismayed, he did arrange to sit in on some lectures and generally
observe Harvard campus life.

On January 16 he penned a note to his mother which skirted the truth
enough to be reasonably truthful. It was about all he could do under the
circumstances and especially in view of his optimistic letter to her of
January 5. He reasoned that he would make it all come true and, in due
course, he did, making letter explanations unnecessary.

Cambridge, Mass.
1/16/1893

My Dear Mother:

I find that the transition into the realm of books has been so gradual with me, that I meet and mix with the best here on a perfect equality; at once I am at home and among my friends and brothers, for who is my brother save him who thinks as I do? If there is any such thing as taking advantage of a tenderfoot here, I have not seen it. On the contrary, I have discovered this—that there are several societies among the students, and these societies appoint committees to greet all new comers and assist them in any way possible. Such a committee greeted me, and they offered to show me anything about the buildings or grounds that I desired to see and to introduce me to any of the professors, and one of the questions they asked me was, "What subject are you insane on?" Which being interpreted means that if I happen to be a crank on Temperance, Socialism, Religion or any peculiar phase of thought, they would introduce me to others similarly affected. Y.M.C.A. also has a branch among the students who greet new comers.

There are men among the students fifty years old and over, so I am simply classed as one of the boys.

The place is more cosmopolitan than I expected—for there are green horns here as bad as any Normalite you ever saw. Then there is the fast set, rich men's sons, who come with their servants, and live in sumptuous apartments, only about 200 of these however and they are not looked on with much favor by either faculty or students. A good many students are working their way through college, acting as waiters, hostlers, etc., but the great majority, say 2000, are here to get all of the benefit they can at the least expense, yet live well, dress well and have all they need.

I see more of the truth of the maxim that God helps those who help themselves. The world does help a man where it sees he is in earnest, and there is a vast deal of kindness and good nature in the rough and tumble life, after all. If I ask any one here the way to a certain place, the answer always is, "Why, I am going there myself."

Will have to return to Aurora in a few days to arrange some loans I am making, but I will write you again as soon as I get permanently settled here.

With much love, my dear mother, to you and Pa,

I am your son,

E.G.H.

Shortly thereafter, Elbert went home for a few days during which he talked with friends about the possibility of needing letters of recommendation so that he could satisfy Harvard's entrance requirements in full by the fall term when he would be signing up for more courses than he was presently taking. There was no rush, he explained.

Returning to Boston, he discussed the Harvard situation with Alice
and it was decided he should enroll as a special student at ECO. There
would be no difficulty there. She had just recently graduated from the
school, was well known by then to Dr. Emerson himself and was currently
taking graduate studies there. On January 31 Elbert signed the enrollment
application at ECO and this substituted for Harvard for the moment.
But he had avowed his intentions to attend Harvard for four years and
would start making it come true in the fall even if it meant fictional
Harvard attendance for the present. And, besides, ECO *was* a college
and he would be better preparing himself for Harvard.

Elbert now had everything . . . and nothing. His love for literature
and learning had swept him into a physical loving of a learned spinster.
His love for his children kept him ever mindful of the love that brought
them into the world. It was now a lingering, yet disturbing, love for
Bertha.

Alice couldn't have believed or understood it, but her ardent Elbert
was lonesome for his wife and sons. Bertha recognized that she had at
least temporarily lost him to a dream but her heart beat more hopefully
when she read the letters he began sending back home—ostensibly to the
boys. His instructions to them were obviously designed to make life less
hectic for her and the awkward endings seemed to carry clumsy but real
words of love to her as well as to the boys. With the oldest boy, Bertie,
being only in his eleventh year, Elbert knew that Bertha would have to
read aloud his letters to them. Bertha understood this too. The letters
were for her and the boys. As he wrote, Elbert was unconsciously trying
to convince himself that he knew the real reason he was in Boston was
to gain knowledge.

On February 1, 1893, he wrote to Bertie, Ralph and Sanford.

24 Mt. Auburn St.
Cambridge, Mass.
Feb. 1, 1893

My Dear Boys:
    Your Papa has gone away a hunting to get a rabbit skin to wrap the
three boys in. Some men hunt for rabbits—some for bears—some for
dollars—and some for knowledge. I am going to College that I may
have knowledge. Men who know many things and who can use their
knowledge are smart men we say. They can take care of themselves
and of others—they should be good men too, for knowledge shows us
what we should do and what not. Bertie can figure up his accounts now
and count money so people cannot cheat him. Walluf [sic, meaning
Ralph] can count to 15 and Sanford to 13 and there are lots of full
grown men who can only count three.
    When Sanford and Walluf go to school next spring they will be
getting knowledge.
    Men who have knowledge can make money and they are respected
and liked by other men. Wherever they go—to any part of the world—

they find friends for people are always anxious to be on good terms with learned men. Now no matter how smart a man is there is something else he should have and that is *system* which is only putting things in the right places at the proper time so you can find them easily when wanted. My boys will be men some day and I want them to be strong, healthy men, but I want them to be good men who people will be glad to know. So I want them to practice *system* now, and I want my three boys to begin now to do this: Put their clothes at night always in one place—each boys by themselves. Wallup at one end of the bewlow [sic, meaning bureau]—Sanford's at the other and Bertie's on a chair— then each boy in the morning get his clothes and dress himself as soon as he gets up. *Mamma has not to say a word to you about what you shall do after you get up.* Wallup is like his Pop wakes up early like the bantam rooster that crows before it is light. Wallup can wake Whutchie [Bertie] and Whutchie can wake the Snoozer [sic, meaning Sanford] who likes to snooze—then each boys dress himself at once without monkeying with each other, and without Mamma telling how.

Now do this boys & please begin tonight to put away your clothes in one place and Bertie must write and tell me about it. With much love to you all.

E. G. Hubbard

P.S. Tomorrow I will write and ask you to do something else. I will be back in just four weeks and I want to see how well you can carry out my wishes.

They had scarcely had time to digest that letter when their father sent this one.

Thursday, Feb. 3

My Dear Boys 3.

I wrote you a letter a day or so ago about putting your clothes always in one place at night, so you can find them at once in the morning. Now Mamma will not scold you nor tell you to dress but just once—that is all.

Each boy, must dress himself 'cept Whutchie and he can take his Klose out to the barn and let Baba [the hired man] dress him if he can't do it himself but then I guess he can. Then after each boy is dressed he must wash his own hands and face good with soap and water and use the towel. Then Mamma will at once comb his hair and part it carefully in the middle for all of the Harvard boys part their hair so. Mamma will not tell any boy to wash his face but just once for that is enough. Why should she say it a dozen times? If I tell Baba something once that is enough so I want Bertie to write me and tell me if each boy is putting his Klose in one place each night and then dressing himself in the morning and washing his hands and face and if Mamma combs each of the three towseled heads as soon as the boys are dressed and parts each boys hair in the middle like at Harvard. When the snoozer comes here he will join the football team and be the biggest and strongest boy in the school. He will have a hand nearly as big as a ham and a foot in proportion. He will not move as fast as Ralph but will be very sure—The boys will all like him and the teachers will like him. When not in school he will wear a sweater—blue with a big red H on the breast. Then when he gets thro school he will go into a lawyer's office in Boston and study law—he will be a Counsellor and a great many men will go to him for advice and he will make lots of money. He will have lots of books and will never chew tobacco nor smoke nor drink beer but will go to church once on Sunday and will read his books and do his work well and people will like him and will say

Sanford Hubbard of Boston—is a great and good man.

The next letter I will tell you something else I want you to do and will tell you what Ralph will do, then after that Bertie. With Much love to your Mamma and you all, I am, ever yours, EGH

In mid-February Elbert moved from 24 Mt. Auburn Street to 98 Austin Street in Cambridge. On the 20th of that month he took a trip to Concord, Massachusetts, where he met the aged Hosmer sisters whose father had been close to Ralph Waldo Emerson and to Thoreau. He dined at their home and enjoyed seeing first editions of Thoreau's works. Concord, Emerson, Thoreau and Hosmer—these names would all play a future role in the lives of Elbert and Alice.

On February 26, just before another trip back home to East Aurora, he sent a long letter to son Bertie (who also would one day know more about Concord—more than either he or his father could now imagine).

Cambridge, Feb. 25

My Dear Bertie—

Once upon a time a little over a hundred years ago there lived here in Cambridge a young fellow by the name of Paul Revere. What is now the United States belonged to England then just as Canada does now, but King George of England had been making it so unpleasant for the people here that they had decided to have a government of their own and let old King George go to the bow-wows. So the folks here got a big lot of guns and shot and bullets and caps and cannons and powder and swords and knives and packed 'em away up in Concord a place just the size of E. Aurora and the same distance from Boston that E A is from Buffalo. The British heard of this and sent a lot of soldiers around to Boston in boats with orders to go up to Concord and grab on to the guns and things. The Americans did not know that the British would go to Concord but they thought they might and if they did they were going to make it hot for them. Well, Paul Revere and his chum a young fellow about 20 arranged that Paul should stay on the north side of the Charles River about two miles from here at a place called Charlestown and his pard would watch for the "red coats" (that is what they called the English soldiers 'cause they wore red coats and tall fur caps) in Boston and when they came he would climb up the steeple of the old North Church and hang two lanterns which would mean—Pally old boy the red coats are here and are getting ready to go for you fellows across the river in Middlesex County.

Paul had a black horse with two white hind feet and a white star in his forehead, and he saddled up this horse and walked along the river to watch for the light. He led his horse back and forth and it was awful dark and cold to [sic] being in April, it rained a little and the black horse didn't like it to be out so late just standing around. And Paul kept looking across the river toward the church. By and by he thought he saw a light glimmer away up in the steeple—then he stopped and looked. Yes he said—but no—what yes—great Scott there are two lanterns. He stared at them a moment and pinched himself to see that he was awake, the two little lights away across there looked peaceful enough but they meant the red coats are after you. Paul reached his left foot into the stirrup and leapt into the saddle at a bound, the black horse snorted and Paul clapped the spurs to him as he never did before and the sparks flew from beneath his hoofs as he ran toward the Lexington road that goes to Concord—Lord how that horse did run. Some soldiers heard him coming before he had got out of Charlestown and they rushed out and tried to stop him, he slashed one of them across the face as the black horse flew past and Paul laid flat across the horse's neck for he knew they would shoot and they did—bang—bang—whiz—whiz went the bullets over his head and on he went, stopping at the first farm house where he pulled up riding right up on the porch and pounding with the butt of his whip on the door and the old farmer tumbled out of bed and called "whose there" [sic]—"The British are Coming" yelled Paul and on he went to the next house and there he just smashed in a pane of glass and yelled "the red coats are coming." This he did at every house all the way to Concord. When he got to Concord the sun was just coming up and at the same time the red coats started to march to Concord—200 of them all armed with muskets. They marched by fours so you see there were fifty of these fours. They hadn't gone far before bang—bang went a shot gun from behind a stone fence and before they could see what was what bang bang it went again and all the way to Concord the farmers that Paul Revere aroused kept giving it to them, about half of them got to Concord however and found the stuff they expected to capture had all been carried off, and then at a red [sic] bridge that crosses Concord River the farmers made a stand and drove the red coats back to Boston.

Now this was the first battle of the Revolutionary War. George Washington was the Commander of the American forces—he lived way off in Virginia but he was a good soldier and smartest man in the Country, so they sent for him to come up here and take charge of the army, he did so and under an elm tree which still stands there is a monument about half a mile from where I write and it says

Under this tree Geo. Washington assumed
command of the American forces

Well, what I wanted to tell you was that there is a large and beautiful statue of a farmer in his shirt sleeves with a musket in his hands near the bridge in Concord. This marks the place where the farmers stood. The statue cost $5,000.00 and was all paid for by

Ebenezer Hubbard who owns the land on which the statue stands. This Hubbard is a distant relative of ours. I rode Snowball over the same road that Paul Revere went over from Charlestown to Concord. Some of the same houses stand yet that Paul stopped at but the folks that lived there have moved away.

Don't you think Bertie that Paul and his pard were fine fellows?

EGH

Elbert found the courses at Emerson College of Oratory interesting enough but he was anxious to write and spent more time at his rooming house working on manuscripts for two novels, *No Enemy But Himself* and *One Day*. In the evenings he would meet Alice and they would go over the plots together. In many respects these stories, like *The Man*, were autobiographical and reflected the thoughts they were thinking about themselves and others.

By early March Alice was obliged to concentrate more on her post-graduate course and Elbert was preoccupied with his writing. He returned home, telling Bertha that he would be returning to Cambridge—and Harvard—in September and in the meantime would fix up a room in the attic where he could work on two novels he expected to sell.

He made considerably more progress on his manuscripts there even though he had to take time out to write daily letters to Alice. Sometimes he rode horseback to neighboring post offices to mail them or would take a trip to Buffalo to do so. Letters from Alice came to him addressed to a post office box in a nearby hamlet. There was no turning back from this entanglement now and he knew it. And the deceit bothered him for he knew he loved both Alice and Bertha.

He spent more and more time in his room and writing was now an escape as much as it had been a dream. He wrote at a furious pace and then, as Alice's letters became more insistent, he decided he had better get back to Boston and talk over their futures.

He told Bertha that he needed to do some research there and also wanted to visit some book publishers. He would be away for a few weeks. By March 31 he was back in Cambridge.

Alice sensed that their deeper sexual involvement, while strengthening her hold on Elbert in one way, was weakening it in another. The urge for more knowledge and the freedom to write had brought them together. That initial motivation was still the strongest urge of *her* "husband" just as it was for Bertha's.

She resolved not to make the same mistake that she knew Bertha had made back in 1890 when the early symptoms were showing. She would now continue to whet and satisfy the physical appetite and continue to whet the intellectual appetite but permit Elbert to satisfy the latter in whatever way he, at the moment, might consider best. After all, even though he was better able than ever before to do his own research, writing, and rewriting, she was still the only close one to whom he could turn for help in such things when that should become necessary. Her Elbert was improving but was by no means experienced as a writer. Immediate physical love was her insurance. Stand-by intellectual help was her best reinsurance. It wasn't cunning opportunism on Alice's part. It was genuine love of a kind that creates a resourcefulness for serving, winning, and holding—legally or otherwise.

In bed, then, she told him of her resolve to give up the idea of romping the Elysian fields with him. She had applied for a teaching position at Potsdam (N.Y.) State Normal School and was accepted on the faculty there for the fall term. He should seriously pursue his Harvard ambitions in the fall, be free to write in the evenings, and they could visit back and forth. She would faithfully help him with his manuscripts and research by mail in between visits.

How sweet and sensible of Alice! How promising the future! Elbert went back home in a confident frame of mind. Somehow his relationship with Alice seemed to be now back on that higher plane where it had started, notwithstanding the now much deeper sexual relationship. Alice was his literary wife and Bertha the wife of his home—the loving and devoted mother of the sons he loved with her.

In May, buoyant with freedom and aspiration, he made a quick business trip to Chicago and while there visited his sisters Daisy and Mary. He arranged to stay, in June, at Mary's home and from there take in the World's Fair.

So it was that, toward the end of May, Elbert, Bertha, the boys and Elbert's friend, Rev. Brown, all took the sleeper to Chicago. It was like a traveling family reunion and it made the long trip to Chicago seem short.

After the family visited the fair together, Bertha and the boys went on to visit her folks and Elbert's. With his aged cleric friend, Elbert stayed at his sister Mary's home for most of the month. They visited the fair by day and engaged in intellectual discussions at dinner with Daisy, Mary, and Mary's educator-lawyer husband William R. Heath. Mary was always especially fond of her brother and was pleased to see how much more articulate and intellectually broadened he had become.

6

"...And We Were Like Bees Drowned in Honey"

Alice was back home for part of the summer of 1893 and she and Elbert resumed their trysts in the hills back of East Aurora and in the hotels of Buffalo although, after returning from Chicago, Elbert devoted more and more time to his writing and to insuring his admission to Harvard in the fall.

On July 1 he wrote to Harvard and told of his successful business career, stating that now, at the age of 37, "I desire to enter as a Special student in the fall term to gain enlightenment in history, law, government and economics." He gave as a reference Dr. Brown, Episcopal Bishop Vincent, 445 Franklin Street, Buffalo and William C. Conwell, President, City Bank of Buffalo.

On July 12 the registrar wrote to Hubbard asking about his scholastic credentials. He wrote back saying, "I never attended any school except in childhood" and then recited in more detail his business success and added that he had organized Chautauqua Circles and had been president of one for ten years. He summed it up by saying, "I now have the leisure but not much culture."

Meanwhile, on July 15 both the Rev. Dr. Brown and the Rev. Mr. John A. Sayles, Jr., pastor of the First Universalist Church of East Aurora, wrote letters of recommendation directly to Harvard.

Dr. Brown said, "He has excellent moral character in East Aurora and Buffalo," and went on to praise Hubbard's mind and writing ability and to state that Harvard "wouldn't be sorry" if they accepted him.

Rev. Mr. Sayles was less detailed, but equally positive in his recommendation. He said "I know him through and through, his moral character is excellent."

By July 19, Elbert had a formal application to complete. It was a sign that he could be accepted as a special student at Harvard that fall.

One question on the application asked, "Why do you want to attend as a special student?" Hubbard put it simply. "I do not care for degrees and the discipline of regular curriculum." He hadn't really known this until his earlier rebuff at Harvard and his brief experience at Emerson College of Oratory.

As if to pique the curiosity of a school dedicated to preparing persons to succeed, he pointed out again and again how successful he had been in business and "having all the money I want" desired their assistance in pursuing a cultural life.

By and large, Elbert belonged more to Bertha and the boys that summer than he did to Alice, but the "off limits" rule that he placed on his garret room caused Bertha to recognize that he had sealed her off from a part of his life. Still, he was at home more now, even if he wasn't as completely communicative as he had once been. If she had bothered to unlock the door while he was out she would have found boxes of letters from Alice and would have unlocked the secrets of the past three years.

Early that warm September Elbert and Alice met at the Broezel Hotel in Buffalo and had their last reunion before she left to take up her duties at Potsdam State Normal as a teacher of reading and calisthenics and he to take special studies at Harvard. It was another deep 1,2,3,4 intimacy that renewed Alice's love insurance on Elbert. Somehow, he felt obliged to pay the premium which was getting higher all the time in terms of self-denunciation and hopeless entanglement that changed his spring buoyancy to inner turmoil that fall. It was heightened by the knowledge that once away in Boston he would miss Bertha and the boys. He would also miss Alice. He would be truly alone.

When Elbert returned to Boston in mid-September he took over the room that Alice had occupied at Mrs. Tyler's. He set himself to the task of completing the details of entering Harvard and bearing down hard on the writing of his two manuscripts as well as shaping up two articles to submit to magazines.

He likened their separation to his being on land, with only his horse for company, while she put out to sea for an exciting voyage.

MWD—

As I write you are on the briny deep—putting [out] for open sea. I sit on this old log and Snowball is tied to yonder tree.

I think of you and wonder why I love you. I have been endeavoring to formulate the reason and can only do so negatively. For your charm for me lies not on the features of your loving face, nor in the tall, agile graceful figure, nor in the varieties of expression that play across your face, nor in your wit and words of wisdom. Nor yet in the faint love perfume that intoxicates, not the thrill that comes warm and flush when we clasp hands, nor in the tropical excess of sublime emotion, but it seems to be that there in your soul for me is perfect truth and having no guile yourself you attribute none to me, thus I am benefitted and strengthened.

Tell me of your trip Dear, and of Potsdam and your boarding place and all the good people you meet.

Alice, an experienced and able teacher—and not wholly without guile—quickly adjusted to her new job and had ample time to fill, by mail, the void she knew existed in Elbert's lonely, uncertain new life.

The recent Buffalo reunion, coupled with an expression of what he had done for her, were the subjects of one of her first letters to him from Potsdam.

At Evening

Darling,

Are there times come to you that you have no words to describe when the Hush of Love takes you into the very gate of Heaven? You drop everything and are unconscious of all but that—the Love that lifts you from all of earth and you are only conscious of the Beloved and the Heaven. You understand and read between the lines all I would tell you, for I have no words at all to express it. I send the thoughts and feeling to you now—6:15 P.M. and I know you feel it. It has come to me several times today with such intensity as I never felt before when away from you.

All day long I have looked for you feeling sure you must be coming. Have listened for your foot on the stairs and then would recollect myself that you *could* not come. I have seemed to live only in the spirit and wholly with you all day and forgot the impossibilities which flesh make. Have you not felt my arms about your neck—my face against yours all the time today? And how peaceful and still and full of Rest the Day is. The Reaction of the week of action is wonderful today. How glorious, O how glorious Life is! Floods and floods of light have come in quick succession this past week, and today I seem to have felt the reaction of it all.

How holy our desires and longings may become. We cease to fear that we may become evil, for the good seems to envelop us so that we have the faith that we shall become like Him.

Custodian quoted in her letter from "Light of the World"—and I read this between the lines, that the old tempest and unrest and tossing was subsiding and that Peace was beginning to be with her.

Dearest, I want to write those same lines to you tonight with a positive meaning. You know, Beloved, that the tossing long ago—more than two years—ceased with me. That in that sense, "Peace began to be" for you and me when your spirit first rushed to meet mine. We did not know what it was, but there was a sureness of life, of God, of Eternal Love, we never had before. We were unconscious that it was so then, but I began to lift up my head into purer air. Do you know, dear, I owe my physical life to you? You put out the rope to a drowning man the last year I taught in E.A. before school closed, and

I should have given up the struggle at Sachem's Head had not your letters come. I will tell you some time. But that "Peace" was in a sense negative—it was getting up on to moving ground.

Read all that I quote intensely for it means laying hold of that which _has_ entered within the vale, beyond the gates—into no. 4 near 5.

> Peace beginning to be
> Deep as the sleep of the sea
> When the stars their faces glass
> In its blue tranquility:
> Hearts of men upon earth
> Never once still from their birth,
> To rest as the wild waters rest
> With the colors of Heaven on their breast!
>
> Love, which is _sunlight of peace_
> Age by age to increase
> 'Til angers and hatred are dead
> And sorrow and death shall cease
>
> "_Peace_ on earth and good will!"
> Souls that are _gentle_ and _Still_
> Hear the _first music_ of this
> _Far-off, Infinite Bliss!_

Our little clock has said 1 2 3 4 all day, so happy and so full of hope and it never stops or flags. I used one spoon and our cup tonight but I hurried for it lacked someone so terribly.

I l y D—I l y D.

Elbert took careful note of Alice's recounting of what he had done for her and the reward of intimacy that had been gratefully given him. And now, she was directing his thoughts to step 5. This would be the completeness that would have her bear a child by him if only he would take the step. Had she been there in his room, saying what she had written, it would have happened that night!

The letters between them that fall were frequent and poignant. They mixed love teases with manuscript exchanges as Alice began to hint at literary aspirations of her own.

On Monday, September 26, Elbert wrote to Alice at Potsdam and told her of his decision to move from Mrs. Tyler's to another boarding house, at 1734 Cambridge Street operated by Mrs. "Mother" Gavin. He also gave her his appraisal of a story "Ginny" she had written and sent to him.

. . . Dear—a minute please—on my knees, there, so—have you noticed that neither you nor yours can write excepting from our own experiences? It is only of ourselves we care to write. Neither of us have [sic] enough Imagination to make John Smith's trials our own.

. . . There is material here for a fine story. The restless groping spirit is well set forth and will find a kindredness in all who read—

for we are all gropers. Well do you ask, "why do we go here or there?"

Yes Dear I think you can write because you have felt and lived. You should not try to do much of it now though. You have enough to do in producing "results." Of course the teachers are plastic in your hands. So are we all, all of us. Hear! Here!

****

I am not at 149 as you see by this heading. Mrs. T. wanted $4.00 and can get it from others. I pay $3.00 here and have cheap board too—but good. Have a room by myself in a nest of law students, several of whom are near as old as me but none so good looking. They have given me a hearty Greeting—Profs as well—I will do little (if any) writing but will mix closely with these men and get as much from the lectures as possible. A year is all I can stand any way—but I will make the most of it.

Elbert, scarcely underway as a college man, was already having second thoughts as to this new way of life and was already cutting down his planned attendance from four years to one. He clipped a Browning quotation from the newspaper and enclosed it with his letter to Alice.

HELPS TO HIGH LIVING

Sun.—Peace means power.
Mon.—Work must stand or stumble by intrinsic worth.
Tues.—He who stoops lowest may find most.
Wed.—Bring new good, new beauty, from the old.
Thurs.—Endeavor to be good, and better still, and best.
Fri.—In the delaying of an ill lurks cure.
Sat.—The great mind knows the power of gentleness.
                                        —Browning

Elbert had told Alice that her writing attempts always seemed to be autobiographical. Now he was being autobiographical himself through his concentration on these somewhat contradictory lines of Browning! Somehow, they seemed to sum up his own mixed thoughts and emotions which wouldn't otherwise add up in his mood of loneliness. These were reasons and objectives, and solace, to two persons who knew Browning better than themselves.

When Alice had left Boston earlier that year she left some of her personal belongings with Elbert who stored them in his trunk at Mrs. Tyler's. She knew she would be visiting him on weekends that fall when she could get away from her teaching chores at Potsdam. In his new boarding house Elbert was unpacking the trunk and, seeing Alice's clothing and packets of their earlier love letters, his despondency deepened for still another day. The next morning he stayed in his room and wrote to Alice. He answered a letter from her in which she had reminded him that she had left the Methodist Church in Boston and might not join any in Potsdam. He also told her of the great loneliness that unpacking the trunk had brought upon him.

There was a banality to the love lines that showed Elbert at his worst; a pathetic low ebb that found him groping for meaning to their affair consistent with a lingering desire to be not immoral.

> 1734 Cambridge St.
> Wednesday AM

Dear One. I am sorry you told the Methody Mufti that you took a letter from the Methody Mosque and then destroyed it. You did not destroy Methodism by leaving it, child, although it lost its best member when you walked down the church steps.

The Mosque did not decay and tumble at once either Dear, for its members, I heard a few weeks ago, were engaged in a very lively fight among themselves—the Mufti wanted baksheesh that was due him and the members were divided among themselves as to whether he should be paid. You did not destroy the letter they gave you either Dear, for I found it last night and read it Dear—it was in a trunk I have and it was the only secular thing in the trunk—all else was holy.

It was the first great pleasure I have known for weeks and weeks, the unpacking of that trunk. There was an Alpha but no Omicron— or Omega I mean. No end was there to the treasures. On my knees I looked and searched and wept over the treasures but Dear—it needs two to unpack a trunk. One to comment on the things and cry over them and 'tother one to hand 'em out. What a Columbus I was on that voyage of discovery through the Love trunk. I warmed my hands in your old muff or tried to and I handled the hats very tenderly and wrapped the red skirt around my neck to keep off all bad influences. Then when I lifted out a coat that looked as if it would fit me a blue dress actually clung to it and insisted on coming too. They refused to be parted Dear. God help us Dear, we not only believe that dumb animals and trees and flowers have souls but inanimate things as well. No wonder Dr. Stowell trembled for his Catholic friends. You would have corrupted the Youth of Athens with your paganism.

Then there was a garment called a "vest" but if I would go to a store and ask for a vest or a "weskitt" I would be given something different. Why do they call it a vest Dear? Never mind. I buried my face in it and will try it on tonight when I take my cold bath. A beautiful piece of white quartz bears simply the mark of "79." Tenderly and reverently I wrapped it in the tissue paper and laid it away.

"... Well Dear I want to go right to the RR and buy a ticket to Potsdam"

That last week of September 1893 was one of deep torment for Elbert. For the first time in many years he was completely alone. He didn't have much in common with the young men in a new boarding house. He missed his sons and his wife. College life was looking sour even before he had officially signed in and paid his tuition. He had Alice's belongings in his trunk but they served only to remind him that she was in Potsdam and that their original bond of literary interest had somehow become a sexual relationship that wasn't being satisfied except through his increasingly unlofty love letters. On Friday, September 29, he mailed a letter that he had pencilled the night before to Alice. His hand had trembled as he dashed it off. The trembling was reflected in both his handwriting and his critical self-analysis.

> Merciful Christ! Thou who didst die that men might live—even Thou, God that canst not breath into *my* nostrils the breath of life.
> Like Lazarus of old—once I was dead. A woman with the sunlight of love called "Arise" and I awoke to life.
> But Lazarus did not live always. Neither could I.
> I am only half a man—a demnition coward at that, afraid of wind and storm and the wild billows roar.
> I have left the last year's dwelling—not for the new, but for none at all but the blue canopy of heaven. I have no home, I have no child, I have no wife, I have no friend.
> I have a patient white horse and she carries my material form and is glad to do it but this is all she can do. My soul is dead.
> I know my weakness. I know yours. On land with my white horse I am partly safe although I can do no mighty work on account of the unbelief of the people. Then there is no one who believes in me save you, and you and I cannot live together on land.
> We could enter the galleons and worship on the sea but who would helm the ship? Not you, for you can barely baffle the storms of the land. Not I, for have I not told you I am a demnition coward and *need* help? We are both weak at the same time, and as for swimming, I have told you many times I cannot swim without some one holds a hand under my chin. In the water we would clutch each other and go to the bottom instanter.
> Spiritually the bond is perfect—physically we are too weak to stand against the storm. Each time we have met you have been undone and we were like bees drowned in honey.
> If you could be strong when I am weak it would do, but see how it was the last time we met in Buffalo!
> I have said I have no friend—better you are my *Friend* and I am yours. True and noble woman that you are you will help me all you can.
> God knows I am yours and there has been no sacrilege—no dishonor. Where Love is there is God. At the final Judgement I will present this love as my sole Credential.

Part of Elbert's mood of wretchedness stemmed from the fact that he and Alice had already been talking about spending the still distant holidays of Thanksgiving and Christmas together: Thanksgiving at Potsdam and Christmas at Boston. It troubled him deeply for he was getting in deeper and already feeling that special lonesomeness that holiday separations from the family always bring. Yet, with it all, he could see no immediate way to change his course. His love for Alice was his despair and yet his only hope. He closed his letter with a decision in her favor.

Yes come on December 23. Mrs. Tyler will have a room for you. *She is our friend.* I have the trunk, desk, chair and lamp. The pictures and things in the drawer I left but she will take care of them for you. She has a high regard for you Dear—*very* high.

Midst the torment of that week Elbert did find some rays of hope with respect to finding the sympathetic ear of a publisher. He visited the Arena Publishing Company on Boston's Copley Square. They published the monthly *Arena* magazine as well as small books known as the "Side Pocket Series."

Elbert was successful in meeting the editor and publisher, B. O. Flower. The latter agreed to look over Elbert's manuscript for his short novel, *One Day,* and to consider any articles he cared to submit for the magazine. At the week's end Elbert's spirits were up again and he followed his gloomy letter with one that was more cheering to Alice. He told of his experience at the Arena.

I called on the Arena people yesterday. Spent over two hours with them. Their offices are in a brown stone building just across from the Art Building on Copley Square.

General Boyce, the Manager, is 55—came from San Francisco five years ago. His daughter first reads all Ms—if good she hands it over to the Editor, Mr. Flower for final decision. She is a bright girl, 25 I should say.

Now listen—"You was [sic] born in Boston Mr. Flower?"

"No, in Illinois."

"Indeed! Where?"

"At Albion, about fifty miles south of Bloomington, in 1856."

"But Mr. Flower, a mud country cannot produce a poet."

"Yes, Mr. Hubbard—they have told me so here so I confine myself to prose."

"So do I for the same reason."

"What reason?"

"Because I was born at Bloomington, Ill. in 1856!"

On Sunday, October 1, Elbert Green Hubbard, a man without a family, arose early and walked across the Charles River bridge to go to church. Appropriately, he was going to hear a sermon by Rev. Edward Everett Hale, a Harvard graduate, pastor of the South Congregational Church and author—most notably of the story "The Man Without a Country." Hale, then 71, had come to that pastorate in 1856 and had become a legend in his time.

Arriving over in the city early, Elbert made himself comfortable at a writing desk in the lobby of the Vendome Hotel and, on their stationery, penned a letter to Alice before church. It wasn't a love letter. It was a more thoughtful critique of Alice's *Ginny* manuscript. This one written with the new-found confidence of an author who had found a new publisher. The mood of the letter was also set by the day. The overtones were religious.

Sunday, 10 AM

MWD

I have come over here to hear Dr. Hale. A splendid bracing walk across the bridge in the stiff cool breeze. While waiting for the sermon time what better can I do than write to you?

Ginny—I have gone over the Ms again. Very sweet and tender are the passages describing the simplicity—the fear—the groping—the unrest. It appeals to *me* just as it is. If I was a publisher my criticisms would be these:

We describe simplicity, fear, groping, etc., not because there is virtue in these things but because we desire to use them as a foil or background to set off virtues. At the last of the story you show how a light came from Heaven—and you thus prove by inference that God recognized the worth of this soul even though men did not. This last touch is the saving salt in the whole narration. But there is not enough of the salt. You have confined yourself too near the truth. The one essential in fiction is *Forward Movement*. This excites expectation—anticipation. Then if you can have your character do the unexpected you succeed. Ginny is simple, dull and fearful. Naturally the reader would look for a simple, dull and weak action on his part. Surprise them by allowing him to rise for an instant and show the God in him and the story is immortal. Dear, tell me, is not the object of literature to show the God in Man?

Glance for a moment at the books that have moulded men. The New Testament (largely fiction says Matthew Arnold. We are shown the ideal Jesus, not the real but fiction is often the purest truth).

We cling to the Man Jesus because he was an outcast, a shadow on his birth—from over the hills of Galilee he came—"Is not this the carpenter's son?"—poor, despised, forsaken, helpless, torn, bleeding. "My God! My God! Why hast thou forsaken me?"—the cry of utter despair —they spit upon him—the crown of thorns—the buffetings by the brutal soldiers when he was bound. Alas, need I tell them? Look at his virtues, his gentleness, his patience, his courage.

If MWD will write a pure work of Imagination and picture by contrast as the New Testament does—the book will live. No man such as Hamlet ever breathed but still he lives.

Read Uncle Tom and Eva—where Tom *listens* and *understands*. *The Hunchback*. Fishing Jimmie and all the rest where weakness proves strength. This is Ideal—such characters are not found in real life. See Maartens "God's Fool." King Lear and Cordelia, Cinderella.

Henry James tells a story of an artist in Paris who was a Realist and wanted his sketches all made from the genuine. ("The Real Thing" is the name of the story.) He finds the "real thing" but is obliged to fall back on the made up beggar as the genuine is wholly unfitted for artistic purposes. You must take the "real" and add to and take off, and if you are strong enough and not too much, the picture will have a place on the Salon walls he says.

My Dear, Ginny has great merit and if you don't look sharp I will absorb it and seize it bodily and work it up as my own. I propose to make Ginny turn to children for companionship—play with them and be one of them—have him shun all grown folks and then have him do a great and heroic act to save a child—and then I'll send you the story and you can add the final touch as you always do to make it right. You are a Dear Noble good girl and I love you very much Dear—more today than ever it seems.

Having thus jotted down a little sermon of his own to Alice, Elbert posted it and went to hear a man he respected; a man who had entered Harvard at the age of thirteen. As he listened to the music before the sermon, Elbert was still thinking about what he had just written to Alice about the real and the unreal, fiction and truth. He mused about his own growing inability to separate the two in his everyday life.

Walking back from church, headed for his lonely rooming house was like a return to reality. His thoughts turned to Bertha and the boys back in East Aurora. Had they been to church too? What might they be doing this very moment? What were their thoughts about their husband and father? What would those thoughts be if *they* could discern between truth and fiction? Where would this whole unreal business end for everyone involved?

Elbert spent a miserable afternoon with his conscience and, as dusk fell, he wrote his second letter of that long, long day. It was to his son Bertie.

Sunday, October 1, 1893
1734 Cambridge St.

My Dear Bertie:

The Dartmouth football team played the Harvards yesterday and the Harvards won—16 to 0. Both sides did a lot of slugging and the umpire sent two men from the field for butting other fellows in the bread basket.

It is an awful rough game though—lots of men get hurt at it. When you come here you can play ball and tennis or row on the river but you had better leave football alone although there is this advantage in it that the men who play football get four meals a day which would suit the Snoozer.

I have been pretty near homesick today. I wanted to see my boys and the boy's Mamma but I didn't cry although I came pretty near it.

I walked over to Boston, to Dr. Hales church and back. It is three miles over and four miles back as the wind was blowing strong from the West and on the long bridge over the Charles River the breeze gets a straight sweep.

You boys must work and look after things well while I am away. Help Mamma all you can and do not quarrel anymore than seems necessary.

I want you to look after the work in the chicken house just as you have been doing. Do not fail to feed the rabbits at least twice a day.

Be a good boy and someday we may live down near Boston; you will go to college and wear a sweater with a great big H on the breast.

Yours Always,
Elbert G. Hubbard, Sr.

The letter was posted at 9:45 P.M., after which Elbert turned his thoughts to the special courses for which he would sign up at the Harvard Bursar's office during the first week of October. By Thursday, October 5, he had done it! There, in his possession, was an official Harvard receipt, issued to E. G. Hubbard and signed by the Bursar. It said simply, "Mr. E. G. Hubbard has given the security required from a Special Student in Harvard College," but to Elbert it was an accomplishment that turned fiction to truth. One by one that week, he had signed up for, and had heard lectures in, English I, English II, English 24 and Philosophy.

The new student was anxious to relate his experiences at Harvard and Alice was thus insured a steady flow of notes and letters. About Professor Kittredge he wrote:

MWD—
Prof. Kittredge today said that "Browning and his wife had separate workshops. Neither ever showed the other his work while it was in progress. They worked in the same line and were rivals for the world's favor and wishing to retain each others they never mixed in a way that might cause literary jealousy for one is as 'touchy' about his poem as a mother is of her child. A mother will receive hints from a woman who has had children but never from a woman whose babe is the same age of her own."
MWD what do you think of Prof K's logic?

Elbert gave Alice a clue about how *he* felt. He slipped in another brief note that said, "Dear, I thought you might prefer to work Ginny out alone so I have only read it and cried over it a bit." Of course, only the week before, he had supplied her with two critiques of Ginny but now he had new direction and, as Alice surmised, new literary efforts of his own to pursue. That didn't bother her just so long as he continued to write letters to her. And he did.

Alice especially liked the note she received about Professor Gates.

MWD—
Prof. Gates is asquiring more pimples. I fear he eats too much pork with his beans and I am sure Dear that he drinks coffee after every meal. Had I better advise him to take suthin' for his blood? He treats me well though for look you, Dear, he beckoned a bony forefinger in my direction today and said, "Hist—you there!" I harkened. "Mr. H I will excuse you from attending any of the lectures in Rhetoric—I do not think you will be benefitted by them. The facts are all familiar— and in calling the roll I will always mark you present anyway." I did not tell him I was about to suggest the same thing but surely I am perceiving more and more that My Wyf is right in her estimation of College Profs and students. I have been rating them too high. In rare cases there is much merit but the instances are very few and the distance is long between. Dear, reading a thing in a book and then telling you about it or you reading and then your telling it to me is

the thing that leaves the vivid imprint. Drowsy lectures by pedants avail not.

I am delighted to know that your work is showing Results and why not? Look at me. You impress me and I know you can others—they respond to your strong spirit and I am glad.

As a letter writer Elbert was becoming as prolific as had been Alice over the past several years that had seen him change from businessman to author to student; from dutiful husband and father to furtive lover of another woman. Alice's letters had done much to bring all this about and she felt confident that Elbert would soon be completely hers. After a week of obvious soul-searching and self-condemnation Elbert seemed to be making the adjustment. His letters weren't totally love letters but were more like those of a person determined to stick with the field of literature, if not to formal studies. No matter which, it was clear to Alice that she would be playing a more important role from now on.

As October moved along at an exciting pace for the both of them, Elbert attended lectures, wrote letters, got the final nod from Arena on his novel and found good company in ministers just as he had back home. He told Alice about every new thing that was happening. Sometimes he gave the whole panorama in a single letter which he held up for a second day's addenda.

Thursday

MWD—

The book [*One Day*] is printed but the cover they proposed to use did not suit me. It was pretty enough in design but the color was dark blue. I clung for pure white and bronze or white and silver and got it.

This put the book back ten days but they say they will have a few bound copies out within a few days. Of course the first one I can put my hands on will go to you my Dear. This sunshine *is* glorious—so wild and hazy is the view. It's not Heaven tho Dear but thank God it is not Chicago.

'A wyf! Ah! Seint Mary, benedicte. How might a man have any Aversite that hath a wyf? Certes, I cannot saye. (Chaucer)

****

Friday PM

MWD—

I wrote Mr. Fuller a letter a few days ago and this morning he walked in on me.

We had lunch over in Boston and Sunday I am going over to Malden to hear him preach and stay with him until Monday. He is quite stout and has cultivated a goodly crop of side whiskers which changes his appearance. He has no governor to his steam chest which means he lacks ballast—is explosive in his methods of work—way up or way down. He will gravitate or evolute into a fat sleek holy man of God but he thinks his life is blasted as far as achievement is concerned and if he thinks so, so is it.

My first honors came Monday when I wrote an essay in company with 120 other men—all candidates for a select class in Literary Criticism. Only ten out of the lot were to be chosen. My essay was marked "B," "A" being perfect and I am told it is never given for fear it will cause the student to swell up and "bust" like the ox in the fable. The names of the successful men were posted in the hallway and we duly met Prof. Wendell who was born in Harvard yard and has never been out of it. He wears the Shakespearian pointed beard as all the literary men here do. Parts his hair in the middle, and smokes a pipe on the street. After the class I stayed and talked with Wendell or *he* talked at me. He told me how he had written a novel but the villainous newspapers in New York had damned it with faint praise. He also told me that Lowell used to smoke a pipe on the street and that Lowell had once assured Wendell that someday Wendell would be *the* prose writer of America. He *loaned* me a copy of his book and I am to read it. I have tried to but my intellect fails to grasp it. The situations are as stiff and wooden as Sitting Bull who stands in front of the cigar store where Wendell gets his tobacco. A volume of Wendell's lectures on English Composition however are good reading. Certes the man knows the technique of writing but he is so enslaved to the method he has no fancy, much less imagination. My Dear Wyf, I am sure that we must *feel* if we would write well. Our hearts must be warmed by a coal from God's altar high. Most writers have mannerisms that should be overcome—their weak points should be made strong—one cannot learn to write in Masterful Manner by studying Rhetoric but we should study Composition enough to know our faults.

Emerson would have been stronger without that continual "Tis." Wendell has no "'tis" but then he has no thoughts. Wendell volunteered to go carefully over anything I care to submit. Shall I tempt him with some of the H letters?

That weekend Elbert went over to Malden to hear Rev. Fuller preach and to stay over until Monday with that minister. Before he left on Saturday he sent a long letter to Alice relating everything he found exciting about his Chaucer studies under Professor Child. When he got back on Monday, October 9, he wrote a detailed account to Alice about Rev. Fuller's sermon, his home and furnishings, his guest room and his housekeeper.

With his little novel, *One Day,* soon to come off the press, Elbert was directing more attention to completing another one, *Forbes of Harvard.* It centered around the trials and tribulations, the labors and loves, of one Arthur Ripley Forbes, a fellow who had to quit college on the advice of his physician "on account of his health." The whole story would be told through a long series of letters. On the weekend following his visit with Rev. Fuller, Elbert told Alice in another letter how Professor Wendell reacted to portions of the letters-manuscript. Almost boy-like, his salutation just had to demonstrate how Chaucer-imbued he was at the moment.

Saturday

My Dear Wyf—

I am rejoiced to know that the teachers are with you—not for your sake especially, but for theirs. Do not bear down on the Methody Dear, it is to be pitied—it thinks it has gotten the thing down fine and to change is to retrograde. Spare oh spare the Methodee. I took Prof. Wendell's book back and he presented it to me—after all it is a pretty good book and Prof. Gates in spite of whiskers, pimples and abdomen is not entirely base. I gave him two of the Forbes letters and The Lady and the Flowers yesterday and went to his office for them this morning per appointment. Quoth Gates: "These letters are neither Narrative, Exposition, Description or Argument. I cannot criticize them for the reason that there is no standard of excellence for such compositions. They are what I call fugitive Prose-Poems. No man by taking thought can write like this—do not attempt it—you will surely fail. A few pages in a peculiar mood of course can be turned off but beyond that the work will be very bad. Such work has made a few men famous for the very faults of these eccentric things are believed to be virtues by many. Carlyle and Browning did this "fugitive" business but the work of neither will stand criticism. In some minds these letters you have submitted would strike a sympathetic chord and people might cry over them—others would turn away. At times they might appeal to *me*—in fact they did, but the peculiar and the eccentric should be shunned by a writer. What he does in this way is either very bad or very good—generally very bad."

Dear, Gates is no fool—he knew better than to make a single mark on the letters—his opinion would not change us anyway but I had a curiosity to see what he would say.

How much time will you have at Thanksgiving? And how much Christmas? I am to go to Potsdam on the former and you are to come here at Christmas. Is that it Dear?

Who wrote "Memories"? Have you read "John Ward—Preacher"?

The plans were being firmed up for a Christmas that neither Elbert nor Alice would forget to their dying day. And Elbert had recorded for posterity one of the best reviews ever to be written, in his lifetime or the decades to follow, of *Forbes of Harvard*. Ably done by Harvard's Professor Gates after reading just two of the manuscript-letters.

However, Elbert was more impressed and motivated by Alice's appraisal of the Forbes letters. She advised him to recognize Gates for what he was, a "gent" but a professor who doted on rules which can crush great things. Of the same letters that Gates had doubted the value, Alice wrote, "I know their value. They are sonnets, pure and sweet as any Elizabeth Barrett Browning wrote or Shakespeare either. They are prose poetry inspired by Love. They are sweeter than 'Memories'—yes it is a fine idea Dear, to separate them into single gems. Bring them when you come. I want to read them to you every one again."

7

"Married—on Christmas Day"

More and more now, Elbert's letters were like a college lad's recitations of each day's lectures to someone back home. They ranged from literature to Egyptian art with a little love or college gossip thrown in. The youth-like enthusiasm was natural even if it was penned by a successful businessman of thirty-seven. This was a part of life he had skipped. Intellectual discovery isn't so much a matter of turning back the clock as it is turning on a mind to a given stage of exciting enlightenment. There is a sameness to the reaction at any age.

In the waning days of October 1893, Elbert wrote of an experience that was moving to him as a man of his age in his mixed up yet real world.

Monday

MWD—

Yesterday at Kings Chapel I heard Sen Chunder Mooraurah—a Buddist [sic] who came to this country to speak at the world's congress of religions in support of Theosophy.

There was quite a long service preceding the address and this Indian sat with bowed head and folded arms as quiet as marble. I never saw a mortal so calm.

His face is nearly black but nose thin, head high, ears small. Hands and feet dainty as a womans. Merciful Heaven! Do we send missionaries to this people? I never saw an American as sufficient unto himself as this man.

When he arose to speak he stood in silence an instant with uplifted face and clasped hand. For an American to do such a thing would have been theatric but this man surely "had his mind on the thought" for the movement was wonderfully impressive—the audience was still as death.

Very slowly he began to speak in low clear voice. He uttered the prayer I have written out from memory for you. My curiosity turned to sublimity while this prayer was being repeated and the tears ran down my cheeks Dear. Perhaps the reason I cried was because I know you would have done the same if you had been there; I did not reason quite this far though at the time but on viewing the action in a cold psychologic light—as I always go back and analyze my feelings (being a college man) I think this must have been the case.

The address this Indian gave was a general statement of his religion. He did not claim for it perfection—only an approach to Truth—the nearest approach he knew of. Absolute truth cannot be formulated or understood perhaps yet. We will abide God's time. We turn our faces to the East and await the sunrise.

"Infinite Parent Thy name is Love! When we attempt to tell *what* Thou art the tongue stammers, thought grows confused—we know only some of Thy attributes.

"But when we think that we do not even know what man is—aye! Or what a wayside blossom is, knowing only the attributes of each, we take courage, and lift up our hearts in thankfulness for manifestations of Thy exalted nature which we behold on every side.

"I am in a strange country, afar from my birthplace, among a people whose ways of life are very different from my own; but I behold the unselfish kindness, the sympathy the beauty of spirit they outpour upon me and I recognize it as being of the same fabric that I have been blest with at home.

"My cottage is in the shadows of the Himalayas—the mountains that have seen races pass away, ideas perish, religions vanish, dynasties decay; but we know that before the mountains were, Thou art.

"I lift up mine eyes at nightfall and I behold here the same stars that I have known at home; I recognize them as my own—I call them by name and they scintillate an answer. The sun that lights this beautiful house of worship is the same sun that gives warmth to my loved ones far away.

"The Ocean which men call the Pacific—the peaceful—caresses the shores of my native land and his waves also kiss the skirts of this. When I go from this land kind friends place in my hands tiny seeds—I carry them away and after months of journeying I plant them in my garden. Behold! Thy rain cometh and Thou sendest Thy sunshine and the seeds spring forth into flowers that delight the eye and fruit cometh in due season.

"Wherever we go we can see the Unity of Thy care; from the inanimate to the animate—from the unconscious to the conscious, from the unthinking to the thinking.

"When we behold these things we know that Thy loving kindness is over all. When again and again in many climes we have seen Thy spirit made manifest in our brothers even so that they have given up this earth-life for Thy glory that others might have life, we say O Infinite—Unknowable—Thy name is Sympathy—Thy Name is Love!"

The Buddhist's prayer-sermon, as repeated by Elbert from memory in his letter to Alice, was really their kind of prayer. It touched upon their love of the great outdoors—the sun, the stars, the flowers and the seasons of the year. It focused upon the sea—something which held a fatal fascination for both Elbert and Alice. The prayer was, to them, a beautiful expression of a religion of wonderment and love as opposed to the doctrinaire, hell-fire religions with which they had been so uncomfortable all their lives. There was no "Methodee" in this man from India! There could have been just a touch of Elbert Hubbard thinking in the reconstructed prayer but neither he nor Alice would have sensed it, for much of Elbert's thinking on religion by now was intertwined with Alice's, and its principal theme was Love.

The harvest that rounded out that October for Elbert was the coming off the press of his novel *One Day*. The Arena Publishing Company had done it up nicely and he quickly sent a copy to Alice. It was duly reviewed by the Boston papers and Elbert sent the clippings on to Alice and to the papers back home at Buffalo. He particularly liked the one that made reference to his earlier novel *The Man*.

"One Day" is the title of a striking little pocket volume by Elbert G. Hubbard, the Buffalo man who wrote "The Man" a couple of years ago to establish the novel theory that Shakespeare was a dual genius and that the inspiration of his work and its literary finish were the contribution of his wife and collaborator, the daughter of an Italian exile in England. The booklet has a second title, "A Tale of the Prairies," but the prairies do not appear, save by reflection in scenes in the household of Deacon Multer and his wife, a work-a-day couple with a hard-featured religion, which is brought in striking contrast with the sweetness of character of a little girl, whose tragedy is the theme of the story. The action of the piece is all limited to one day's events. The farm house scenes are lifelike and full of the keen, sympathetic humor that shone through "The Man" gloving the steel hand of the author's crushing satire. It is as a satire that the book serves its chief purpose. The cruelty of some people's religion is powerfully set forth. "One Day" will be read and will set many people thinking. The Arena Publishing Company have given it a pretty setting, in a narrow pocket edition.

The advantage of such a review, indicating that Elbert Hubbard had been published before and was now out with another book "that will be read and will set many people thinking," was that Elbert could now let it be known that the author would be available for lecture appearances. He figured he might very well get some invitations that would add to his income . . . and add to his exposure as a writer and emerging lecturer.

Elbert's days were getting too full. Work on *Forbes of Harvard,* putting together lectures for the few engagements that were beginning to materialize, attending lectures, writing daily letters to Alice and a few back home each week—all these things were making a poorer student of him. His attendance was good, though, until mid-November, when he had to go back to East Aurora to straighten out some business matters. While it was good to see Bertha and the boys, a week back home served only to widen the growing breach between him and his wife. It didn't help any when Elbert announced that his school, lecture and writing efforts would keep him from getting back home at Thanksgiving. And, of course, one could hardly expect Bertha to wax enthusiastic about the novel *One Day* and its favorable reviews. After all, she had not been involved in its writing and its success meant only one thing to Bertha—her husband was now all the more certain that he had done the right thing when he sold out his Larkin Soap interest. He would be chasing the literary rainbow all the more and that meant more time away from her and the boys. Elbert's feeling of guilt and helplessness concerning his already laid plans to spend Thanksgiving with Alice at Potsdam caused him to assume an air of polite casualness with Bertha and, all in all, it was an uncomfortable reunion for both of them.

He told himself that what he planned wasn't wrong because, thanks solely to Alice, he was now twice-published and she was helping him with *Forbes of Harvard,* his most ambitious effort to date. Arena wanted to get it on the press early in 1894 and only with Alice's help could he take this next step toward literary success. He owed something to his collaborator too didn't he? And wasn't he adequately providing for Bertha and the boys, who would also someday benefit even more when full success came to him?

He wished it could have come about some other way but Bertha couldn't have helped him with his writing—or at least had made no effort to—so that was that. But deep down he knew that Bertha *had* helped him, and was continuing to, in an indirect but important way. She was running the home and raising the boys. The train ride back to Boston was a long, lonesome tour of his conscience.

Elbert's attendance at his Harvard classes now became spottier and more and more the professors were marking him absent from class. He was concentrating on putting the finishing touches on his Forbes manuscript so that he could have Alice go over the whole thing at Thanksgiving. They spent several days together at Potsdam and, midst a routine of love and letters, found a timid unorthodox thankfulness in their stolen moments of happiness.

After the Thanksgiving visit with Alice, Elbert was in a position to turn the manuscript over to the Arena people and await galley proofs. Meanwhile he was finding his studies at Harvard to be more difficult and less interesting. He attended lectures there only when he felt he didn't have something better to do. Even as a special student, the professors expected *something* from him, and when it wasn't forthcoming they chided him. College was fast losing its appeal for Elbert and he started to give some thought to taking a tour of England and Ireland to broaden his knowledge in a more practical, pleasurable way.

Early in December of 1893 Elbert went back to East Aurora for another visit—and to announce that he wouldn't be able to get back home for Christmas. While there he talked with his old friend Dr. Mitchell about maybe going to Europe the next year and asked him to think about going along. He also had a chance reunion on the Boston to East Aurora train with William Faville of the neighboring village of South Wales, New York. They hadn't seen each other since the two of them were regular daily commuters to Buffalo during Elbert's Larkin days. Will was elated to hear that Elbert was now a college man going home from Boston for a few days because he was planning to take up architecture at Massachusetts Institute of Technology. Will explained that he had just signed up and was going back to South Wales to pack up and head right back to the Boston school. Elbert explained that he would be spending eight or ten days in East Aurora but that Will might as well use his room at Mother Gavin's until he got back himself. He scribbled a note of introduction to Mother Gavin and told Will to give it to her when he got back.

Elbert's announcement to Bertha that he would not be back for Christmas was almost the last straw. She chided him for his growing lack of interest in his home and family and wondered aloud about when he was going to settle down and act his age. Bitter words passed between them and it was strangely reminiscent of what had happened several years before when Alice was invited to leave the Hubbard home though Bertha did not actively pursue her renewed suspicions.

On December 9 Elbert was riding the train back to Boston. He wrote a little note to Alice enroute.

> Saturday—on train for Boston
> (Thank Heaven)
>
> MWD—
> I love you very much Dear and thought I would take this pencil and this piece of paper and tell you so. You are a dear good Lady—in fact the best and most patient and the bravest I ever knew. You have a heart as big as all out-of-doors and yet there is in it no room for hate. That is 'cause it is so full of Love ain't it Dear?

Back in Boston that night Elbert went to his room at Mother Gavin's to find that Will Faville had moved in as he had suggested. In the front hall he had picked up his mail—a letter from Alice—and luckily had read it down there before going to his room, which he had forgotten he had offered to his old friend.

Elbert insisted that Will stay and share the room with him for the rest of the school term and Will accepted. The next morning Elbert went down to the parlor and wrote another brief note to Alice to add to the one he had written on the train but he didn't bother to tell her that Will was going to share the room with him.

> Sunday AM
>
> MWD—
> You (The Letter) greets me before anyone else—the letter was here on my table.

The foine auld Irish gentlewoman who owns the house had the love lamp lit and a glowing fire for me and this morning all Boston smiles in the brilliant sunlight that gleams over the snow. Surely Boston is a good place to be when love letters wait one and all is warmth and sunshine and light for where the sunshine fails the love lamp does the rest.

1,2,3,4

The next day Elbert went over to Harvard and, as the records there still testify, withdrew as a student. The date—December 11, 1893. He didn't bother to tell anyone else at the time.

He was a bit despondent for the next couple of days and was in the mood for the warm love letter from Alice that was awaiting him Wednesday at Mother Gavin's. She was reminding him of their planned Christmas reunion. She would come to Boston and stay at Mrs. Tyler's, remember?

Wednesday PM

MWD—

The letter of Monday PM is here.

I will go over and see Mother Tyler this evening and write you again tonight.

Fate has already cut me off as much as it ever will or can. As I told you I will have to go back there occasionally to see the boys and look after my investments—beyond that here I am. In May I have arranged to take a tramp thro Ireland with Dr. Mitchell—starting at Killarney and going up to Scotland about 200 miles. Will be gone from May to August. Come on the 22nd—but there is no need of you writing Strykersville where you are—only tell Mrs. Pierce. I suppose your vacation is about two weeks. I am anxious for you to help me on the new story. I have written 36 chapters or about fifty thousand words and it is only half done. My plot is clear and distinct and cannot be shortened without deliberate homicide—it is the boldest thing we have attempted, but whether good or ill I am too submerged to say. It is original, that is all but originality is not necessarily good. Enclosed explains itself—if I failed I was not going to tell you.

No money in lecturing tho, only gggggglory.

What was enclosed was a brief but favorable newspaper account of Elbert Hubbard having given an interesting talk in a nearby community. The new story on which he was working was another novel which would be titled, *No Enemy (but himself)*.

Elbert didn't write again that night as he had said he would. But he did get a letter off again the next day to let Alice know that everything was set for their Christmas reunion.

Thursday Noon

MWD—

I was over to see Mother Tyler last evening. She was very glad to see me and opened the ball with "Do you know—I just got a letter from Miss Moore. She is coming the 22nd, ain't you glad?"

I acknowledged it.

She has not a woman in the house and all the rooms are full but she says she will give up her room to you and the parlor too and that I must come every day, etc., etc. I told her we wanted her to go with us to several of the Music Hall lectures and she gladly accepted.

Bishop Vincent is here and dined with me yesterday and also the day before. He has come to my room and we have had some very pleasant talks. Forbes proof is coming along and I am making a good many changes—shortening it up. My "Style" is changing I think—brevity and epigram are having a larger place. Have I a style Dear? Where did I get it from—you Sweety. You are to blame.

Bishop Vincent, a leading Episcopalian figure in Chautauqua circles and the same good gentleman who was among Elbert's Buffalo recommenders when he applied to Harvard earlier that year, was sufficiently impressed with Elbert's growing literary promise that he wouldn't have been dismayed had Elbert told him that he had withdrawn from Harvard. However, Elbert wasn't ready to divulge that information to someone who might inadvertently mention it to Rev. Brown back in East Aurora and he to others there. There would be time to announce that when and if another possibility that Elbert was weighing should come to pass. He told Alice of that possibility when he wrote to her on Saturday, December 16.

Saturday

MWD—

The message Dear—thank you. Tell me when you will arrive—hour and day and route so I can meet you.

Dined with Mr. Boyce yesterday and today. Mr. Flower's health is very poor. He can scarcely walk a block. It's the grind and he has not known my secret that a galloping horse can shake off and leave behind all care. Well both Boyce and Flower want me to take the management of the Arena. Do you know what that means? $5000 a year and loss of all "art impulse."

The man in that position must hustle and he can produce no literature, nothing but advertisements.

Their book department has increased very much recently and demands more of Mr. Boyce's time. Tell me Dear can we afford to exchange liberty for dollars? Dollars are well but we must have freedom too. A fine little note came to me tonight from Dr. Savage—the story is vivid and valuable he says.

On Monday, December 18, Elbert posted two short notes to Alice. He mailed them in an Arena envelope, indicative of the time he was spending in their offices.

Monday

MWD—

You say well that Heaven is a state of interest. When we are interested we are a part of our surroundings. To a degree when interested we lose our identity and are fused with Nature. (What interests us in things like love, what disintegrates like loneliness!)

A man at work is interested and *is* his work. A man out of his place is a sliver in the thumb of Nature—no wonder there is a fester.

Enclosed is a "galley" proof. Page-proof will not be ready until Christmas. Correct enclosed and return at your convenience.

Monday PM

MWD—

Thank you very much for the sweet and tender poem, Dear. I never felt its force before. In your handwriting it appeals to me more strongly. I met Dr. Savage today at the Arena and had a very pleasant visit with him. He offered me a cigar but as I had just smoked and prefer a pipe anyway, I was compelled to decline.

Friday at 10:30 Huntington Ave. Mrs. Tyler is anticipating your coming with much pleasure—"We must make her rest and have such a good time," she said.

The period between Thanksgiving and Christmas always seems short to shoppers but to parted lovers it can seem an eternity. Elbert and Alice had spent the interim amply feeding their intellectual work appetites and there would still be an abundance of both to feed upon together in Boston. They were hungering more for sheer physical togetherness. They could scarcely conceal it as they embraced at the railroad station and parting that night after seeing Alice to her room at Mrs. Tyler's was torture for Elbert . . . and Alice. But tomorrow was another day, and then there would be Sunday and on Monday it would be Christmas . . . *their* Christmas!

Mrs. Tyler was spending Christmas with relatives. Her boarders, save one, had also departed. The lone boarder, Alice Moore, would spend the day at home with her beloved Elbert. His estrangement with Bertha, his disillusionment with Harvard, his literary success still in the hands of Alice—these things, plus the warmth of the season and the excitement of utter privacy, seemed to give new meaning to the 1, 2, 3, 4 love symbol of these two strangely attracted souls. Step five, to which Alice had often alluded, going beyond the veil, was inevitable. As the winter sunlight gave way to twinkling stars that for once held no fascination for Alice and Elbert, a maiden was no more. Hours later, Alice reached over her lover to lift from the desk the page proofs of "Forbes of Harvard." She scribbled a brief final chapter that they had that day lived into being.

She wakened Elbert and read it to him. "Married—On Christmas Day, at the residence of Mrs. Tyler, No. 217 Magnolia Street by the Rev. Dr. H. M. Brown, Arthur Ripley Forbes to Miss Honor Harold." He gave his approval by clutching her to him for a kiss of final collaboration. And it all seemed so proper that it went to the printer the next day as written. And it was to be so published for the world to see, if not to understand, for years to come.

8

"The All Too Fortunate Winner of Her Affections"

The popular, pocket-size Excelsior Diary for 1894 was full of those little gems of printed information that intrigued Americans of that era.

Eclipses, 1894: There will be four eclipses this year, two each of the Sun and Moon, and a transit of Mercury.

For Elbert, Alice and Bertha there would be more dark days and nights in 1894 than those pinpointed by the astrologers. There would be startling parallels in the times of nature's eclipses and the personal eclipses engulfing them and hiding them one from the other . . . yet revealing things about themselves they had never before known. But the year's start provided no clues to any of them.

Following the Christmas holidays Alice went back to Potsdam where plans were underway to mark the first quarter century of the State Normal & Training School. Founded in 1869 for the purpose of training teachers, it was now among the finest in the State of New York and Alice Moore was a highly regarded member of the faculty.

The principal of the school was Dr. Thomas Blanchard Stowell, a native of Perry, New York, a small western New York village not too distant from Alice's birthplace. He was only 48 but looked much older because of a heavy greying mustache and a beard that began at the ears and grew downward to his vest top. He had headed the school since 1889.

Dr. Stowell's Ph.D. had been granted in 1881 by Syracuse University. His views of teaching had a marked effect on Alice, for in the main they coincided with hers. Thus his enlarged views, developed through broader experience, were eagerly adopted by Alice. Dr. Stowell found her views equally stimulating.

He had set forth criteria for determining professional qualifications and he measured professional spirit by these signs:

1. Devotion to Preparation of Work.
2. Willingness to assume extra tasks.
3. Power to awaken in pupils an ambition to study.
4. Ability to make pupils think vigorously and logically.
5. Ability to develop use of technical terms, elegant and correct constructions in recitation.
6. Ability to enable pupils to *use* as well as to comprehend subject matter.
7. Loyalty to Authority, Punctuality, Professional Courtesy.

Alice was, and had been, doing much of this on two fronts—teaching teachers at Potsdam and, in her way, teaching Elbert, even as far back as their collaboration on *The Man.*

Many of Dr. Stowell's criteria would thus find their way into the future writings of Elbert Hubbard.

Potsdam's *Courier-Freeman* was the popular weekly newspaper and Alice could subscribe to it, plus the *New York Weekly Tribune* for a special combined price of $1.25 a year. It carried much news about the preachings of Rev. DeWitt Talmadge, who was particularly prominent in the news of 1894. That January, Former President Rutherford B. Hayes died and everyone knew it but, unknown to Alice, Elbert and Bertha, a new life was forming in Alice's womb from a seed planted on Christmas day.

The *Courier-Freeman,* in March of the previous year, had carried an excerpt from the *London World.* It was a little truism called, "When A Woman Loves." It wasn't something that Alice would have clipped and sent to Elbert for she wasn't in Potsdam at that time. Even if Alice had been there, it was unlikely that she would have appreciated it or sent it, for it was too near the truth of the nature of her relationship with him.

When a woman loves severely, she begins to be unlovable, for she begins to be unreasonable and, for her great love's sake, to do her best to make miserable the all too fortunate winner of her affections. She insists upon accusing him of virtues which he knows are not included in his character and taxing him with failings of which he is just as completely innocent.—*London World*

Periodically over the previous two years she persisted in trying to convince herself and him that he was God-like and, at the same time, chided him for his inability to make a decision about which woman he loved. But, in fact, his principal failing was that he loved both in different ways and for different reasons.

The "all too fortunate winner" of Alice Moore's affections was indeed feeling miserable that January. His need for Alice's help in putting the finishing touches on *Forbes* had led him once more into a physical intimacy which always troubled him when the warmth of togetherness gave way to cold self-appraisal.

As always, when alone with his conscience, he would write to Bertie and lose himself in that uncomplicated affection of a father for a little son who seeks little from you beyond a friendly smile or a simple story. Also, a letter to Bertie was an indirect way for him to patch up things with Bertha for he knew she read the letters. And Bertha, also troubled by their estrangement, helped Bertie with lines in his letters to his father that would get her own indirect messages across. She had regretted their early December quarrel and let it be known, through Bertie, that she would like to come to Boston to see him. Elbert promptly got off a reply to Bertie's letter.

Saturday, Jan. 14, 1894

My Dear Bertie

You have written me a very nice letter indeed. Not a single word misspelled and all arranged and punctuated properly. I thank you for it.

For the past week I have been walking over to Boston every morning. Mr. Faville you know is rooming with me. We walk together and get our breakfast on the way at a restaurant.

It is about three miles over and we cross the Charles River over a bridge that is half a mile long. This morning the tide was high and the water came nearly up to the bridge but tonight when we came back the river was ten feet lower. The tide comes in this way twice a day. On the beach at Revere where we went last Sunday the tide throws up lots of funny shells and sea weed and not long ago it brought up a whale and dropped him in water so shallow that he could not swim away so the boys went out in boats with sling shots and things and killed him and they cut him up in pieces and made a big fire and fried out the fat. They got forty barrels of oil which they sold for ten dollars a barrel and it wasn't much of a day for whales either.

When your Mamma comes down here we are going to the sea shore and will pick you up a big lot of shells.

With much love to you all, I am

Sincerely yours,
E. G. Hubbard

He mailed it in an Arena Publishing Co. envelope for he was now on their payroll. "Might as well earn some money while getting an education," he had explained.

Bertha and Elbert were together in Cambridge by the time the father next wrote to his son. Bertha's mother was keeping the boys.

Cambridge, Jan. 27, 1894

My Dear Bertie

We have just received your very nice little letter and must thank you for it. I noticed that you directed the envelope yourself which is the first of your writing I ever saw on an envelope.

It is just as plain as I can write.

The pictures Jim McCreary took of you are very fine indeed. I am going to use it in a book. We will be back one week from today.

With love, your Papa,

EGH

With Will Faville's presence to be considered, plus the natural awkwardness of a reunion of a married couple long-estranged, Bertha and Elbert were satisfied with sight-seeing and dinner with Will. Nothing would really be resolved between them during that short visit—they both knew that—but at least they weren't quarreling and Bertha could see that Elbert was busy and was in good company. She knew and approved of his plans to go abroad that summer. He would have to abandon the college idea and leave the Arena firm, she felt, and maybe after the trip he would settle down again in East Aurora with her and the boys. He hinted at someday starting a print shop there.

At the end of the week's visit, Elbert accompanied Bertha back to East Aurora where he had business to attend to. In a few days he headed back to his work in Boston. They both felt better about everything but there was no rekindling of their original love.

In February this item appeared in a Buffalo paper:

The Arena Publishing Company of Boston have in press another book by Elbert G. Hubbard of this city. The title is "Forbes of Harvard." It is a tale of college life in the 30's. Emerson and Thoreau figures as characters in the plot. "Forbes of Harvard" will be handsomely gotten up and bound in the Harvard colors.

Elbert Hubbard's short story, "One Day," is a series of vignettes of prairie life. There are four of these, each picturing a pathetic scene in the hard pilgrimage of a child from earth to heaven. They are drawn graphically and there is a great deal of truth in them, although the satire on the Christian ministry is bitter and not faithful to the generous Christian spirit of our day.

While Alice was extremely busy at Potsdam with her teaching chores in a year that was also filled with many extra activities in connection with the school's anniversary celebration, Elbert was also busy at the Arena, giving lectures and working feverishly on his next book, *No Enemy*. Will Faville was good company. Sometimes he would go with Elbert when the budding lecturer had an engagement in a nearby town. Other times Elbert would join Will and his M.I.T. friends for a gab session at their favorite haunts.

Elbert would not be privileged to know what Will would write, years later, about their winter together.

Hubbard was a delightful companion, and boredom never hovered.

His mind was alert and receptive. He was writing incessantly that winter what seemed to me atrociously bad stuff . . .

We often went when he delivered a lecture at some nearby town. He had been hired by some circuit that provided lecturers at an honorarium of, I believe, $20 per lecture. It was always difficult for him to keep to the facts of his discourse, the audience seeming to wish, and he more than willing, to introduce the dramatic at the sake of veracity.

During the winter we hunted out rather cellary, smokey places that served strange things to eat, or at least strange to us,—frog legs, then taboo, snails, queer concoctions, musty ale into which a red hot poker was plunged, and other delicacies. He did not smoke and drink had no appeal beyond the fellowship accompanying it. I met few of his acquaintances, and he few of mine; I think we were both too intent upon our own development to wish for the glitter that hangs around some phases of college life, and our roads of learning were divergent, although sympathetic.

He was not a woman chaser, as scandal suggests, was clean mouthed; there was always too much of interest that held us otherwise for he had a keen wit and a deep penetration. I do not think he could be called profound, and his writings show a charm and sort of naivete, an acting up to his audience, as it were, arising from a wish to be liked. The future will seriously evaluate his work.

By March Alice found herself to be unusually moody and not feeling up to par physically. She tried to tell herself it was because of the cold winter, the extra activities, and the fact that she and Elbert had both been so busy since Christmas that she was just terribly lonesome. But she was experiencing physical irregularities and lapses from her usual straight thinking. In her calmer moments she thought of something else—she might be pregnant. Whenever this possibility entered her mind she was at once overjoyed and frightened. How she wanted to bear his child! But if it was true, if she was pregnant, how would he react? What would her family say? How could she expect compassion from Bertha? Could she expect Bertha to say, "He's yours, go in peace and be happy"?—hardly!

Each time she fell to wondering about her true condition, these thoughts and the whole panorama of her past with Elbert would race across her mind. If this was the end of their romance might it now somehow be just the beginning of a wonderful family life together? The warm thought would then be quickly followed by the chilling realization that, in her way, she had carefully taught Elbert to put family second to a burning desire to be a writer!

She resolved to not tell him of her suspicions about her condition until she was absolutely sure and, in any event, not until he had realized his dream of going abroad. If she was pregnant she would not be alone. Their child would be with her. The loose-fitting attire that was in vogue would be her ally in keeping her secret from Dr. Stowell and the faculty until the summer vacation. If Elbert followed his plans to leave on his trip in May he wouldn't find out either for she wouldn't see him until his return. She would let him know that she wasn't feeling well, though, for he had always seemed to be especially concerned and affectionate over the years whenever she had talked about her health.

May came and Elbert finalized his plans for leaving, little suspecting that his rhetorical "wife" was well on her way to becoming a very real mother.

Blissfully unaware, he wrote of his plans.

Thursday, May 10, 1894

My Wife—

I have bought my ticket and have the upper berth in Cabin 46. . . . With a Methody preacher downstairs who is going to the Holy Land.

This is a first class cabin but they put us in it because there are not many people going anyway—-35.00. It's all right of course and I do not wish to find fault. You will not think me presumptuous nor unduly fastidious or exacting—that is to say not arbitrary, but Dear it *would* be all right if that Methody preacher had stayed in Podunk and you had the other berth. That is what it should be and what the Captain of the Pavonia desired. It will be so the next time I cross. I met the preacher in the ticket office and the Man introduced us becaws as we was going on the same boat and the preacher was afraid of strangers and awful suspicious for he has always lived in Podunk, but he said, "I know you are a good man—and God fearing." He has stuck to me like a burr all the morning.

I enclose proof of Mr. Flowers review of Forbes that will go in the June number. I have ordered them to send you a copy. You will see several choice things in this number. One article especially I can recommend as I wrote it myself.

The uneasiness, etc., is caused by the "anniversary"—Nature gets in a habit I suppose. I hope it is all gone now. Tomorrow I will think of you, also the next. Sunday you must lift the dipsy chanty.

"So far is there any money from our books?" No Dear. There is not much of a fortune in bookwriting. If a book gets a run—sells 10,000 or more in a year, then there is money in it. I kind of think we have not written any books yet—only studies. Nothing we have done deserves immortality. What we will do remains to be seen. No line I have ever written seems just right—it looks better in Ms than type.

Mr. Flower says that my article in the June issue is very choice in a literary way, but as I read the proof yesterday it did not seem so to me. Perhaps this dissatisfaction with work done is to urge us on to better things—on, and on and on.

Will make out the new route tomorrow and send you, then another Saturday. And no more can I mail you for eight days. But one week from Monday I will whisper under the sea one word—Browning— and it will contain more love for a beautiful and gracious lady than was ever before packed in so small space.

Through tears Alice read the letter and clutched it to her abdomen as if to let their baby read it. Aloud, she said, "How can men be so unknowing? Dear Husband, my uneasiness is more than you think. I almost told you and you still don't suspect!"

On May 12, 1894, Elbert received a letter from Bertha, similar to one that would also be received by Alice in a few days.

Bertha had been hearing disturbing rumors that were filtering back from Boston to the effect that her husband was still "carrying on" with "that school teacher who used to live with the Hubbards." She had decided to check his locked attic room to see if there would be any evidence that this was so. She knew what kind of evidence she was looking for— letters—and she found a bundle from Alice in his desk.

Hurt, dismayed and angered, she sat down and wrote scathing letters to Elbert and Alice and she was particularly pointed in her remarks to Elbert about his preaching virtue with his pen and behaving the opposite. She pointed out, with more fevered fantasy than fact, that the whole town knew about it and had nothing but loathing for him . . . and for Alice.

Elbert knew he deserved the vitriol that Bertha heaped upon him and felt strangely relieved that he had been found out. So be it. There would be no need for subterfuge from now on, he thought. But, as he put the letter away in his room, safe from discovery by roommate Faville, and prepared to leave for Boston Harbor to board the *Pavonia,* he had no idea as to how wrong was his appraisal of the future.

Later that Saturday Elbert was on the deck of the S.S. *Pavonia* as the tugs began towing her out of the Boston Harbor a little after 2:45 P.M. Dr. Mitchell had elected some weeks before not to join his old friend on this trip, so Elbert had gotten the idea to persuade Will Faville to join him. He almost did go with Elbert but changed his mind that very week. He was there, though, to see Hubbard off—a detail that Elbert overlooked telling Alice in a letter, chronicling the 10-day voyage, which he posted from Queenstown on Tuesday, May 22, the morning after his ship's arrival there.

Will told a friend about seeing Hubbard off.

I was carrying his luggage. As we approached the steamer he distressingly embarrassed me by seizing his luggage from me, among which was a steamer chair, a folded steamer chair, and following behind me, saying sotto voice, "Yes, my Lord, No my Lord, where will you have your chair placed, my Lord," as we climbed the companionway.

The daily diary of the 10-day voyage didn't reach Alice at Potsdam until June 12. It was in an envelope which Elbert had appropriated with foresight from Boston's Twentieth Century Club to duly impress the curious among the Queenstown postal employees. Alice anxiously ripped it open. She lived the voyage over with her beloved Elbert as she read it.

On board Pavonia
Saturday May 12
8 PM

My Wife

At 2:45 the bell rang sharply and a voice sang out more sharply
still—"All visitors ashore!"—There were hurried Good byes and many
tears. Every passenger seemed to have a dozen friends to see him off
and as the little tugs puffed busily along the great black ship the hand-
kerchiefs waved a Chautauqua salute from the docks.

Out past the islands we slowly steamed down toward Nantasket—
past the white light house and in sight of *sacred sands where lovers
strayed.*

Then the coast faded away into a line of hazy clouds and night came
down on this great ship whose prow was headed for the East. America—
my country and my wife were behind. The black waters rolled up and
smote our good ship but they were dashed into foam—onward we went.

The moon shone bright and the stars came out and we were alone
on the waste of waters. On my heart is a strange sadness. Only thoughts
of Her I love crowd upon me and I have even ran [sic] the risk of being
unsociable to good meaning people, by offering scant courtesy to their
advances.

You feel the uncertainty of life—the frailness of man when on the
sea. Yet one notes the throb of the engines, the lights high aloft in the
rigging, the black figures on the bridge keeping watch and orders
shouted in hoarse voices and one says how great is man that he should
thus defy the elements and wage war with wind and storm. The absolute discipline among the crew, the good nature of the officers, the
courtesy of all gives confidence. Good night Dear Wife—Good and
Gracious Lady you are thinking of me as I write. Good night Beloved,
Good night.

Sunday 2 PM

My Darling—A clear sky, but cool strong breeze. Have made the
acquaintance of a dozen or more passengers who try very hard to be
friendly.

The Captain read prayers at 10 o'clock in the main cabin. Very impressive. I hardly expected it would be so. Have watched the sea,
day-dreamed and thought of you. Only one ship have we seen all day.
Am well and happy.

Monday 10 AM

Cold rain and fog. The dull moan of whistles sounding every five
minutes on acct of fog. Makes melancholy music. Two men were on
the bridge on watch and one in the "crows nest," clear at the top of
the foremast. Well and appetite good. Thought of my Dear Wife and
wafted messages of love back to her constantly.

Tuesday 4 PM

Bright clear and cool. At noon the bulletin on Captain's door showed
958 miles from Boston. Four meals a day. Breakfast 7 AM. Dinner 12.

Tea 5. Supper 8. Ship rolls considerable and many passengers paying tribute to Neptune. Am well and on deck most of the time. Have to cling to rope for safety. Sails set and the stars say it is fine weather.

Wednesday 10 AM

I am happy and give thanks that I know no one on board. You are the only comrade I wish and any other but you would break in on my sweet content. Yet I talk with many and today paced the deck for an hour with the doctor, as fine a young Irishman as ever kissed the blarney stone. A ship's doctor should cure by personal touch, not medicine. All he wants is to get his passengers safely ashore. He does not treat chronic diseases nor cut off legs, nor operate on tumors. So he tells me he gives bread pills and sometimes sea water but mostly Good Cheer. A good many are sick and I went with him on a round of calls among his patients. He jokes the men, plays with the babies and blarneys the ladies. Looks at their tongues, feels pulse and orders 'em on deck or gives sensible advice as to diet and exercise.

Yesterday the temperature dropped fourteen degrees in an hour. "Icebergs" said a sailor. Sure enough we shortly made out a white object away off on the horizon. Soon we plainly make out its outline. Glistening white, as high as a church steeple and covering in surface ten acres. Yet four fifths of the mass was below water. A "white tramp" the sailors call an iceberg. A derelict is a black tramp. Nothing is so feared at sea as a tramp. He gives no signal, answers no salute. He is dead yet he is full of stubborn hate. Wind and storm are naught but to strike a tramp in a fog means death.

We gave the shining white sullen monster a wide berth, buttoning our overcoats about us and praying we should not meet his brother.

Our ship rolls in the waves and great masses of water yesterday dashed across the decks but it is on and on and on. Never a pause of the piston's stroke and all the while the crew works steadily and good naturedly and the bells ring out the time every half hour.

Yesterday I was down in the furnace room where the real heroes of the ship toil. The fireman's task is the most severe on board ship. The temperature is always above 100 and the men work naked, save for overalls strapped about waist and hobnailed stockingless shoes. I thought of our moulders and of how you would enjoy the sight if I was with you, as of course I would be. All young men and *little* men but superbly strong. But I am told it is death—that no man can stand it for more than three years. Yet the high wages tempt and these heroes go down to death each one proud in the thought that *he* can endure even if others have failed.

The sea, the sea, you and me Dear!

Friday AM

Dear and Gracious Lady, I love you very much and thought I would drop you this line to tell you of it. Fine clear cool weather. Four meals a day. Breakfast at seven, Dinner at 12, tea at 5, supper at 8. I have not missed a meal so far and never felt better, save for the fact that I am constantly looking for sheltered nooks by the smoke stack or near a lee scupper or abaft the mizzen where we could sit and hold sweet converse or sit in silence and watch the sea. The waves dash up against the prow and are broken into foam. Yesterday the sun shining through the foam made dainty rainbows that kept us company all day long.

Dear One, it seems to me now that you cannot do better than tell Dr. Stowell you will go back next year. The work is hard but the pay is good considering the fact that talent never does get fit recognition. Next year will not be near as hard as this has been. Now it is settled that I am not going back to Egypt, you will have additional strength that horrid uncertainty is what robbed you of life but now we can keep our eyes fixed on Canaan-land. Your going back there will relieve you, and *me* especially, of much of Mrs. Grundy's spleen.

I will be with you all of the time—you will have your daily letters and love will give you strength. Simply tell Stowell you will go back and we will have plenty of time down by the sea to make plans for the future. As for pay Dear—the Boston life gave me valuable knowledge about the income of scribblers. Writers live on a crust or less unless they have an income outside of their profession. We work for glory, God save us, and generally fail in getting it. After we are dead it may come but he who pens his highest thought must not hope for present gain.

Of course it is possible to write a book that will become a fad, then a fortune comes easily but this is a miracle. After 20 years you and me [sic] may be the victims of a miracle but we need not expect it now. We must live on love and the thought of being true to each other and our highest light. Can you do it Dear?

****

Friday   Fine weather. I love you and am well and happy. Miles are naught.
Saturday   The good ship rocks and rolls but I go with her and am happy. I long for a genuine storm. Tomorrow we reach Ireland and I will at once mail this letter.

Alice, who by now was having considerable difficulty keeping breakfast down, found little consolation in Elbert's twice recording that he was enjoying four meals a day. It pleased her that he was so well and happy but at the same time she wished he knew how miserable and unhappy she was. Still, as she read each day's entry in Elbert's running commentary, she was impressed with his reportorial style and passed off his constant expressions of content as being her own fault for not having come right out and told him before he left that she was certain that she was pregnant.

She hadn't needed to see a doctor. An undressed look at herself in the mirror revealed the telltale body contours. While he was crossing the ocean, writing to her each day, she had written three letters to him, on May 17, 21 and 24, gradually building up to and finally telling him of her condition. He found them all waiting for him at the Bedford Hotel, Russell Square, London when he arrived there on June 4.

It was too late now to undo anything but Elbert wished as he read

Alice's letters that he had not sent that final one of his voyage, announcing the delay in their flight to "Canaan" and suggesting she continue teaching at Potsdam. He knew it would strike terror in her heart when it would arrive. He sat right down to pen a letter that would be more in keeping with the situation as he now knew it. He wanted it to be reassuring to her in two ways. First, that he loved her and would take care of her. Secondly, that he would remain calm so that solutions to the myriad problems that would now face them could be solved. In the latter he was writing to convince himself as well.

Bedford Hotel   June 4 2 PM
London, W.C

My Dear One—

Have hastened a trifle to get to London for *My Letters*. Here they are—three, postmarked 17th, 21st and 24th. All devoured and pored over, and now I feel I must write you at once and tell you how much I love you, Dear Lady. You have no cause for fear in any way.

You are *mine* and I intend to take the best possible care of you and God will care for us both. We will be reviled of course, odds bodkins! But I guess we can stand it. Yesterday at Stratford I attended "Divine Service" at the church where rests the poet's ashes. Did I worship? Not I, Dear One, nor would you *there*. We would have gone down on the bank of the lazily flowing Avon amid the daisies, buttercups and wild poppies and there under the shade of melancholy boughs we would lose and neglect the fleeting hours of time.

But let me tell you something that is not in the books but which I *know*.

Shakespeare was a bad man Dear. His mother Mary Arden was a Catholic and he never went to church except to see how they did it. He was a "play actor" and as such was well hated by church people. Then he did not live with Anne Hathaway (no one ever called her Anne Shakespeare) to whom the priests say he was married. She lived at Shottey, two miles from New Place where he died. The church people kicked up a great row about burying him in the church but he had a few friends who stood by him. One of them was Dr. John Hall who married his daughter Susan. Ingersoll says every man is dual—that he looks both backward and forward.

This was the way with Hall. He reverenced the Church and he loved Shakespeare, so he insisted that the tired body should be placed in the Church and at midnight he and two friends buried the poet beneath the stone floor of the church and over the dust they put this inscription (which you know so well)

> "Dear friends for Jesus sake forebear
> To dig the dust enclosed here
> For blest be he who leaves these stones
> And curst be he who moves my bones."

That's all they put Dear, no name, no date, no nothin'; only this request and threat. Shakespeare never wrote that doggerel verse at all.

Dr. Hall wrote it and it worked. When the Rector and church folks came around the next morning they were frightened—it was the voice of the dead and the dead man inspires much more fear than the live one. They were going to order the body removed but they didn't. They let it stay and now they charge six pence to see the spot. All around are the names and the opined virtues of nobodies and nobility but there, with nothing but this request and curse above it, sleeps the poet. A hundred and fifty years after his death a bust and tablet were placed on the wall opposite.

Of course he should sleep out on the banks of the Avon, near one of those great elm trees and a great boulder should mark the spot but this is not what I was going to say—only this—He was reviled but he reviled not again. The great and good are always spit upon by the mob. They will buffet you and crown you with thorns. You are not so very great and I am not near as good as you are great but still if we try to live for the highest we will be spit upon. Perhaps not even the threat of a curse will protect us; never mind, we will live as we believe is right.

The day I left Boston I got a letter, the mate of the one you mention, calling attention to the fact that I had "preached" from the sacred desk and set myself up as a model of virtue (which of course I have) but now I was detested by all good people in Aurora.

So be it Dear, they have cut us off widout a shillin'.

This is a great town but someway I feel at home here, more so than any place I have been since I left Boston. Do not write after you get this. I will see you the 28th.

1, 2, 3, 4

Enclosed with the letter were little flowers that Elbert had picked in the garden at Shakespeare's birthplace and had pressed flat in a piece of yellow notepaper.

As Elbert posted the letter he thought again about his final shipboard letter and how he had told Alice that by her going back to Potsdam they could both avoid the spleen of the legendary Mrs. Grundy, the social arbiter created in 1798 by Tom Morton in his *Speed the Plough*. By Hubbard's time the popular way to ask, "What will our proper and straight-laced neighbors say?" was to ask, "What will Mrs. Grundy say?" They would surely be saying plenty *now* if they knew Alice was going to have his baby!

Lines that would have summed it up for Hubbard were these by Locker Lampson in London Lyrics:

> They eat, and drink, and scheme and plod,
>   They go to church on Sunday;
> And many are afraid of God,
>   And more of Mrs. Grundy.

But the truth of the matter was, he had a healthy respect for Mrs.

Grundy himself. She couldn't be completely ignored and he knew it. God was important too, and he knew it, but neither he nor Alice had ever warmed up to the God that Mrs. Grundy worshipped.

While Elbert's June 4th letter was making its slow way across the ocean to Alice, his earlier letters, written as he journeyed through Ireland and England enroute to London, were preceding it to Potsdam. It would be a while yet before his reaction to her startling revelation would reach her.

The other letters, more travel reports than love letters, would become the notes from which he would write the first of his "Little Journeys" series of biographical, tour-guide pamphlets in which he hoped to interest a publisher upon his return to the States.

From the Royal Victoria Hotel in Cork he wrote to Alice, alerting her to the fact that all of his letters wouldn't be love letters and asking her to keep them for their later review together:

May 22, '94

My Wife

If I write you mere news letters you will resent it. Instead of keeping a diary I will tell you about it—and afterwards we can look over the notes together if we have nothing better to do and we likely will.

Head winds kept the Pavonia back so it was ten o'clock last night when the tender came alongside and carried fifty odd souls to Queenstown five miles away. I went to a funny little stone hotel where the porter lighted a candle and gave me to carry while he led the way with my baggage to a room near the roof. An iron bedstead piled high with feather tick and immaculate linen looked very inviting. A canopy top on the bed made it look like a picnic wagon about ready to start on a voyage. I quickly undressed, blew out the candle and plunged in. An how I slept—dreamed of you and when I awoke the sun was shining and I gazed about for some moments before getting my latitude and longitude. A dainty pretty room it was with lace curtains and chintz business around the mirror tied on four sides with blue bows that would suit you exacter. No carpet, but a rug or two and no pictures but those painted on the wall and ceiling by an indifferent artist. Never mind that though—they made me smile and I thought if you had been in that big bed too how we would have criticized Irish art and Irish furniture and of how you would have tip-toed to the window and taken a peek out and said, "Oh, what a glorious view!" as you looked at the sea all dotted with sails. Then you would have hurried back to bed cause the uncarpeted floor was awful cold on your feet and the window was open so the sea breeze came in a wee bit and I would have hugged you up very close to get you warm.

But "the boots" spoiled my dream by bringing in my "shaving water" and asking for the gentleman's ordher for breckfast sorrr! It seems each man orders just what he wants and states when he wants it and when he goes down to the coffee room there it is on a little table all smoking hot and a big bunch of yellow roses on the table as well, and a girl in a lace cap and big white apron who curtsies and informs you "it's a foin mornin', sorrr."

Queenstown is built on four terraces rising above the other. All of the houses are in long blocks all snow white, built of stone or stucco and whitewashed.

The terraces are the greenest of green, and made up of tangles of rose bushes and ivy, giving the appearance from the sea of wide boards of green and white alternating. I did the town this forenoon and then sent my valise here by sail, walking to Kilmurray five miles away and then taking the jauntrey car here—paying a passage of a shilling.

The trip was the quaintest experience I have known for years— *one thing only I lacked.*

Oh the beauty of these hedge rows of flowering yellow, the climbing rose bushes all in bloom the greenest of grass and every foot of land jammed right up to the stone walls! The air seemed laden with the perfume of the flowers and every little thatched cottage seemed half covered with the running ivy. The tropic cannot be compared with this for beauty, for there is often a waste of land and stretches of dismal swamp but here all is smiling health and beauty. I am speaking of the country but here in this city of a hundred thousand people there is another side.

At Killarney, a letter from his mother caught up with Elbert. Confused about his actual departure date, she assumed that he was already in mid-ocean as she wrote:

Hudson (Ill.) May 6

Dear Bert,

I have thought of you often today, and we have said, "he is out of sight of land now." How strange to think that you will get this in the Old Country. It is the first letter I ever addressed there. We are hoping you will have a safe and pleasant voyage. Mary is here with Wm. and the children. He was most sick and thought a few days outing would bring him out all right.

We are having lovely weather, and everything is growing finely.

We get along all right, and thank you for *your* interest in us. You know our wants are few, and with what your Pa earns and your generosity we come out even. We make *no* debts and *pay* as we go. Your Pa has a few old friends who will probably always stick to him, that is as long as he is able to serve them. Then he has a regular set of customers for his medicines who nearly always pay down, and he gets pay for about all he does. (He has been today called out to Moot's) and while I don't think he feels able to do much more than he does, still it is better for him to do what he does. We have our garden and poultry and *home* and I think we have much to be thankful for. Your Pa seems far happier than when he was a younger man and I feel very thankful for that.

Then we have real good neighbors and friends, and I believe enjoy life as well as the majority of people our age, and more so than some we know who are far better off financially.

Lawrence's start tomorrow and will stop in Ohio a few days and sail the 16th. He is in hopes of meeting you in England. We made a surprise farewell visit to him and he was much pleased about it.

I think you will enjoy seeing the castles and all the old places you will visit. Will want to see you on your return and perhaps we can plan to do so, as it will be about the time of the cheap excursions.

I think your Pa and I can live comfortable on 300 dollars a year from account of our expenses kept the last six months and have all we need. I feel very glad of the health and strength we have, and though I have sometimes felt sorry we could not have provided more for our last years, still I think we both did the best we could and that is all that the Lord requires of anyone. I know I am thankful that we have *good* children who are kind and thoughtful to us, and are honors to us, all for which I often thank the good lord.

Honor is better and begins to go out, and I think of soon going to see her. With much love and many thanks to you I am as ever and allways yours.

J. F. Hubbard

In his room at Johnson's Hotel on the Lakes of Killarney, Elbert put down the letter from his mother and brushed the tears from his eyes. He gazed out the window and thought about good and gracious Juliana Francis Hubbard. "A man is never better than his mother," he mused, "and how could any man be as good as she?" He picked up the book, *Chords in a Minor Key,* and read these lines:

> Though I be shut in darkness, and become
> Insentient dust blown idly here and there,
> I hold oblivion a scant price to pay
> For having once held against my lip
> Life's brimming cup of hydromel and rue—
> For having once known woman's holy love
> And a child's kiss, and for a little space
> Been boon companion to the Day and Night,
> Fed on the odors of the summer dawn,
> And folded in the beauty of the stars.
> Dear Lord, though I be changed to senseless clay,
> And serve the potter as he turns his wheel,
> I thank thee for the gracious gift of tears!"

He clipped the lines from the book and then pencilled a letter to Alice, telling her more of his experiences during his hike from Queenstown to Killarney. She was his refuge and his hope now more than ever before. To her he sent his mother's letter for safekeeping, along with a little advertising folder put out by Johnson's Hotel, a booklet on Killarney he had appropriated from the more expensive Eccle's Glengarrif Hotel, and the lines from *Chords.*

More of Elbert's "Little Journeys" letters, from Dublin on May 28, Grasmere on May 31, Warwick on June 2, etc. were wending their way to Alice as he approached London and that shocking news that was awaiting him upon arrival there June 4.

From June 4 on, Elbert's jaunts about London and Paris, soaking up history and culture, were conditioned by his predicament back home. Unconsciously, and perhaps consciously, he delved into the backgrounds of famous persons whose lives had been touched by meaningful love affairs, the attendant scorn and final rising up above the storm.

From London, on June 6, he wrote to Alice about Ouida.

"Ouida has been well spit on by society. They say (who are "they"?) she is a "bad" woman. Never mind, perhaps she is, but she is near seventy now so let us hope the worst is over. She has made a fortune and Henry James, who is a most conservative critic says her "Bebe, or Two Little Wooden Shoes" is the sweetest and tenderest story ever writ in any language by any mortal.

He enclosed with a June 8 letter a little 4-page leaflet titled, "Beliefs of a Unitarian" by the Rev. S. Fletcher Williams. With vertical lines in the margins, alongside portions of the dissertation, he called Alice's attention to Williams's observations which particularly impressed him. One such was this:

I believe that God has been manifest in the flesh in holy men and saintly women, saviours and redeemers of the race, since the world began, but most richly and clearly in Jesus Christ, who is the "chief among ten thousand, and the altogether lovely"—who is, with us, one of God's Children, the holiest and the best—whose life, character, and teachings are a revelation of and from God; but I am wholly unable to conceive of him as identical with that Being who fills immensity.

One day in the future Elbert would write a book about Jesus and some of this same thinking would run through it. But that was yet to come. The immediate future was of more pressing importance.

On a postcard addressed June 9 to Alice at Potsdam but bearing no salutation nor signature, he penned these two stanzas of the hymn, "Lead Kindly Light":

Lead kindly light amid the encircling gloom
Lead thou me on.
The night is dark and I am far from home
Lead thou me on.
Keep thou my feet, I do not ask to see
the distant scene.
One step enough for me.

So long Thy power hath blest me
Sure, it still will lead me on
Oe'r moor and fen oe'r crag and torrent
Till the night is gone
And with the morn the Angel faces smile
Which I have loved long since
And lost awhile.

On June 13, another postcard to Alice. The salutation MWD, but no signature:

I have arranged passage on the 'Berlin' from Southhampton on the 23rd. This boat usually makes the run to N. Y. in seven days; it may take eight. Will wire 'Browning' on arrival, to 149, and will be in Boston day following.

I am writing on the street as I see there is a boat for N. Y. today. 1, 2, 3, 4 more than ever

Still in London on June 12, Elbert wrote a long letter to Alice. It was another from which he would later write "Little Journeys" biographical sketches. In this one he put down the background material on Thomas Carlyle and George Eliot. After setting the London scene for Alice, he wrote:

I looked through the iron fence at No. 4 Cheyne Walk, and admired the pretty flowers where some woman of taste must work several hours a day. I rang the bell which is an old pull out affair, with brightly polished knob. A pompous butler in awful black came slowly down the steps and eyed me as he came to see if he could detect what sort of wares I had to sell. "Did George Eliot live here?", I asked.

"Mrs. Cross lived 'ere and died 'ere, Sir" came the solemn and rebuking answer. Then as he unlocked the gate he continued—"You wish to see the 'ouse I s'pose. We have many visitors—the Missus does not like it much, but I will take 'er your card." And so he gave me a seat in the pretty hallway and disappeared up the stairs with my card (and a shilling for himself). Soon he came back, his dignity quite softened.

" 'Er says to hexcuse 'er for not seein' you but that I was to show you the rooms that wasn't occupied, Sir."

But there was little to see, only this easy comfortable big house, not a mansion but all well kept and well to do with spacious double parlors, dining room with big bow window opening out on a little garden in the rear. Geo. Eliot's library and workshop was upstairs, a large square room looking out on the Thames. The ceiling was painted a light blue with designs of flowers and vines for the border. The sides yellow running down into brown near the floor.

It is now used as a library and one pretty case is filled with George Eliot's books alone. Evidently the Missus is a woman of means and taste.

Back of the library is a large sleeping room—the one in which the great woman breathed her last. Several of the bushes and vines in the little garden in the rear were planted by George Eliot herself. She was rich you know and respectable (for she kept a carriage). This butler worked for her when she was Mrs. Lewes. He did not know Mr. Lewes but he did Cross and did not like him but his admiration for Mrs. Cross was very profound.

"She traveled quite a bit you know and I kept the house while she was gone. She used to write me a letter nearly every week—tellin' me what to do."

"And you have the letters" said I eagerly.

"No, no, I sold 'em for two shillin's each after the funeral. I should ha' kep 'em sir—I could get a pun for every one now!"

****

One block up the river—following Cheyne Walk brings you to a little alley-like street called Cheyne Row. It is just four hundred feet long and has fifteen houses on the North side and twelve on the South. These houses are all built right on the street and are very plain and dingy. No. 24 faces the South and is the plainest of the lot for it has never been painted and has solid dark shutters while some of the other houses have fancy cornices and blinds. A marble tablet, freshly inserted, is in the front with a bas relief profile and beneath it these words, 'Thomas Carlyle lived in this house from 1834 to 1881'.

The house is three stories and about the size of 149[1] except that the third story is not as high as the others. I stood in middle of the street and looked up at the loose shutter that swung and creaked idly in the wind—at the swallows making a nest in the chimney and the sparrows over the door and the dust and the cobwebs that covered all and I said, as Thomas the Uncanny has said: "Brief brawling day, with its noisy phantoms, its paper crowns, tinsel-gilt, is gone; and divine, everlasting night, with her star diadems, with her silences and her verities is come."

So I rang the bell and clanged the knocker and scraped my feet on a well worn and very ancient scraper made years ago by a very awkward blacksmith and as I waited on those steps where Emerson had stood a woman put her head out of a window next door and said "Don't you see—sir—there's nobody livin' there sir, don't you know."

"I know it Madam that is why I rang the bell."

"The key is over to Mrs. Browns if you want to get in."

Mrs. Brown keeps a little bakeshop and grocery diagonally across the street and was very willing to show me the house as she showed it last week to three Americans who gave her a sixpence each. "Only Americans care for Mr. Carlyle" added the old woman plaintively as she produced a big bunch of keys.

We walked across the little street and the rusty lock was at last

---

1. A reference to Mrs. Tyler's house at 149 W. Canton St., Boston

made to turn. Cold, bare, bleak indeed was the sight of those empty rooms. The old lady had a touch of rheumatism so I climbed the stairs alone to the third floor and in the back room overlooking the little arbor and garden down below, I flung wide the shutter and stood before the fire place where he of the Eternities and the Immensities used to sit and watch the flickering embers. Here he sat in his loneliness and tried to recall the hard words he had spoken to a great and tender woman. Here he cursed curses that were prayers and here for half a century he wrote and thought and studied. Twice over in this room he wrote the French Revolution. The wind whistled down the chimney gruesomely as my footfalls echoed through the silent chamber and I thought I heard a voice say in a sepulchral growl—"Thy future life! Thy fate is it indeed! Whilst thou makest *it* thy chief question, thy life to me and to thyself and to thy God is worthless. What is incredible to thee thou shalt not, at thy soul's peril, pretend to believe. Elsewhither for a refuge! Go to perdition if thou wilt, but not with a lie in thy mouth—by the Eternal Maker No!!"

Watery clouds scudded athwart the black and smokey sky, the shutters banged against the brick walls and then swung to and shut me in the dark.

He is gone. He sleeps at the place of his birth by the side of his father, James Carlyle, stonemason at Ecclefechan in bleak yet bonny Scotland.

"In Westminster where the mad mob surges, cursed with idle curiosity—in the babble of tongues—never! Take me back to rugged Scotland and bury me out under the stars by my honest father."

He refused a baronetesy [sic] because he says 'I am not the founder of the house of Carlyle. My father was not a robber and I have no sons to be pauperized by a title."

Something of Elbert's inner turmoil came through in the final two pages of that long letter to Alice. He sensed that at long last he was on the threshold of sorrow and shame. He wondered why they always seemed to have a common door. As if to dispel any fears within himself, he closed his letter with these observations which were perhaps more applicable to himself than to Carlyle:

Hard headed man of granite and heather, of fen and crag, of moor and mountain and bleak east wind, hail! Eighty six years didst thou write and work and curse and mutter and pray. One hundred years— lacking fourteen—didst thou suffer and enjoy and weep and dream and strike thy hairy breast; and yet methinks that in those years there was much peace and quiet and joy and serene content. For constant pain benumbs, and worry and vain unrest summons the grim messenger of oblivion. But thou didst *live* and work and *love,* howbeit thy touch was not always gentle nor thy voice low. But mark you, on thy scarred and battered shield there is no crest. Thou camest out of obsenity [sic], thou deserted all to follow truth and on thy lips there was no lie, and in thy thoughts there was no concealment and in thy heart there was no pollution. Thou didst not apologize for crawling imbecility nor proud pretense. Thou hadst no *Past* but thou hadst a Future. Yet thou didst leave no sons to mourn their loss nor fair daughters to bedeck thy grave. Over thy grave with its clay sheets so cool and its coverlet of whited snow, or blowing daisies I lean and say I am the youngest of thy ten thousand sons and thy memory will we keep green so long as men shall work and toil and strive and pray and hope. Sleep, perturbed Spirit sleep.

Elbert's emotion of the moment was evident in his handwriting and the obvious extra pressure he applied to his pencil as he brought the letter to a conclusion.

As he sealed the letter he mused about the oddity of Carlyle. Spoken of as England's chief philosopher, he subscribed to no creed and had formulated none. Would it possibly be also true of him one day? He would try to make it otherwise.

Though he mailed the letter to Alice at Potsdam, she had already left there and had taken a room at Mrs. Tyler's. It didn't reach her there until June 28.

The same was true of this letter which Elbert posted in Paris on June 15:

MWD

Paris is very wicked Dear. So they say. I do not know whether it is so or not; perhaps "they" know. But when you come we will go on the search for wickedness and seek it out in the holes where it skulks, that is if you are not afraid of getting your hands bedaubed. (That's a fine wurred—"bedaubed" Dear—better than soiled—don't you think so?)

But what I do see on every hand is order, politeness, courtesy, sunshine, flowers. Music greets me everywhere and all is light and life. "Ninety three" pulled from their pedestals the statues of generals, warriors and politicians and in their places put the works of Greece—coupled with the faces of artists, poets and benefactors.

In England one sees Wellington, Nelson, Havelock, Gordon and other fighters. Here it is Moliere, Corneille, Grevy, Hugo, Dumas, Rubens, Millet, Diderot, Rousseau.

The palace of the Louvre has *seven hundred* (700) statues of artists (the broad sense) and works of imagination on its outside. Within are 2000 canvases and 1500 pieces of marble—and all are free for the people. Here the people are supreme. They have bought their freedom with the price of "ninety three" 1842 and 1871 but they have it now to an extent America does not guess.

Art here is for all more than it was ever in Athens of old so I am told by one who knows the history of Art. He tells me that the world has never seen such beauty as exists in the Louvre. The Luxemberg and the Palace at Versailles. Neither now nor ever before have such treasures been thrown open to the public without money and without price. The Government of France supports it and pensions her great sons. If you live in France you are taxed (indirectly) to support art and here it is—come help yourself—fill to the brim and carry away all you can hold.

He who works for art, beauty and truth must out of his very limitation stop at times and ask himself "Is it worthwhile—is it worthwhile?"

Here you get your answer.—*Yes, Yes,* a thousand times *Yes.*

How little one person can do! But come to Paris and discouragement will take flight and despondency will die and Ambition will take the reins and Hope will ride on wings of light! It is worth the while Dear, Yes it is worth while!

On every church, on every prison, on all public buildings and many private palaces are the words Liberte, Egalite, Fraternite. In bold letters and all alike as if one man carved them all. It looks a trifle queer in front of some of the old Catholic churches—churches built in the Sixteenth Century.

On one such I saw the mystic trinity of words over the door and once on either side and on entering it was carved high up over the altar, cut deep in the stone and then painted in black. This was the work of the Commune of 1871 and any man who objected was shot and one priest who protested against the words being on his church had the whole building pulled down over his head. The Commune was put down with a strong hand (as it must needs be) but it did good. Every so often it seems necessary for men to arise and put down arrogance and greedy wealth. Then wealth becomes useful for a time.

The Louvre and Tuilleries join each other enclosing forty eight (48) acres of space. All belongs to the people. There are seven miles of galleries in the Louvre. To walk through without stopping to see a thing takes two hours; to inspect may take weeks. It is the richest art gallery in the world. The Vatican, the British Museum and the Louvre hold the art treasures of the earth. The "Elgin marbles" are in London, but the original of the Venus de Medici, the Discobolus, the Gladiator and great numbers of those we have seen represented by casts are here in the originals.

Many houses in Paris are built in blocks that enclose a square where a fountain plays and where flowers, ferns and palms give their pleasing effect. There may be eight separate residences surrounding this square which is entered only by one big gate where a Concierge keeps guard and only allows the elect to pass.

All of these houses have "Apartements A'lours" or rooms to let. Everybody in Paris rents a room or has rooms to let. If you rent a room your landlady serves chocolate and rolls or coffee to you in your room at eight o'clock. Then you breakfast in a restaurant at twelve and dine at five or six where you please. There are restaurants at every turn, good and cheap. There are wide awnings over them and tables are set outside, for the side walks are sometimes forty feet wide and there the folks dine—miles of them.

The "Quartier Latin" is filled with thousands of students from all parts of the world who are here to study music or art. Many of them I have met as I had a letter to one, an architect, who deposited me in a room next to his, all at twenty five francs a week. And as my meals cost only one franc each you see I live cheaply. One can safely calculate that a franc (20¢) will go as far as a quarter in Boston.

I have gone over the whole city alone and have quite surprised myself by the ease with which I have gotten the geography down so fine.

On top of the bus only costs 3¢. I guess that is where we will ride mostly, Dear. It gives one a chance to see the people and the funny sights. As to the language, I think we could get it down in six weeks so as to argue fine points of theology with the tonsured priests I see on the street. Leastwise I only know eleven French words so as to speak them but they allow me to order what I want at the cafe. And I can read heaps of French Dear—I'm a linguist, I am, and you will be very much afraid of your husband, Dear cause I'm so smart. I'll just chatter and gabble and you will have to listen and say, "Wee, Wee, Monseer."

I have written this much in the gardens of the Trocado Palace right in the shadow of the Eiffel Tower.

I love you very much, Dear One, and think of you always and only wish you could see all these beautiful things with me, now, but then I am only prospecting and finding the way *now*.

This is the last letter I will send to P-d. The next will go to 149.

1 2 3 4

Adding an unthinking touch to his enthusiastic letter about Paris, Elbert enclosed two little purple London omnibus tickets that he was still carrying on his person. On the reverse side of the tickets was printed an advertisement of Cockle's Antibilious Pills, "for liver, indigestion, etc." Alice would enjoy the information about Paris, the words of love that were intermingled but, bothered with the nausea of pregnancy, she would have rather had the pills than the reminding advertisement. But then, hadn't Carlyle once taken his beloved wife Jeannie to the theater and forgotten to take her home?

By June 18 Elbert was recrossing the English Channel from Dieppe to New Haven aboard the ship *Tanise*. Paris was behind him and he would soon be checking with Thomas Cook & Son. in London to make certain that the *Berlin* was still scheduled to set sail for the United States on Saturday, June 23. Aboard ship he scribbled some final thoughts about France on sheets torn from a pocket memo book. He wound it up by talking about visiting the tomb of Victor Hugo and his thoughts about France and Hugo:

The history of the place is one of strife and it seems meet that the dust of the agitator should be laid amid the scenes where he struggled. Not in a church—no, no, no: not in the quiet of a mossy churchyard like the one at Grasmere nor the church at Stratford where priests mumble unmeaning words, nor alone on the mountainside, for he chafed with solitude. But he should have been buried at sea. In the midst of storm and driving sleet the sails should have been furled, the great engines stopped and with no requiem but the sighing of the night wind through the shrouds, and the moaning of the waves as they surged about the great ship, the plank should have been run out and the body wrapped in red, white and blue of La Belle France. The Sea—the infinite mother of all—the Sea-beloved and sung by him, should have taken him to her arms at last and there should he rest.

But if this was not possible—then the Pantheon—once a church now a place devoted to the memory of the work of genius.

****

This morning I bought a ticket for "London, Bretagne." Saturday I sail on the Berlin. She should go through in eight days but it may take ten if there is bad weather. France with its scarlet poppies and quaint stone houses and all its courtesy and kindness is behind. Long will I remember my visit there. It was all pleasure and quiet peace.

1 2 3 4

Elbert, deeply troubled by certain adversity back home and at the same time feeling the excitement of just finding the intellectual life, wasn't sure whether he wanted to live or die. But of one thing he was certain— in a strange and mystic way—the sea brought him solace and whenever death might come it would be solace eternal if he could die in her arms whether as a Hugo or as Hubbard.

Back in London Elbert found a letter waiting for him at the Histon House on Thornhill Road, Barnsbury Park. It was from Thomas Cook & Son. and was dated June 15. It informed him that the American Line had found it necessary to substitute the S.S. *Chester* for the S.S. *Berlin,* on which he had been originally booked. Moreover, the *Chester* wouldn't sail until Monday, the 25th, instead of Saturday, the 23rd.

Elbert turned the letter over and penned a quick note to Alice:

MWD

May Pluto smite ThoS. Cook & Son with an east wind. I planned first to sail on the 20th, then the Berlin offered better terms so I waited. Now it is the Chester on the 25th but they say she is a fast boat. Let us pray hard for fine weather.

Your letter is here and it must last me many days. But it is a fond letter so very full of love and all good things. I thank you very much. I am to hear Mrs. Humphrey Ward lecture tonight. Please read Marcella for me and tell me of it as you did the other.

On Friday, June 22, Elbert reported to Alice his reactions to the lecture by Mrs. Ward:

London, June 22nd

My Dear Lady

Mrs. Humphrey Ward made $20,000 out of Marcella—she probably will get as much more, but you will be rejoiced to know that she is human. When the wooden chairman had finished his fibrous speech wherein he told us that Mrs. Ward was the author of Robert Elsmere, David Grieve and Marcella, and we had all pounded the floor with our sticks and called " 'ear, 'ear" the lady began to read her ms. in a voice showing considerable agitation. But she soon got under way and read for an hour, very sweetly and very charmingly. No one was thrilled, a few went out, an attorney called "louder, louder" but we sympathetic souls listened and were well pleased. She is serious, earnest and looks as if she carried a burden that was at times a trifle heavy. There is a certain amount of ballast required to give the necessary poise; none gives the look of careless vacuity; too much makes dark lines beneath the eyes and puts the minor key in the voice. There is almost a plaintiveness at times in Mrs. Ward's voice but when she smiles, it is a beautiful set of teeth as well as a charming soul that she shows. Yet in the argument there was nothing new—you and I, My Dear One, have said it all again and again—a plea for spirituality that is not bound by set forms. A privilege to deny all tomorrow that are believed today—a sympathetic imagination that can clothe the dead form of ritual in beautiful garments and breathe into its nostrils the breath of life. "As a man advances in intellect, so much his faith in the Unseen keep step." "To deny the unknown is recession." "They tell us to search the scriptures, but demand that we shall come to Sixteenth Century conclusions."

This last perhaps was the sharpest thrust she gave. Aged 42—say. Nearly as tall as you. Dressed in simple brown with bonnet to match, tied under her chin in a big double bow, gloves held in her hand. Brooke Hereford was on the platform and made a brilliant little speech (on request) after Mrs. Ward had finished. Then the chairman who wore white gaitors, one eye glass, long side whiskers, hair parted in the middle and white gloves, referred pleasantly to Mrs. Ward as the Mother of Robert Elsmere, etc., etc. We gave her a vote of thanks then all of us pounded on the floor with our canes and the audience dispersed.

The Chairman, Dear, stepped out of one of Dickens books just long enough to preside. 'Ow you would have larfed and larfed in your puffed sleeves and then we would have gone 'ome on a broad grin and a tram (which reminds me that I have tossed you a similar joke before). But they are a polite folk are these English—howsomever not so polite as the French. But surely I have been treated everywhere with rare courtesy.

The London policeman is a fellow of considerable sense (so is the French gendarme), far ahead of our policemen, and they seem o'erjoyed to assist you or give information and take you quite into their confidence —imparting historic knowledge of a very Baedeker sort and all free or for the price of a smile and a thank you. If however the thank you is too pronounced the "bobby" gives you advice all over and repeats the information with variations.

Two weeks from today I will be with you, My Dear and well Beloved. What a long, quiet, peaceful love-feast it will be!

This is the last letter I will send. I love you Dear Lady.

With the letter Elbert enclosed two bits of philosophy clipped from the London papers:

There are few things more beautiful than the calm and resolute progress of an earnest spirit. The triumphs of genius may be more dazzling; the chances of good fortune may be more exciting; but neither are at all so interesting or so worthy as the achievements of a steady, faithful, and fervent energy.

—Dr. Tulloch

The second clipping again had Elbert looking toward the heavens and the sea:

We are to know that we are never without a pilot. When we know not how to steer, and dare not hoist a sail, we can drift. The current knows the way though we do not. . . . The ship of heaven guides itself and will not accept a wooden rudder.

—Sovereignty of Ethics

9

"I Wish to Do Right"

The trip back to the States took 10 days and Elbert needed all of that time to think about the hard realities of life that had only occasionally gripped his thoughts while the wonders of England and France fought for his attention. All that was behind now and, in addition to his obligations to Bertha and the boys, he now had an obligation to Alice where before to her there had been only the call of comradeship.

He resolved to tackle the problems in the order of their acuteness. Bertha was occupied back home and was already alienated from him as the letter he received from her before sailing to England well told him. He had every intention of keeping her amply supplied with funds to raise the boys and so there were no immediate problems back in East Aurora. Alice would bear his child—there was no other way to that situation—but would she insist that he find a way to marry her? In New York State there was then only one way for him to get free to do so and that would be by confessing all to Bertha and have her, in turn, file for divorce on the only legal grounds permissible—adultery. Mrs. Grundy *would* have a field day then, and so many innocent persons would be hurt. Enough were hurt already, he felt. Well, the first thing to do would be to go to Alice's side in Boston. Her hour of need was at hand. He would get her settled somewhere away from prying homefolk until the baby arrived and then see where the current would take them all. Certainly he dared not hoist a sail until the storm on the horizon gave some sign of the direction it might take.

Of one thing he felt certain. He would need to get some income rolling from his writing because Alice would not now be teaching in the Fall at Potsdam. He would have to provide for her support and that of their child when it would arrive. The freshest in his mind were his experiences in France and England. If he could interest a publisher in putting out his "Little Journeys" biographical sketches in monthly magazine form it would provide a steady income he could turn over to Alice. And then too, his latest novel, *No Enemy,* was in G. P. Putnam's hands and would be published by late summer. Maybe it would pay off better than his earlier efforts. The sale of *Forbes of Harvard* might pick up but, at the moment, he was wondering who might pick *it* up and sense the real significance of that final reference to a marriage that took place at Mrs. Tyler's on Christmas Day.

Elbert arrived in New York City with his thoughts, on July 5 and promptly sent a wire to Alice at Mrs. Tyler's. It was brief, as wires should be, but to Alice the nine words were like a book of Browning poems:

BROWNING MANY TIMES WILL BE WITH YOU TOMORROW MORNING

The next day Elbert and Alice were together again at Mrs. Tyler's who having always felt they belonged to each other in a romantic if not legal sense, understood their plight. She was "Mother Goose" and Alice and Elbert numbered among her children. She could be trusted and would help them any way she could.

With the ever present possibility of some of Elbert's or Alice's acquaintances from back home visiting historic Boston and seeing the pregnant spinster, it was quickly decided that she had better find a secluded spot miles away from there. Searsport, Maine, should be about right, they concluded, and Elbert and Alice would together go there at least for several weeks until they could chart their future course. A little reckoning back to Christmas 1893 told them that they would *have* to be settled somewhere by mid-September.

It was further decided that Elbert had better put in an appearance at East Aurora before heading for Searsport. He wanted to see the boys but dreaded the certain confrontation with Bertha over her point-blank letters of accusation to both him and Alice just before he sailed for England. If his reception at home would be cool, all the better—he would try to keep it that way. He was hardly in a position to win a debate on the subject now and so why get one started?

Things worked out pretty much as he had hoped and after a day's visit—much of which was spent in Buffalo on business—he announced that he would need to go back to New England for several weeks in connection with the *Forbes* and *No Enemy* books.

He sent Alice a note at Mrs. Tyler's:

I am looking forward to those weeks we will spend up on the seashore. Ireland is naught and England is only English but Searsport with you will be my Haven.

The note reached Alice scarcely a day before he did and they were off to Searsport. It was not wholly an Elysian fields sort of experience for either of them. She was far from feeling well physically and he was alternately sweet, distracted, worried and occupied with correspondence about his books. But, so long as he was nearby, Alice was content and unworried about the future, as uncertain as it seemed to be beyond the certainty that she would soon give birth to their child.

Elbert was pleased with a letter he received from Putnam's Knickerbocker Press on July 20. It was addressed to Elbert G. Hubbard, Esq., Searsport, Maine. It read:

Dear Sir:
　　We have received back the cover and will give due attention to your wishes.
　　The writer thinks that a brighter color on the back would be a decided improvement, and we will see if we cannot make a more attractive looking cover than that submitted to you.
　　We are waiting for the return from you of the proofs of the illustrations and also of the list of illustrations. Pray hasten the return of these with all dispatch, that we may get the book on the press.
　　　　　　　　　　　　　　　　　　Yours truly
　　　　　　　　　　　　　　　　　　G. P. Putnam's Sons

Elbert proudly read it aloud to Alice with special emphasis on Putnams' desire to please him with a more attractive cover and their "pray hasten" plea.

Alice smiled. "And notice, they call you 'Esquire' too!"

"Oh! So they do," he said, "I hadn't noticed it as I read it!"

"Well I did as *you* read it," she jibed. And they both laughed one of the really few laughs of their harried sojourn at Searsport.

They did manage a little time to go over his letters from England and France and agree that with some embellishing they should be marketable in the "Little Journeys" form that Elbert had envisioned. He would whip a couple into shape and try several publishers—particularly Putnams, who were the first really long-established and important publishers to put out one of his works.

When Elbert had visited briefly back home he did receive word that, it being the "time of cheap excursions" mentioned in the letter he received in Ireland from his mother, she and Dr. Hubbard planned to visit him and Bertha in August. Also, from mail he picked up in Boston on a trip there from Searsport, he learned that Bertha was not feeling at all well. He suspected that it might be more a brooding over the much widened breach between them but with her condition, whatever the cause, and the impending visit of his parents, he determined that he would just have to go back there for a while or all sorts of hell might easily break loose, which wouldn't be good for anyone and particularly for Alice in her condition. Alice agreed.

They located a rest home, operated by a Catholic order, near Concord,

Massachusetts, and, with the good Sisters promising to look after Alice, Elbert went back to East Aurora the first week of August. He resolved that he would at first take a room at the Hotel Broezel in Buffalo and not plan to move back into his home until he and Bertha could arrive at some understanding that would let him stay there and help without getting into a discussion about Alice—at least until the old folks had come and gone in peace.

He stopped at Mrs. Tyler's on his way back, picked up some personal belongings he had left there and dropped a note to Alice from Boston: He praised her courage and wisdom under stress and reminded her to send her letters, and any for him to be forwarded, c/o General Delivery, Buffalo—any wires directly to the Hotel Broezel.

On the train from Boston to Buffalo he wrote another reassuring note to Alice for he knew she would already be missing him and it was essential that she remain as calm as possible in the trying weeks ahead:

On train, 6 PM

My Wife—
  I am partially at peace to think you are in the very best and safest spot I could leave you in. The Sisters will be such in very fact to you. Please give me an inventory Dear of your daily doings. You must get acquainted with others in the place and see the children and let your loving presence minister to them. Do this Dear and tell me all about it.

  The more I think of you (and I think of nothing else) I bless God that I know you and that your heart's love is mine. Such a wealth of thought and suggestion you have bathed me in for a month—each day I have looked at you in astonishment as you seemed to reveal new sides of your nature.

****

In the Munsey magazine is a little article on Ouida. It named two sweet stories she wrote. Send me the names please and I will try to get them. I love you only My Darling.

When Elbert got back to Buffalo it was late at night and he checked in at the Hotel Broezel. The next day he went out to East Aurora and found that his mother and father had already arrived and planned to stay two or three weeks. Bertha was sick in bed with a severe headache and general discomfort. How much of it was real and how much feigned, Elbert couldn't be sure but it troubled him deeply to see her wan and unhappy. Under the circumstances he resolved that he would have to stay at the house rather than in Buffalo but would wait a few days before doing so, using the interim time to find someone in Buffalo to go out home and do the housework. Bertha had simply been unable to do it.

On August 9 Elbert penned a letter to Alice on Hotel Broezel stationery and brought her up to date on the situation at the Hubbard home:

My Wife

O, My Beloved—it is dark, very dark and yet there is hope for me for your dear letter does lift the clouds a little and it did look an hour ago as if the sun would send a ray through some rift but now I am down again. Was out to E. A. yesterday and came in last night to look for a woman who could scrub and clean things—as for cooking I can do that myself. Bertha is in bed most of the time and Miss Hutchins has been there caring for her. The boys are ragged, rough and unkempt. They hang about the creek fishing and swimming, making bonfires and eating with neighbors or where or what not comes in their way. I envy you your quiet and seclusion and could I get in such a place and hide away for a month I might get back my nerves. The Dear Old Father seems twice the man that I am. He is quiet, sober, calm and takes all that comes in the most patient manner.

It is all "Jes' so, jes' so—exactly" and nothing disturbs or troubles. Is it because he has loosened his hold on earth and that *things* matter little?

God help us—I pray for a dull indifference or a deadness—I wish to do right and I do scorn brutality—and yet the *desire* to do right undoes me. Your letter tells me of a poise and steadfastness that seems like the Dear Doctor's and surely it is not for want of example that I am not a man in very fact.

Write me care General Delivery here and tell me you love me Dear and that you are always my own Dear patient wife—my tall, dignified gentle Lady who thinks good and speaks good and who has struck sparks of goodness even from me.

All my heart's Love is yours—yours and our Trilby's.

Later the same day Elbert wrote another letter to Alice after receiving two from her—in one of which she told him that the food was not good at the rest home and that she wasn't getting as much attention from the Sisters as she had hoped for and wished he could get back with her as soon as possible. He told her that things looked a bit brighter in Buffalo because he had found a woman who was going out to East Aurora with him at six o'clock to stay and do housework. Then he addressed himself to her reported problems:

. . . it wrenches me to know you are getting such poor food and attention. You better get a trained nurse Dear to be with you all the time— do this and she will then get you good food and answer your ring.

The Father will be here for two weeks and I cannot leave while he is here—what would he and Mother think of me to leave this wreck to wash away on the rocks or sink. All my heart's love is yours. I am in a prison with bars of cruel limitations on every side. Be brave my Beloved. Let the Sisters get your check cashed. Another or all you need. Write to Gen'l Delivery here.

Alice was feeling miserable and sorry for herself and similar emotions were gripping Bertha and Elbert that miserable August of 1894. But how much worse it would have been for all of them if Bertha had known the whole truth! In a way, Bertha's misery was the most lamentable because she could turn only to her lonely bed and her inner self whereas Elbert and Alice could turn to each other by letter and there bare their thoughts of self while at the same time consoling each other. And yet, midst consoling words to each other, the lovers seemed always to add new worries, each to the other.

For instance, Elbert had been away from Alice scarcely a week when she wrote, saying:

Could you not get good help so as to come next week? You can scarcely wait until Mrs. Crawford comes. Where is Myrtilla? Will not Dr. Mitchell help? For your own sake, Dear, you must get away. You are strong but no mortal flesh can endure such torture. Darling, I will be just as brave and strong as is in my power. Give me normal physical conditions and I can hold on and be strong. But we must have freedom, Dear One, and a shelter from this fierce storm. You need it as well as I—and our Trilby, Dear One. I keep as active as possible—in one position but short time and go out on the veranda as you said—then I stitch, stitch for Trilby and think of you all the time and that means very much love fastened into the garments. Yes, Dear One, it is your Love that keeps me. All that I should otherwise turn from with revulsion is now made beautiful and sweet thru your love and because it is *Yours.*

Such was the tone of their daily letters all that August. Certain in their minds that their child would be a girl, they had fallen to calling her Trilby after the heroine of George Du Maurier's book of the same name. Elbert had called Alice's attention to the story in one of his letters from London that June just after it appeared in serialized form in Munsey magazine.

Time was running out for Elbert and Alice as the end of August approached. The baby was due in mid-September if their calculations were right. Fortunately for them, things began to straighten out at East Aurora. Bertha's sister, Myrtilla, came back, after a rest, to stay with her. And their mother, Mrs. Crawford, had agreed (with Elbert offering to pay her fare from California) to come and help also. Dr. and Mrs. Hubbard were heading back to Hudson a bit earlier than planned.

Elbert quickly got the good news—with a little bad mixed in—to Alice:

Have just got a telegram from Mrs. C—in answer to one from me. She will be here August 30th or 31st. I will be with you on September 2nd, leaving here on the 1st.
I have good help but such as need an overseer to secure attention to duties.
Mrs. Goldsmith died yesterday suddenly from a brain lesion.
My eye is better but my nerves are wrong and ears buzz so I cannot think very straight. Yet, I am pretty well—as well as could be expected.

A few days after Elbert was back at Alice's side, and while they were making plans to remove her from the rest home to a cottage at Hingham, Massachusetts to await the birth of "Trilby," this little news item appeared in the "Normal Notes" column of the Potsdam N.Y. *Courier-Freeman,* issue of September 5, 1894:

> With the exception of one member, the faculty of the school will be the same as at its close in June. Miss Moore has been ill nearly all the time since her departure in July and is now reported as being seriously ill at her home in Boston with nervous prostration.
> The elocution department will be under the supervision of Miss Ola Esterly, a graduate of Emerson College of Oratory, Boston, where she spent three years under instruction

Nervous prostration wasn't what was ailing Alice, of course, but that was the best thing she could think of to tell Dr. Stowell. And as a matter of fact, now that Elbert had moved her into the Crosby Cottage at 32 Lincoln Street in Hingham, she was not "seriously ill at her home in Boston," but supremely happy miles away from Boston—and the serenity *was* heavenly at Hingham that autumn!

Within a day or two after getting Alice settled in Hingham, Elbert made a final visit back home to gradually announce that he would be going back to Boston to do some more writing for Arena, Putnams', et al, and to take a few more courses at Harvard. Though he would be back for brief visits, it would probably be late in January or early in February before he could get back for a long one, he explained to Bertha, Mrs. Crawford and the boys.

Meanwhile, assured by constant letters from Elbert that he would be back for her hour of need and was taking all necessary steps to insure his being able to stay with her afterwards, Alice was enjoying her stay in Hingham with a calm that had not been with her for many months.

While back at East Aurora, Elbert looked through some old issues of the Buffalo Medical Journal. He was particularly interested in those containing information about childbirth. His father, who had been one of the founders of the Buffalo Medical Society, had been a frequent contributor to the Journal during the 1850s and some of his articles were on the subject of conception, delivery, etc.

Dr. Hubbard had left Buffalo in 1855 to practice in Bloomington, Illinois. It was there, on June 19, 1856, that Elbert was born. Now, 38 years later, the doctor's son needed a doctor's advice.

With all of his troubles, Elbert couldn't avoid chuckling to himself as he read several particularly pointed passages in his father's articles in the April 1855 issue titled "Theories of the Production of Males and Females."

> Now as I shall have occasion in my discourse to refer to some of the foregoing statements of authors, I will here give some of my own observations, to which I shall also afterward refer.

I have observed that those women who are strong and exercise the most on foot or on horseback, as a class, give birth to a greater ratio of males than those women who are sickly, or feeble, or sedentary in their habits or employments.

"What will Alice's baby be?" Hubbard mused. "She has always walked a lot and has been riding horses all her life . . . but she's sickly, too!"

What other theories did Dr. Hubbard have that might be more accurate as to the probable sex of their soon-to-be-born baby? After all, he and Alice already knew it would be a girl!

There it was, a few paragraphs later, but Elbert didn't like the terminology!

As for the opinion of some statisticians, that the ratio of female births is greater among those born illegitimately than those born in wedlock, it may possibly be accounted for on the supposition that women are more susceptible of seduction shortly after than before their courses.

Well, one thing sure, their baby *would* be legitimate in the eyes of the Divine Presence and Elbert would lash out with his pen someday at Mrs. Grundy's cruel habit of so branding innocent babes. Indeed, he told himself, the word "illegitimate" should be striken from the English language. No matter, their baby would have a proud and proper place even in a petty society. He would see to that, he vowed, if he did nothing else.

Armed with sufficient information about how to deliver a baby, Elbert arrived in Hingham to spend the September waiting days with Alice.

They had not long retired on September 16 when labor pains visited Alice. It was a normal birth and salesman, executive, college man and author Elbert Hubbard had now added midwifery to his growing list of experiences.

The baby, weighing 10 pounds, *was* a girl. Elbert promptly informed Alice.

"I know!" she said. *"We* knew, didn't we, love?"

There had been a partial eclipse of the moon visible throughout North America the night before the arrival of Elbert's and Alice's baby, but it shone brightly that night.

By careful planning though, the family scene at Hingham was eclipsed from the view of far-off Bertha and Alice's sister, Emma.

10

"She Has Been Born in a Jungle of Man-Made Laws"

The difference between married and stolen love came into sharper focus for the two lovers with the arrival of the little girl. She had to be loved. That was no problem. But she also had to be given a name and her birth duly recorded in the official records of Hingham, Mass. Mother and child had to be provided for.

Alice had her "husband" at her side, her baby at her breast and a comfortable roof over her head. To her, all seemed as it should and forever would be. But her Leander was just beginning a Hellespont swim that would last two decades and end as bittersweetly for them as it did for Hero and Leander of Greek mythology. Already Elbert sensed this but he joined Alice in the joy of the moment.

Laughingly, they agreed that settling upon a name could wait a while. In the meantime, "Howlums" seemed most appropriate.

The first of Kipling's *Jungle Books* made its debut in 1894 and one of the characters was Mowgli, a boy baby who was brought up by Mother Wolf with her own cubs. Following a rugged and hazardous boyhood among the animals of the jungle, Mowgli became a man looked up to by other men.

Elbert told Alice that she was already demonstrating the fierce, protective love of Mother Wolf. "Then I shall call her Mowgli," Alice replied, "for she has been born in a jungle of man-made laws and mores from which she will emerge unscathed and respected!"

Elbert nodded assent. "But she's not a he and so you had better think of a better name before we make it official."

There was no need to rush the recording of "Mowgli Howlums's" proper name. No doctor had officiated at her birth so Elbert could handle this detail to suit his own timetable. He needed time: time to think about how he was going to support two families and time to think about what might happen when the birth of a baby, born to Alice Moore and Elbert Hubbard, was officially recorded at Hingham. Local newspapers reported the vital statistics. Would everything now come out in the open? What would Alice's family do or say? What would the revelation do to Bertha, his relationship with his boys, his parents and his sisters? The disgrace, the spitting upon—what would all of this do to his new-found publishing connections and, indeed, to his just-beginning-to-hatch literary career?

Well, he had unnecessarily crossed such bridges before, hadn't he? Best course now was to be ready for whatever might come rather than to waste time on mental crossings! The realization came to him, though, that writing would have to be his salvation now, even as it had been the instrument to bring him to imminent downfall.

He had tasted forbidden fruit and already some small measure of literary acclaim through the gentle magic of that comely schoolteacher who now rocked their babe to sleep in old Crosby cottage. The wide pine floor-boards yielded arthritic snaps, one after the other, as the rockers massaged them over and over but across the room Elbert re-worked his first "Little Journey" biographical sketch, unannoyed by the rhythmic noise. He was strangely content and surer than ever that he would carve a niche for himself in the annals of American literature.

Not strange was the fact that much of what he now was "smoothing out" in his George Eliot sketch was lifted verbatim from his letter to Alice just after he had visited No. 4 Cheyne Walk.

But some of the other passages sprang to his mind solely because he was now with Alice and Mowgli:

> She corrected more proofs, and when a woman begins to assist a man the danger line is being approached.

and,

> Once there was a child called Romola. She said to her father one day, as she sat on his knee: "Papa, who would take care of me—give me my bath and put me to bed nights—if you had never happened to meet Mamma?

Elbert spent the first two weeks after Mowgli's birth assisting Alice, checking with Putnam's on the publicity to announce the availability of his newest novel, *No Enemy,* and on the George Eliot and other Little Journeys.

He felt the best way to sell some publisher on the idea of issuing one Little Journey a month in magazine form would be to have one sample issue printed. He would leave enough space on the covers to individually proof-press the name and address of each prospective publisher just so each could more readily identify himself with the concept.

However, a point he made early about these proposed sketches was to become lost to Hubbard critics of the distant future who were to dub them as shallow, incomplete and inaccurate biographies. Yet they were thus forewarned:

> Little Journeys does not claim to be a "Guide" to the places described, nor a biography of the characters mentioned. The volume, at best, presents merely outline sketches: the background being washed in with impressions of the scenes and surroundings made sacred by the lives of certain "Good Men & Great."
>
> Stray bits of information, "the feathers of lost birds" are here set down; various personal incidents are lightly detailed and some facts stated which have been told before.
>
> If these random records of beautiful days spent in little journeys may brighten the pleasant recollections of a few of those who have already visited the places described, or add to the desire for further knowledge on the part of those who have not, the publication will have fully accomplished its mission.

Elbert felt that, explained this way, a sample journey done up in print would surely find a publisher. Alice agreed.

"Well then, now all I have to do is to get with a printer who will let me get in the back room with him to set it up the way I want it . . . and do it as economically and quickly as possible!" Elbert excitedly explained.

"There's only one answer," he added. "I'll have to go back to East Aurora. My best bet is to work with White and Wagoner Print Shop on this. And while I'm there I'll sell off some livestock and get some extra money to tide us over here."

Alice's heart sank but she had long since learned that the best way to keep her impetuous lover was to let out the rope and then temptingly tug at the right time. And besides, little Mowgli could now add a tiny but compelling extra tug.

So early in October Elbert was back home. It was a heartening sign to Bertha but she concealed it because there was no way to express a ray of hope and that was all that was left of their marriage by now.

Elbert was kind and considerate but at the same time more distant and distracted than she had ever seen him. He made it a point to be out with the boys as much as possible when he wasn't up at the printers' working on the proposed "Little Journeys" magazine that he only casually explained to Bertha as the reason for his temporary return home. Nonetheless, his presence lightened the boys' hearts and she took her own heartlift from the happy father–sons reunion. Then, too, her friends and neighbors could see that Elbert was home and hear that he was working on still another literary project. At least the outward appearance of an intact family was renewed, which always helps to reduce tongue-wagging in a small village and Bertha was grateful even for this.

She and Dr. Mitchell's wife, along with the wives of 15 other prominent East Aurora men, had formed the Woman's Club of East Aurora
in March. It was a reading circle, the objectives of which were "mutual
improvement and the advancement of the interests of education and
philanthropy." By the time of Elbert's October return the club's member-
ship numbered 30 and Bertha, its first president, was in the midst of
planning its first large social function. It was to be a "banquet" for
members and friends "at the home of Mrs. E. G. Hubbard." Yes, it was
nice that Elbert was back at this time for it conveyed to all the appearance
of family well-being at the big Grove Street home!

Elbert thought of the letter he had mailed from the Back Bay Boston
post office on October 11 to Alice as he was heading back to East Aurora.
It was, of course, addressed to "Mrs. Elbert Hubbard, Hingham, Mass.":

Thursday noon

My Own—

We have tried Life for near six weeks, tried it under conditions
supposed to be hard and amid circumstances that men say are trying
and what does my Dear One say? Yes I repeat what does my Dear One
say—more—what do *I* say—yes I'll tell you what we both say, tell you
boldly, frankly, truly and well—but you know what we say.

You and I gentle lady have philosophised much and spoken again
and again of the ideal and through it all you have been firm in your
belief that the ideal could and should be real. So have I but my faith
has been misty at times while yours has always been clear. So often
have I seen my expectations turn to ashes at the touch that I kind of
thought that the world was not our home. Now we know it is. We
are at home here. We will be at home anywhere for love makes paradise.

Because you loved me very much and because I loved you very much
Little Mowgli came and Little Mowgli knows all the bears and wolves
and she is not afraid and neither are we.

Alice received the letter the next day—the day Elbert arrived back in
East Aurora—and lost no time in getting a reassuring reply off to him:

Friday Night (Oct. 12)

My Husband,

Thank you, My Beloved One, for the Letter of Love that I found
at the P.O. at 10:30. It made my step quicker and the sunshine brighter
and the responsibility lighter—and if possible it made Love greater.
Yes, yes, Dear One, the Ideal is the Real and Heaven is our Home and
wherever you are, there is my Heaven. I want no other. My Soul rests
in you and I am at Peace. Little Mowgli grows more precious to us
each day because each day we realize more and more that she is an
expression of our Love—one of the many, but *The One.* And this little
child* has led us and will lead us—yes, into much truth if not all the
truth.

* (Elberta Alicia or Alicia Elberta? or Mowgli or Love Babe or what? Ali-
berta, Elice, Ellicia)

After thus letting Elbert know where their mutual Heaven could only be, and then suggesting names for Mowgli that would firmly remind him of the dual parenthood, Alice deftly switched to Elbert's other consuming love—literature:

> The Librarian was very kind. I found in the English Men of Letters series the life of Thackery by Anthony Trollope but have had no opportunity to peep into it. Also found With Thackery In America by Eyre.
> Crowe and I think we shall find something there. I asked him of the bushy, fierce eyebrows about Oscar Wilde and he gave almost a snort (it was the funniest kind of a noise) and every bush of his eyebrows and hair stood up. "Oscar Wilde, brrrrrsph, sph, sph—he's too dude for us!"
> I laughed outright and said we had thought him very aesthetic but had found several short sketches lately that were most charming and wanted to read one of his books.
> "Ah is that so!" No hope of their getting them tho—only a small fund for books he said. I notice they have Marcellus tho.

Elbert sent the letter back without comment except to write "This is extremely funny" across that portion of her letter that related her discussion of Oscar Wilde with librarian Crowe. But he enclosed sayings clipped from his desk memo sheets for October 12, 13 and 14. They told a great deal of his dilemma and the constant prodding of his religious upbringing:

> Peace I ask—but peace can be but in being one with Thee.
>
> ********
>
> Soul must rise superior to environment, dominate the body, and free itself. The law of the Infinite never fails, and by compliance with its provisions we enlist its unlimited might in our behalf.
> —Henry Wood
>
> ********
>
> Only the man who supplies new feeling fresh from God, quickens and regenerates the race, and sets it on the King's highway, from which it has wandered into byways—not the man of mere intellect, of unkindled soul that supplies only stark-naked thought.
> —Hiram Corson, LL.D.
>
> ********
>
> God stooping shows sufficient of His light for those in the dark to ride by.
> —Browning
>
> ********
>
> Because thy loving-kindness is better than life; my lips shall praise Thee.
> —Psalms 63:3
>
> ********

We must live nobly to love nobly.

—Chas. Kingsley

Elbert added his own comment to the latter of Kingsley's philosophy— "With you it's easy!" But deep down he knew better. That could only be if he had been an unmarried man when first they met.

Now, back in East Aurora, he was again in the real world and was obliged to realistically measure the price of paradise in Hingham and of peace in East Aurora.

In terms of guilt and moral obligations the total cost was incalculable. Away from Alice's infectious calm, his faith in himself and in their ability to maintain the "ideal" was becoming misty again. Worse, he had to fight the inner turmoil alone.

The only way he could turn his mind away from visions of ruined lives and dashed expectations was to bury himself in his writing or abandon all thinking in favor of fast-paced frolicking with his boys. He did both and then tried to erase any lingering unpleasant thoughts by penning daily letters to Alice. Her daily letters to him brought him both peace and torment.

Ashamedly, he had to occasionally speak disparagingly of Bertha for he knew full well that the only thing that might unhinge Alice was the thought that Bertha might win him back while he was back home under her roof.

Thursday, October 18

My Beloved—

I went with Dr. Mitchell this morning to see a patient who gave birth to a baby ten days ago. She had not been up and will not be for some days yet. And the baby! Well, well, it gave no grunts of satisfaction neither could it lift up its voice and howlums, howlums—nor claw the air, nor stretch. Only moan and lift one thin little hand. The Mowgli is the princess of all babies—God bless us'n.

Was talking with the Dr. about bathing babies and he does not believe in putting them in a tub but believes in the least possible washing that is compatible with cleanliness.

Have sold two cows and the folks will keep the other as Bertie can milk. My customer has promised to come for the horse on Saturday. Have prospects of selling one piece of land in Buffalo but don't know— will see.

Have letter from Mrs. Crawford saying she will be back early in November. B— is ill and scarcely moves out at all. Sits stupid and pretends to paint at china but accomplishes little.

I am well and rode horseback from Buffalo yesterday. Am doing some writing on the drama—it is being copied on the typewriter.

You are in my thoughts all the time Dear Good Wife—I dream of you and of our baby and live over again all of our love prattle and in it all I cannot recall anything but pure love and joy.

You better see the Mother Goose and have her go out anyway and then again when I come.

I enclose key to Box No. 6 Cambridge P.O. Please go over when you are in Boston and get mail. Open it and keep it unless it demands a reply and then perhaps you can answer it. Open all my mail that comes of course.

I will be with you November 12th. Heaven bless my wife and baby (which is a measly stiff expression but I've no imagination away from old Smarty, Smarty and my little Howlums, Howlums).

Elbert's spirits were subject to quick change as he was buffeted by the emotions of Bertha and Alice. He couldn't effect the sale of livestock and property as quickly as he had hoped and the longer he witnessed Bertha's pretended buoyancy but obvious depression the sorrier he felt for her and the more disgusted he became with himself.

All of this was evident to Alice in the letter he penned to her on October 20:

Saturday (October 20)

My Blessed Wife—

Have just received a letter from the man (professor) whose ad we saw in the Clipper. He says he will be here next Tuesday and will take the horse if he is pleased with him. Have sold one of the cows and could sell the others for $6.00 each but do not care to do it. By taking a little time though I am sure a purchaser can be found.

Here's the situation Dear One, not so bad as 'twas a few weeks ago but hardly pleasant. Mrs. Crawford and B— had a quarrel and Mrs. C. left for Maryland ten days ago. B— is ill and therefore is to be pardoned for many shortcomings. So Mrs. C. will return Myrtilla says if I write and request it. This I have done.

Myrtilla came out this morning and will stay until Monday but no longer. It will take fully two weeks to get matters into leaving order here. Blackman (the hired man) leaves today and the boys know very little of work. Blackman has never shown them how and would not. But they are strong and willing. They have 100 ducks that Blackman has raised and 200 chickens. The ducks I will sell, in fact have sold pairs @ 40¢ each.

I am feeling well and am facing the problem as we must. Of course my heart goes out to you and the Mowgli—God bless 'er. I have been reading a few Shakesperian Sonnets—please read the first two and smile with me.

Dear Good Gentle Lady—how my heart goes out to you. But you are brave and strong and the Dear Blessed is hearty and we have money enough to buy food and clothes and you have plenty of milk for Mowgli and I wrap you both much with my love. Goodnight my Dear Ones—

When Alice received the gloomy letter she was vexed by his delay in getting away, worried by his turnaround sympathetic attitude toward Bertha. Hadn't he only recently observed to her that she "sat stupid" and "accomplished little" in her china-painting pretense?

She would give him something else to think about! She shot back a letter pointing out that her sister Emma was writing prying letters that indicated suspicion as to why she was in Hingham and not back at Potsdam teaching. Shouldn't they maybe best make a clean breast of things with Emma since she would probably not stop her prying until she saw Alice herself and knew all was well? Why not, since Elbert, she and Mowgli would be soon living together permanently at Hingham? And hadn't they better therefore give Mowgli a proper name and record her birth?

That letter, received on October 23, brought Elbert up short and brought a quick reply on Hotel Iroquois stationery. He tried to indicate calm and to be reassuring:

October 24, 1894

My Wife and My Baby's Mawmee—
   I went to P.O. to mail the letter to you and there it was. I am delighted that you did not tell good Grandma Goose to wait—delighted. Yes it shall be Miriam Crosby Hubbard (Crosby—yes of course—even if he is near and raises our rent next May; if he does we will go to London and teach Miriam Cockney and Paree-Francois).
   About your sister (777) I think we will have her come down towards Spring. We will both meet her in Boston. If she is with us a week or two by the Sea we can teach her a little truth. She will go back pleased—to remember your handsome face (and when you look at me it is handsome for it beams love and joy and Heaven). You are ever and always good looking. Anyone would pick you out of a crowd for an extraordinary woman, but you are only *beautiful* when you look at me.

To give further assurance he enclosed a note to his little daughter, addressed on a Western Union Telegraph blank from the Iroquois lobby writing desk to Miriam Crosby Hubbard c/o Crosby Cottage:

   Your name is no longer Mowgli but Miriam cause you were borned on Lincoln Street and Lincoln was the goodest man in the White House. They killed him 'cause he pulled thorns out of "niggers" pads. You too will always rise like your Mawmee to the level of events.
Your Papa

Such was the nature of their letters all through October—give and take, testing of each other's love and the ever-present cross references to a togetherness soon to be for ever and always.

On November 3 he told her:

   Putnams are getting out the "Little Journeys" on a plan that will surely pay us $30.00 or more a piece and give us a tuppering worth o' fame. (It will not be long!)

Alice felt a bit ashamed at the impatience she had shown. Here was evidence that Elbert's work back home, getting out the printed samples at White & Wagoner's, had paid off! And she hadn't made it any easier for him. Dear Elbert! Dear sweet, patient husband!

There were more delays and the necessary explanations by Elbert. The long-awaited November 12 came and went. November 17 was the next date set by Elbert for his departure for Hingham. He didn't quite make it. At 1:30 P.M. he proudly mailed her an order list "To the Trade" published by G. P. Putnam's Sons. It was a listing of their publications "for the Autumn Season of 1894" and there in boldface type, along with offered titles of established authors, was *Little Journeys To the Homes of Good Men and Great* by Elbert Hubbard with the further explanation, "A series of literary studies, published in monthly numbers, tastefully printed on hand-made paper, with attractive title page. No. 1—'George Eliot.' Oblong 24 mo. Price per copy, 5 cents; yearly subscription, 50 cents."

By 4:00 P.M. that same day he sent this wire to Mrs. E. Hubbard, c/o Crosby Cottage, Lincoln Street, Hingham:

I LEAVE HERE MONDAY.

(signed) BROWNING

He had shipped two coops of chickens to Hingham and had told Alice to order in coal for the winter.

The plain but persistent school teacher had won another Thanksgiving with her beloved Elbert and *this* Christmas would be theirs again. They would together play with the little girl they had conceived on Christmas last.

On November 19 Elbert left East Aurora for "business and work in Boston" that would keep him there "until spring for sure this time." It was a departure mixed with relief and regrets but there was no other way now. As he rode the train to New England he thought about how much the title of his just-published, not-so-good novel fitted his personal circumstances—*No Enemy but Himself.*

After Thanksgiving Elbert became a near commuter between Hingham and Boston. Studying and writing in the library there, shooting off letters to Putnam's from there and trying out article ideas at the Arena, he buried himself as much as possible in literary schemes, dreams and work. He *had* to become a success in that field. There was no turning back to the life of a businessman, even if he wanted to—and he didn't want to.

He corresponded from Boston with his oldest son, Bertie, now going on 12, from the American Unitarian Association Building at 25 Beacon Street, using their stationery. He picked up letters there from Bertie, too. To write from Hingham would have set Bertha and Mrs. Crawford to wondering why he was lodging so far away from his work in Boston and this was certainly no time to arouse more suspicions than might already exist.

There were the ever-touching aspects to his letters to Bert and their between-the-lines messages for Bertha:

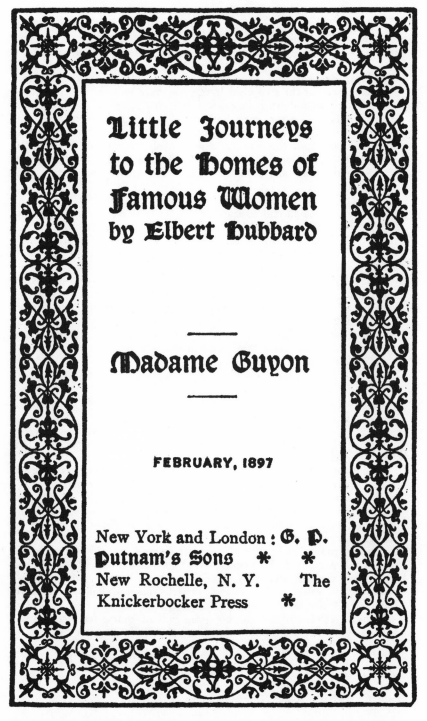

Little Journeys to the Homes of Famous Women
by Elbert Hubbard

Madame Guyon

FEBRUARY, 1897

New York and London : G. P.
Putnam's Sons * *
New Rochelle, N. Y. The
Knickerbocker Press *

On his first trip abroad Elbert's letters to Alice were 90 percent travelogue. She saved them and they became the basis for his first magazine effort. He sold G. P. Putnam's Sons of New York the idea of putting out a brief "Little Journey" biographical sketch on a monthly basis. Later, when he established his own print shop, he took over the whole project.

Boston, Mass.
December 16, 1894

My Dear Bertie Boy

Thank you for the two good letters you have sent, or was it three or four? You are my little business man; you forward the letters and pay the bills and do the work, and feed the chickens and give them hay, and curry the dogs, and milk the geese, and drive the rabbits, and wash the wood, and split the grass, and whitewash the cat, and kerosene her roost, and dig the apples, and pick the turnips, and read the furnace, and paint the road, and plough the fence and shovel the potatoes down your throat.

In fact you are a real good boy and I am very proud of you.

The letters Ralph and Sanford sent were well written and very nice. I will write them both soon. But I cannot come back now. I have important work to do here in the big library and at Harvard so I must attend to it. I get along very slow though and the days pass and it seems I am doing very little indeed.

Then I get only a little money for my articles in the newspapers and not much for the books but someday I may do still better.

Anyway you and the boys and Mamma shall always have all you need. I will send money every week and nice things too perhaps.

I have written Mr. Maur to have him take care of Columbus for us until next summer. So I think he will get him in a week or so.

With much love to you all.

E. G. H.

Then, just a few days before Christmas, another letter to Bertie:

Boston, Mass.
December 21, 1894

My Dear Bertie Boy—

I suppose that the white horses have gone and the Baba has gone too. Please write up his account so I can mail you a check for him.

Fred Maur will come for Columbus soon as he is going to take care of him for us. If Columbus is there yet put him in the box stall and when he goes keep Juliet in there, leaving a bucket of water in the manger for her.

I want you to look after things just as well as you know I would and I will pay you $1.00 a week. Your good Mamma will let you keep the money yourself and with it you must buy all your own clothing— red neckties, shirts with scratchy, scratchy bosoms, long pants, derby hats and all nice things that a young gentleman needs.

When I send mail for the boys you will of course let them open it themselves as no one should ever open other folks letters or papers.

With much love as ever.

E. G. H.

P.S. Bertie Boy—

Up in my little room in the garret is a package of books (Forbes and One Day). Ask Mamma to mark it

G. P. Putnams Sons
27 W. 23rd St.
New York City
Then you take it to the station and give it to Mister Barkaleck for to go.

There is always a false feeling of Peace around Christmas—even, it seems, for the most troubled of persons. One puts despair on the shelf for a few days to better enjoy the general make-believe of the season, but it was an uneasy calm for Alice, Elbert and Bertha this Christmas. It did little to prepare them for the trying events that would unfold for all of them in the coming year.

Elbert made one firm New Year's resolve and kept it. On January 1, 1895 he registered the birth of his and Alice's daughter. In the record it read:

DATE OF BIRTH: September 16, 1894
FULL NAME OF CHILD: Miriam C. Hubbard
SEX, COLOR: Female, white
PLACE: Hingham, Mass.
NAME OF FATHER: Elbert Hubbard
MAIDEN NAME OF MOTHER: Alice L. Moore
RESIDENCE OF PARENTS: Hingham, Mass.
OCCUPATION OF FATHER: Journalist
BIRTHPLACE OF FATHER: Illinois
BIRTHPLACE OF MOTHER: New York
RECORDED: Jan. 1, 1895

11

"With Much Love to the Boys and Yourself"

At 777 Front Avenue in Buffalo, Emma Woodworth gazed out the window at the January snow. Her thoughts went back to her childhood and the snow-blanketed countryside that surrounded the farm where she and Alice had grown up. She wondered what Alice might be doing, at that very moment. She turned to her lawyer-husband and repeated the conjecture aloud to him.

There was something amiss, she feared. Alice's letters were too circumspect. Wouldn't he maybe be able to arrange a business trip over Boston way and do a little checking for her?

Wayland Woodworth was characteristically direct in his reply. "I suspect that the easiest way to find her is to locate Hubbard up there through his publisher. I'll go up as soon as I can arrange it but don't be surprised if I come back and report that he has her in the family way by now!"

The thought sent cold shivers through Emma and she didn't care to look at the snow anymore.

Late in January, Attorney Woodworth did arrange a meeting with Elbert in Boston and his suspicions were confirmed. He came back and reported the situation to Emma. Alice had a beautiful four-month-old daughter and was radiantly well and happy living with Hubbard in Hingham.

Emma was stunned, notwithstanding the fact that she had prepared herself for the worst after her husband's candid remarks before traveling to Boston.

"Well, what are they going to do?" she asked. "It is an impossible situation. He is already married and you know adultery is the only grounds for divorce! We've got to protect Alice some way."

Woodworth calmed his wife. "I know! I know! Hubbard has agreed to come here to the house in a couple of weeks and we'll talk it over with him then."

At Hingham Alice was in a mood of deep depression. What was happening to the Ideal? When Wayland had hinted that she and Elbert couldn't possibly continue to live together, her "husband" had not raised his voice in protest. Nor had he commented negatively when Wayland suggested that perhaps she and the baby should remove to the Woodworth home in Buffalo until a solution could be worked out.

"My God, Dear One, how would that have helped?" Elbert asked. "Things are going to be bad enough when Emma hears about Mowgli. They found out before we were ready and we don't want them doing anything about it until we've had time to think!"

Alice had to agree. The thing she had feared most was Emma's reaction at whatever time she learned the whole truth about her and Elbert. If tempers were allowed to flare now, Bertha, too, would know too soon because the Woodworths would logically want to bring down additional wrath upon Elbert's head. Perhaps, after all, he had handled the confrontation the best way under the circumstances and his agreeing to go soon to the Woodworth home to face Emma's scorn would set things right.

Alice was wrong, of course. It wasn't going to be that easy.

It wasn't long before Bertha was hearing ugly rumors about her husband, Alice and a baby. She had the rumors investigated and soon found they had a basis in fact. Yet she was strangely relieved, for while the hurt was deep, it was like the final pain to a heart that had been aching too long to still be overly sensitive to yet another blow.

Not unpredictably, her greater anger was directed toward Alice. She knew that Mrs. Grundy could easily now be beckoned to her side against "the other woman." The Woodworths were equally aware of this aspect of the situation. Rightly or wrongly, Alice's reputation was hanging in the balance, more so than anyone's at the moment. Emma would have to make Alice see that, and if Elbert, who had more influence over Alice than anyone, could be made the instrument to drive home the message, all the better. If he had to be the one to convince her that going their separate ways was the only answer, surely this would cure her once and for all of her infatuation with him.

The day came for Elbert's visit to the Woodworths. The chill in the air wasn't all because it was a mid-February day. The Woodworths plainly didn't like Elbert Hubbard. They sent their curious youngsters upstairs when they saw him approaching the house. His reception at the door was icy but the conversation in the parlor soon became heated.

Had he been in a court of law he might have tried to argue his case but, anywhere, his wisest approach would have been "no defense." Certainly in the Woodworth parlor that was the *only* plea that would be accepted. Having made it, the only matters left to resolve were his assurances that he would deliver Alice and the baby to them, promise to stay away from them, and provide funds for the baby's support.

The only solace in all of this was that it made it easier for him to face Bertha. He would have to endure scorn there, too, but the promises as to his future behavior were already forced upon him by the Woodworths and these would, he knew, be identical with the wishes of Bertha.

He confessed to her what she already knew about Alice and the baby and told her about his visit with the Woodworths. Amazing Bertha! She told him if he had learned his lesson and was sincere in all of his promises to the Woodworths she would help him in the promise to them of child support by agreeing to adoption of the baby into her own family.

It was a chastened Elbert who headed back to Hingham. He felt better now that Bertha had found him out and heard him out. Her seeming willingness to try to pick up the pieces of their marriage perplexed him but he conjectured that it was dictated more by a desire to avoid scandal than by any possible lingering affection for him. But his doubts about his own deep feelings toward Bertha or Alice troubled him more than anything now. If he had ever really loved Bertha, how could he have become so deeply involved with Alice? And if Alice was his soulmate, how could he even consider a promise to put her and their baby out of his life?

Well, at this point he had only agreed with the Woodworths and Bertha to go back and try to convince Alice that this was the only sensible choice for her own sake. Looking at the whole proposition from the viewpoint of protecting her and Mowgli from public scorn and hurt it did seem to be the only logical solution. But their love wasn't born in logic nor had it been fed by it. In truth, it was the lack of logic or common sense by the conventional definition that lit the flame and kept it burning.

Alice had been anxiously awaiting Elbert's return and looked for an alleviating sign in his eyes. It wasn't there as they embraced in the biting breeze that swept across the front porch of Crosby Cottage.

Elbert hurried her inside and seemed unusually preoccupied with hanging up his overcoat and suitcoat which he usually quickly pulled off and carelessly tossed over the back of a chair. He fondled little Mowgli and inquired as to how they had both been while he was away.

Finally he took Alice's hand in his and led her to the sofa, drawing her close to his side as they sat down.

"They want us to separate. Just as you have suspected ever since Woodworth was here," he said.

Alice began to protest and he quickly put a finger to her lips. "But I haven't agreed or disagreed. I've said we would talk it over and let them know, so let's not do it tonight when we're tired. All right?"

Alice nodded assent for tonight she wanted his arms more than his thoughts.

Elbert knew that he couldn't fulfill any promise to either the Woodworths or Bertha unless Alice was in full agreement. Stay away from her? Possibly he could but, just as it was back in 1890, one innocent letter and then more and more letters would ultimately bring them back together. And now Mowgli would add power to the magnet.

Yet, in the waning weeks of February, the only way Alice would even think of "giving it a try" by going to live with the Woodworths was with a hint from Elbert that they could correspond for a while to relieve the hurt of separation.

It was a dangerous concession for him to make and he would have to live with it. So would the Woodworths, he told them.

Reluctantly, in early March, "Mr. and Mrs. Hubbard" and daughter left the Crosby Cottage. The lease didn't expire until May so they didn't have to hurry about removing their books and the pieces of furniture they had added to the furnished dwelling. To the neighbors, they were just going to their Buffalo home for a few months. But of course, they were going back to separate lives as Alice Moore and Elbert G. Hubbard— going back to reality. Or was it that?

One thing was certain. Now that they were back home Elbert would be obliged to keep his part of the bargain with the Woodsworths. Alice was under their ever-watchful eye. As he had anticipated, Alice had absolutely no interest in Bertha's offer to adopt the baby. As might be expected, she even regarded the offer as a deliberate and ultimate *coup de grace* by Bertha but such was not to be the case. For all of her faults, Bertha was not a vindictive person and, indeed, her greatest fault was her abiding, trusting love for Elbert. If it was a fault then Alice, too, had that weakness.

The Woodworths and Mowgli kept Alice busy that March but her heart was in East Aurora. She wondered how Elbert was managing to accomplish anything now that he was back in the midst of chattering boys and in-laws, the disruptive social activities of Bertha and the inevitable intrusions upon his time by Dr. Mitchell and his other friends. He had hinted that this might all become too much just at a time when things seemed to be breaking right for him in the world of letters.

Actually, in the beginning this was so. Getting back into the old pre-Alice routine was filled with awkward situations, stilted conversation, hesitant glances and clumsy courtesies toward a wife who had become almost a stranger. It was equally difficult for Bertha, this business of getting reaquainted. Yet, they had once been everything to each other and there was an element of flirtation to their new, forced togetherness.

Elbert had much writing to do and she had resolved not to stand in his way. If possible, and if he would let her, she would this time try to help him for he *was* making good progress in his pursuit of a career she had once thought an imprudent choice for him.

One March evening he was going through a box of old letters in his garret writing room and he came upon a letter he had written to Bertha when she was away with two of their boys, on a vacation trip in 1888.

She had saved it! The J. D. Larkin & Co. stationery he had used first attracted his attention and sent his thoughts back over the years to that long-since-abandoned career. Then he read the letter:

Buffalo, N. Y.
September 3, 1888

My Good Wife—

Your letter from Wilton Centre reached me this A.M. and I am grateful therefor. Mail every other day did you say? And here we are raising a disturbance because we get mail only three times a day. Mr. & Mrs. Nichols and their daughter went out with me Saturday and came in this morning greatly pleased with Aurora and their visit.

Yesterday was a perfect autumn day. It rained several days last week so the grass and flowers look fresh and delightful and the sun coming out warm made the weather all that could be wished for. I think our flowers never looked quite as well as they do now. We picked a large bunch of sweet peas but it looked as if we left the vines full.

Ellen just layed herself out on the cooking and an excellent dinner (fried chicken, etc., etc.) was the result. Mr. Nichols complimented her on her skill in cooking and she made a large oval Irish smile and was greatly pleased.

Your quotation from Haven and remarks thereon pleased me. It seems recent writers take a little different view of the faculty of Imagination from what Haven does although he is in the main correct. Imagination is first cousin to memory. Memory consists of two distinct acts of the mind. First the *Impression* and then the power to recall that impression at will. In Imagination we use the same impression which has been stored away in the mind for memories use, and then we combine and arrange and sort out what Impressions we need in the particular fabric and Imagination weaves them together.

But there can no more be Imagination without the mind is stored with Impressions than there can be memory without a first impression. Webster I see defines Imagination as a creative faculty, but it is the poverty of language that compels him to use the word "creative" in this place. One can no more create an image of the mind than I can "create" soap. When I wish to make soap I go to the storehouse and select the needed materials and combine them into a fabric. If I wished to write fiction I would first take good care to store up in my mind's warehouse impressions relating to the intended story.

Before Edwin Arnold wrote "The Light of Asia" he traveled through that country with eyes and ears open and read everything to be found (in Gorko?) relating to Oriental customs. All simply to get his mind in good condition to "imagine an imaginary tale."

The reason we should cultivate the imagination in children is to give them strong memories—power to recall impressions. "Some people," says Loisette, "have poor memories because they receive indistinct first impressions. Others because they have not the power to call up an impression at will—slight and nervous people cannot recall impressions. Such people should cultivate the Imagination which consists in recalling and rearranging first impressions."

How necessary that we should store our minds with beautiful and useful impressions. The mind should be a gallery of beautiful pictures from which should be excluded all that is base and unworthy.

There was much more to the long, long letter and Elbert scanned through it, noting he had quoted John Milton and a later poet he hadn't bothered to name. He twice re-read to himself his closing line, "With much love to the boys and yourself, as ever, Yours, Bert."

He closed up the garret and carried the letter down to the parlor. Everyone had retired except Bertha. He sat down beside her without looking to see what her mood might be. "Listen to what I just found," he said, pointing to the old letter.

Bertha listened and studied him as he read. His profile was as handsome now as it was then, she thought, but lines of strain and worry have been added.

And, somehow, those words and thoughts of 1888 seemed more significant now than they had back then.

Yes, how necessary now "that we should store our minds with beautiful thoughts and useful impressions" and "exclude all that is base and unworthy."

And what were those closing words he had just uttered again? "With much love to the boys and yourself, as ever, Yours."

Little more was spoken that night. They caressed and summoned up beautiful impressions of their first togetherness as newlyweds. Unknowingly, they thus imagined a new fabric of life.

12

"Individuality Is the Thing"

Now the tables were turned. It was Alice who was experiencing the loneliness of separation from the man she loved. Imagination was nothing new to her. She knew full well that this faculty had much to do with her present predicament. She and Elbert had permitted the platonic impressions of *The Man* to conjure up for them an ideal marriage outside the bounds of convention. The Woodworths and Bertha had abruptly disturbed the dreamers.

Alice awakened to a nightmare. Now *she* was a mother and a homebody; tied down, but with more time than ever for the same kind of imagining she had once seen as simply a petty failing in Bertha. Alice now saw Bertha as the "other woman." Ironically, that woman was *legally* living under the same roof with the man Alice had claimed as "husband."

Against formidable odds Alice still clung to the belief that she, Elbert and Mowgli would eventually all be together again for ever and ever. Elbert was pledged to dissuade her from that belief. Of course, the inherent weakness in assigning this major role to him was that he had never been stronger than Alice. Even since their paths crossed she had, in fact, somehow been at once his major strength and fatal weakness.

Thus in their allowed correspondence of that spring's transition period, Alice constantly reminded him of what they had been and should ever be to each other.

To keep her from going off the deep end he gave her implied assurances that he still loved her. At the same time he tried to convince her that they had no choice but to go their separate ways from now on. To her it was as though he were waving her off with beckoning arms and, in truth, a part of his nature *was* doing just that. Such was the strange, inexplicable bond between them from the very beginning—the one they had called the Divine Presence.

Elbert had taken upon himself the unwise and impossible collateral task of convincing two women that he loved them. He did, in this strange way, love them both, and the hopelessness of his predicament was all too evident in his letters to Alice that May and June:

> Tonawanda, N.Y.
> Saturday (May 18, 1895)
>
> My Beloved:
> Thank you for the pictures. They are most beautiful. The child has improved beyond my hopes or expectations.
> My Dear One I cannot do what you ask—I have no nerve force to make this fight.
> We have followed the advice of Mr. & Mrs. Woodworth so far— let us continue it—on practical affairs perhaps they are better than we.
> I am on a tramp tour with Bertie—to Lockport, etc. We will be gone two weeks.
> With great love but in the depths.
> Yours

By now there was a special urgency in trying to convince Alice once and for all that they must forget each other as the Woodworths had insisted. Bertha was with child. Alice's undying hopes for a future with Elbert *had* to be dashed in a kinder way than telling her this! Elbert's best course now seemed to be to invite her scorn early enough to lessen the shock when she did eventually learn about Bertha's condition.

Elbert, with shaky hand, penned a long letter designed to invite scorn and drive the wedge. He mailed it to Alice in care of the Woodworths:

> Friday A.M.
> (June 7, 1895)
>
> My Beloved:
> The wringing and tearing away from these three boys, together with pressure from various points, is a thing I cannot do and live.
> As it is, I "live the lie" and choose one kind of death rather than another. Yet I am *trying* to work at my history, I am *trying* to read, and you too must try to work. And perhaps now, as it has been before, the sorrow-stricken children of earth will yet have a message for those that live at their ease.
> I have no nerve and no courage to be bold away from you. We tried to do without man's consent and had not the strength; and so I will not see you again unless I can make you my legal wife. I tell you this for your own good and to satisfy your sister.
> Mr. & Mrs. W— have stood by you manfully and showed an extent of sympathy and appreciation of the untoward conditions that I would not have thought possible in people not given perhaps to much sentiment.
> Again my Dear One let me confess my weakness and say that I cannot face the tears, threats, entreaties and maledictions of these dozen pen-

sioners. I am drifting. You will despise me and your heart will grow bitter towards one so weak, and I will not blame.

As requested by Mrs. W— I have destroyed my will where you are mentioned but there is a life insurance policy of $5,000 payable to you. I will send you through Mr. Merritt ten dollars a week.

Go to Martha's Vineyard as you proposed—you will find companionship and new scenes that will do you good. Keep a journal and write on every and any subject.

Alice was little convinced, even by this, that the end of their romance had come. Desolate, but still resolute in this conviction, she planned a vacation, began thinking about where she might resume teaching in the fall and continued sending letters to Elbert—letters he let pile up before answering as part of his continued effort to sever their relationship without breaking her heart and spirit.

The truth was that Elbert couldn't long face "the tears, threats, entreaties and maledictions" of Alice either—or those of anyone he loved. A frailty, perhaps, but not unique with him, nor among men, great or otherwise, down through the ages. And, like others who faced with problems stemming from a weakness double their efforts where they do have strength, Elbert delved ever deeper into his writing projects.

With a firm commitment to Putnam's Sons for one Little Journeys biographical sketch per month, Elbert at least had his work assured even

Cabin in the woods back of East Aurora where Hubbard wrote many of his later "Little Journeys" biographical sketches.

if he did not obtain a substantial income from writing. He had a two-fold need to expand his writing revenues notwithstanding the fact that he was reasonably well-fixed with properties and the residue from the selling of his partnership in the soap company. But he had the agreement through the Woodworths to contribute to the support of his and Alice's baby. Moreover, since his source material for the Little Journeys was mostly in the pages of his European love letters to Alice, it was well-nigh impossible for him to keep his thoughts from drifting toward the romance he was supposed to be trying to forget.

He resolved to clear his mind by undertaking a biography of John Brown, the complicated character of the nation's anti-slavery and Civil War era. He planned to enter it in a book-writing competition which promised a $1,000 guarantee by fall, if accepted, with an advertised long-range potential of $10,000. But even this effort tended to bring back memories of that other world in which he had too long lived with Alice and the work went slowly as he tried to find the free and independent author, Elbert Hubbard.

Always there seemed to creep in the kinds of Elysian-fields thoughts that possessed him and his forbidden love:

Birds and babies go to sleep at sundown, and like Solomon's ideal woman, arise while it is yet night.

The ecstasy of forest birds at the first flush of summer day-dawn is a thing to remember long. But to hide their song away in your heart so that you shall keep it forever and a day, you must have heard it in childhood. For then hopes beat high, and a belief in the celestial, the mystical and the miraculous were living things like the song-birds themselves; then you never doubted but that the magic potency of the thyrsus would yet be yours, and at the waving of your wand spirits would start, and men would do your bidding.

As he plodded forward in his independent efforts, without the heretofore frequent rehashing of lines and chapters with Alice, he was coming up with a better style even if the thoughts were basically unchanged at the root source.

Inevitably, he found comparison (where there was really no parallel) between John Brown's two loves and his own and permitted it to find its way into the biography:

Love gives wisdom, and although John Brown was moving straight-forward to his union with this girl, and while there was an attractive side to it all, in his more sober moments he felt there was an inhuman side as well. The young man knew what he was doing; the young woman had no conception of it. She was a blind, passive party to a plan. Fate was pushing her forward and she in her innocence and ignorance knew not where. But someday there would be an awakening. Rachel was capable of love, but John had not awakened her to it: to marry her would be a sin.

Besides all this, when the warmth of young blood ran quiet, John knew that Rachel's spirit did not match his. He had suffered, been disappointed; sorrow and care had come to him in varied forms; he felt deeply. Concerning these things she knew nothing, and could not comprehend, should he explain. So all their conversation was quite in a minor key and on trivial topics. He knew deep down in his heart that no man should attach himself for life to a woman who could not sympathize with his every mood. To marry outside of one's mental sphere was to curb and stifle and hold in check one's highest thought. John knew all this for love of Margaret had made him wise.

Three ways seemed to open before him.

The first and easiest was to drift, and in a year marry Rachel Crosby; he need do scarcely a thing, all would be planned for him. All he had to do would be to hold her in his arms just an instant some Sunday night when she gave him that little parting peck, and kiss her in earnest, right before her mother. Then say a few words and all would be arranged as a matter of course, and he would move over and take up his abode at the Crosby cottage just as he used to—only different.

The second plan was to go straight to Zanesville and claim the woman he loved: claim her in the name of an exalted and all-absorbing passion, and then fight it out with the world, the flesh and the devil.

The third plan was to marry just as nine-tenths of all the men in the world marry: pick the girl that pleases, and provided she seems good natured and strong and will look up to you, pop the question some moonlight night and have it all over with. If she says yes, all right, and should she say no, don't forget there's just as good fish in the sea as ever were caught—fol de rol, la la la la te da! And as for talk about affinities, it's all in your eye. People who are willing to cultivate two bears can get along alright—pish!

But in certain moods it is very easy to dispose of great questions. In the mellow light of evening, for instance as the soft music plays, life and fate present no serious difficulties. On the morrow when we start off to our day's work and alone face the cold realities, things appear different.

This portion of his John Brown biography was really Elbert's soliloquy on his past, present and future. Rachel Crosby was his Bertha Crawford and Margaret Livingston his Alice Moore. But Elbert had already married Rachel before he met Margaret. And the Freudian slip about the Crosby "cottage" only proved the magnitude of his dilemma as opposed to that of the man he was writing about. Incongruously, or ironically, Elbert had slept with the wrong woman in a Crosby cottage of a latter day. And, at the very moment of his present writing, was tempted to go straight to Buffalo, 15 miles away, and "claim the woman he loved: claim her in the name of an exalted and all-absorbing passion, and then fight it out with the world, the flesh and the devil."

But there was more to write about John Brown and, the soliloquy aside, Elbert recalled his already accomplished inhumanity to Bertha, the rude, cruel awakening he had handed her. He was busy at work, alone, and needed to face the cold reality to which he had just referred.

Uptown at White & Wagoner's, where Elbert had run off the sample copies of the Little Journeys pamphlets, a newspaperman named Harry P. Taber was kicking around a publication idea with another newsman, William McIntosh. They discussed it with their up-and-coming author friend Elbert Hubbard and he saw it as another opportunity to display his talents. None of them saw it as an income venture of any consequence.

The idea was to come out with a little pocket magazine in which they could write what pleased them—no rejection slips from publishers to contend with and no blue-penciling of their gems. They called it the *Philistine.* As Elbert pointed out, "It was Leslie Stephen who said, 'The term Philistine is a word used by prigs to designate people they do not like.' When you call a man a bad name, you are that thing—not he." So here, then, were three self-designated Philistines dedicated to the delightful task of taking pot shots at prigs and, at the moment, they felt that way about a lot of publishers. Elbert felt that way about others—social bores, old-fashioned preachers and Mrs. Grundy.

The first issue went out in June 1895 and it caught on like wildfire.

McIntosh set the tone with his opening issue editorial, "Philistines Ancient and Modern" and Elbert particularly agreed with one passage:

> It was a Philistine, a despised player and holder of horses, who gave the modern world its literature. It was a heretic monk who threw ink stands, not only at Satan, but at embodied and enthroned religion, who gave the modern world its impetus to freedom. The imaginative authors who most strongly sway mankind today are Philistines. Thackeray smilingly lifted the mask from aristocracy and exposed its sordid servility. Dickens threw down the idols of pretentious respectability. Hugo taught the democracy of virtue. Tolstoi dethroned convention in religion. Ibsen divorced morality from law.

Elbert's contribution to Volume 1, Number 1 was titled "English Monuments" and dealt with some observations he had made during his 1894 visit to England as to how that country regarded its men of letters. He struck hard with his lead paragraph and never let up:

> England relegates her poets to a "corner." The earth and the fullness thereof belongs to the man who can kill; on this rock have her State and Church been built.

But where he really hit his stride was in a section titled "Sidetalks with the Philistines" in which he interspersed little barbs at other magazines of the day with kind words about people and publishers he wanted to cultivate. The readers loved it.

The June issue had been in preparation during most of May, the latter part of which month Elbert learned from a blushing Bertha that she was with child. What had he said in his John Brown manuscript? "When the

THE PHILISTINE

Vol. 1.   East Aurora, June 1895.   No. 1.

A Periodical of Protest.

———

Those Philistines who engender animosity, stir up trouble and then smile.   —JOHN CALVIN.

PRINTED EVERY LITTLE WHILE FOR THE SO-
CIETY OF THE PHILISTINES AND PUBLISHED
BY THEM MONTHLY.   SUBSCRIPTION, ONE
DOLLAR YEARLY; SINGLE COPIES, TEN CENTS.

The first issue of The Philistine, *June 1895.*

warmth of young blood ran quiet, John knew that Rachel's spirit did not match his." Well, the warmth of Elbert's young blood had not been quiet that March night of reconciliation and now, though quieted by the work at hand, his spirit and Bertha's would have to match. And he sensed that once Alice learned of the new development in an already complicated triangle she would surely call him "Philistine" in the most derogatory sense—and so too would the Woodworths.

But Alice was not to know for many months. She passed the summer in lonely vacation and applying for teaching positions, finally landing one at Whitby College in Ontario which kept her busy and out of personal touch with the goings on at East Aurora though she was an avid reader of the *Philistine* magazine. She did manage weekend trips home to the Woodworths, always arriving with an armful of presents for her daughter and Emma's daughter, too.

By the time the August *Philistine* was rolling from the presses of White & Wagoner's "Pendeniss Press—Printers of the *Philistine*," Elbert's intriguing "Sidetalks" had wooed Boston's Walter Blackburn Harte into becoming a contributor and was working through the same medium on Richard LeGallienne, Stephen Crane and many other known or emerging literary figures. Crane came into its pages via a poem in the August issue and then became a "regular" that fall.

By November Elbert, Taber and McIntosh were even laying plans for the author of *Black Riders* and *The Red Badge of Courage* to come to Buffalo where the three would arrange a press and personages dinner in his honor. The October appearance of *Red Badge* had brought much wider acclaim to Crane than had his *Black Riders* collection of poetry, but he could use more publicity and so could the Philistines. The date of December 19 was set for the affair. The place, the Hotel Genesee in downtown Buffalo.

Elbert was kept busy all that November and early December laying plans for Crane's visit. He had always abhorred the silly teas that the Larkins and Bertha delighted in back in the days when he drifted from such things toward his association with Alice. Now he was learning that there were teas and teas—like literary teas.

Julia Ditto Young, a Buffalo poetess and wife of a bank executive, had come to know Elbert and Bertha, as did Mr. Young. Elbert was interested in publishing some of her poems in the *Philistine* and later possibly publishing a book of her works at the Pendeniss Press. She was similarly interested.

The Hubbards visited the Youngs and Elbert and Julia corresponded, perfectly properly, about these aims and coincidentally about their views of Stephen Crane as well as a possible tea at the Youngs' for Crane when he arrived in December.

Elbert had also been giving little lectures and Browning readings at the Youngs' home and the homes of Mrs. Young's friends. It was not financially rewarding in a direct way but it gave him added exposure and usually resulted in new subscribers to the *Philistine*.

He managed time, too, for a few public lectures, mostly—and oddly enough—for church benefits. The September 5, 1895 issue of the *East Aurora Advertiser,* the village's weekly newspaper, carried this item:

> "A Tramp in Ireland" will be the subject of a lecture given in the Universalist Church (Cowlesville) at 7:30 P.M. by Elbert G. Hubbard of East Aurora. Admission to lecture 15 cents.

Elbert's whirlwind pace was dictated as much by conscience as by ambition. Religion-related thoughts dominated his writings. The emphasis was on suffering and difference between man-made laws and morality. Because he and Harry Taber had decided in September to publish a book—he writing it and Taber setting it up in type—Elbert had to set aside his John Brown biography for the moment and forego entering it in the literary competition.

The book that now consumed Elbert's every spare moment was his study of Solomon's Song of Songs, which was to be published together with a reproduction of the Biblical text.

Elbert's study had his familiar self-vindicating ring to it but there would be readers who would find solace in it for he was not the only person in the world who had sinned:

> To me The Song of Songs is simply the purring of a healthy young barbaric chief to a sun-kissed shepherdess and she, tender hearted, innocent and loving, purrs back in turn, as sun-kissed maidens ever have and will. The poem was composed, we have reason to believe, fully three thousand years ago, yet its impressionistic picture of youthful love is as charming and fresh as the color of a Titian.
>
> An out-of-door love, under the trees, where "the beams of our house are cedar, and our rafters of fir . . . and our bed is green" is the dream of all lovers and poets. Thus the story of Adam and Eve, in the Garden of Eden, "naked and unashamed," has been told a score of times, and holds its place in all Sacred Writ. Shakespeare in As You Like It and The Tempest shows the idea. Paul and Virginia give us a glimpse of the same thought; so does the Emilius of Rousseau, and more than once Browning suggests it in his matchless poems. Stevenson has touched deftly on the beautiful dream and so have several other modern story tellers.
>
> And surely the love of man and woman is not an ungodly thing, else why should God have made it? "God's dice are loaded," says Emerson, and further he adds, "All natural love between boy and girl, man and woman, is a lovely object for the richness of its mental and spiritual possibilities are to us unguessed."

Elbert was well-read and well equipped to put down, for others to read, this and more advanced defenses for the day when his affair with Alice might become known. For the present, and for the unknowing, it seemed as though here was a man possessed of a daring and unusual compassion for lovers who had erred against convention.

The party for Stephen Crane was quite a success. It helped boost Crane toward a permanent niche in the annals of American literature and the articulate, colorful Elbert Hubbard gained new stature and wider personal notice through the well-planned and executed exposure of Crane.

It was just another step in his own career-building, even though he had considerable respect for Crane's ability. A letter to Julia Ditto Young after the event put his mood in focus:

East Aurora, Dec. 28

Dear Mrs. Young:

Thank you very much for the check—such things are quite useful. The five subscriptions for both publications have been recorded and the booklets will go forward in due course.

Mad at you for not liking Mr. Crane? My, my, my! Why, Gentle Lady, look you—that's just why I like you—because you have opinions of your own and express them. *Individuality* is the thing. To it I remove my hat.

Here are poems sent in by the Great Obscure. Pray do read them carefully and in three days return them telling how they impress you. Do you like Mr. Heaton's sonnet in the Jan'ry Philistine?

As for Crane, lets give him time. His power should surely find right direction yet.

E.H.

An otherwise gloomy year, filled with torment, heartbreak, problems and work ended on an optimistic note.

13

"Breathed on By Awful Fears"

Julia Ditto Young, interested in getting her own poetic works published, promptly responded to Elbert's request that she review the poems sent her on December 28 and sent along a piece of her own called "For Once." Alice's counsel was no longer available to him and Bertha wasn't a writer. She approved of Julia's help.

On the fourth day of the new year he sat down at his desk and pencilled this note to Mrs. Young:

January 4 (1896)

Dear Mrs. Young:

I've been reading For Once for an hour and this is to notify you that on no account must you accuse me of plagiarism when you see the Song of Songs which is Solomon's and mine. For hark'ee! I've written some of the same thoughts you have written, and if I wrote 'em first how can you as a sensible woman (and excellent) accuse me of seizing on your ideas?

No you must not do it, for if you do I'll have the Philistines blow Thistle Down down the winds of obliquy [sic]. I send you with this a page proof from the Song of Songs which are mine (and Taber's) to show you typography and margins. Oh, oh, oh! and what if Mrs. Young should turn Bibliophile and "collect" rare editions and dainty-leaves uncut—wide margins, deckle edges; Goat skin bindings with odd stamps, vellum and all—oh, oh, oh! It would be sweet satisfaction in the vengeful heart of her sincere

John Hillard

(The poems I sent you for criticism rec'd. Thank you very much for your frank words.)

The John Hillard signature was tossed in just to remind her of his recent book *No Enemy* in which a principal character was one John Hillard. The remainder of the letter was designed to enlist her aid in promoting sales for the Song of Songs—his first thrust into the field of special typography on imported paper in limited editions, à la William Morris. He thus introduced a new fad to the United States—one that would grow and grow and become lucrative for him, others, and collectors for decades to come.

He didn't mail the letter until January 10. His calm and purpose were interrupted by agonizing cries from Bertha's bedroom. Labor pains had suddenly seized her. On January 5, at home, she gave birth to a baby girl who was given the name of Katherine.

There was no reason to keep this birth a secret. In fact it would have been impossible because Mr. and Mrs. Elbert G. Hubbard of East Aurora were more widely known by now than they had ever been since moving there in 1884.

The irony of it all was that a woman who had dropped into obscurity had carefully nurtured Elbert's latent talent into a new career and in so doing placed him in a position where return to her and their daughter now seemed virtually impossible.

When news of the new addition to the Hubbard family reached Alice, she was shattered. She had been under the unyielding impression that she and Elbert were playing a waiting game; that he lived a sterile life with Bertha, just waiting with her for the miracle of freedom and reunion. No wonder she cried out in her lonely discovery, "Tell me you never touched her!"

Nearing a nervous breakdown when the full impact of the turn of events sank in, Alice was in no condition to resume teaching. She secluded herself in her room at the Woodworths' and was inconsolable save for the soothing words of her old college classmate, Maud Husted, who first wrote her these words and then made frequent visits to help her back to mental and physical health:

> The shepherd knows what pastures are best for His sheep, and they must not question nor doubt but trustingly follow Him. Perhaps He sees that the best pastures for some of us are to be found in the midst of opposition or earthly trials. If He leads you there, you may be sure they are green for you, and you will grow and be made strong by feeding there.
>
> Perhaps he sees that the best waters for you to walk beside will be raging waves of trouble and sorrow. If this should be the case, He will make them still waters for you, and you must go and lie down beside them and let them have all their blessed influence upon you.
>
> I thought of you, dear, as I read this in my little book this morning. It seems to me that is just the way you are accepting the sorrows and trials that come, and their blessed influence has entered your pure life.
>
> *Maud*

Alice needed more than Maud's approach to the power of positive thinking. She had always had a confident and special approach of her own. She would have to recover it her own way or not at all. Still, Maud's visits helped her unburden herself so that she could start life afresh as one who has been to confession. She well knew the special weapons of women in love and the possibility of Bertha's having retaliated in kind did not escape her. But her greater fear was the possibility that Elbert and Bertha had simply rediscovered the love that had seemed to be theirs when she first met them. It had been blissfully so for a night at least.

Her fear seemed to be particularly well founded when she saw a copy of the Song of Songs which was off the press in mid-January and advertised for sale in a limited edition of 600 copies. Bertha had designed the title page and initialed it! Had she found the help-secret that had been Alice's special technique all these years? "No," she told herself, "with us it was more than that. There was a Divine Presence!" And, in truth, whether or not it was precisely that, some special aura had and still hovered over Elbert and Alice. She sensed it as she read Elbert's study of Solomon's poem. Bertha had already dismissed his study as nothing more than a romantic outpouring, not dissimilar from the writings of Mrs. Young and others she had seen since the *Philistine* emerged.

Her Elbert was arranging to buy out McIntosh and Taber and henceforth copyright the *Philistine* in her name and it wasn't just talk. By April the contents page of the *Philistine* carried this footnote information: "Copyright, 1896, by B. C. Hubbard."

In the May issue Elbert, feeling the success of the magazine that was now centered around him, save for the copyright, lashed out at Harvard:

> I have examined many compositions written by Harvard students, and they average up about like the epistles of little girls who write letters to Santa Claus. The students are all right—fine, intelligent young fellows—but the conditions under which they work are such that they are robbed of all spontaneity when they attempt to express themselves. Of course I know that a few Harvard men have succeeded in Oratory and Literature, for there are those so strong that even Cambridge cannot kill their personality, nor a Professor reduce to neutral salts their native vim.

In the same issue Elbert printed a poem by his Cambridge roommate, William B. Faville. Readers of the *Philistine,* other than Alice, had no idea how appropriate it was for the mood of the separated pair in their moments of solitude.

Life's Voyage: A Mood

Dark and tumultuous seas
Have quenched the lurid sun.
Vapors, flame riven, writhingly ascend,
And night comes wringing on
'Cross sullen waves,
While Death upon the bowsprit waiting sits.

Bereft of hope,
Life's running sands low spent,
No rudder steers—nor beacon's flame
Tells us the course to sail.
Alone, alone, breathed on by awful fears.
Groping amidst life's way for light, we drift. . .
—William B. Faville

"Breathed on by awful fears" Elbert wrote more feverishly than ever and read more and more to fill the well of personal knowledge—a well that heretofore Alice had kept amply filled. A month's trip to Europe with his son Bert also helped fill the well. Father and son covered much of England and Ireland on foot. They kept a diary, mostly in Bert's handwriting. More Little Journeys source material.

The *Philistine* and Little Journeys were continuing projects. He was getting more offers to lecture and was accepting many, mostly close to home. Having bought the presses of White & Wagoner, he moved them to a building several yards away from his home. He named his enterprise the Roycroft Press (after the Roycroft brothers, 17th-century English printers) and from there began to fill the growing demand for Roycroft books. His Song of Songs had done the trick!

His second offering that year was his *Journal of Koheleth,* a study of the Book of Ecclesiastes. It was offered to the public in May, in a limited edition of 700 signed copies. Again, Bertha did the illuminating and her B.C.H. initials stood out more boldly than in the Song of Songs.

Elbert's thoughts in the study showed him to be still at odds with preachers' interpretations of God but genuinely aware of His presence. It was a philosophy that had long been with him and would be to his dying day:

> The burden of the Preachers' thought seems to be: We are unable to fully reconcile the events of life with any satisfactory theory of the government of the Universe.
> Let us be frank: For all we know this life is the sum of existence for us; there is no proof of a future life. True, we feel a certain confidence in Eternal Justice, and loving our friends we hope to meet them again after death. But God's ways are past finding out, and all we can do is to make the best of this condition that surrounds us. Whenever any good comes our way let us enjoy it to the fullest. It is better to be absolutely honest and admit that we do not know. Speak today what you think is true and contradict it all tomorrow if necessary. Of all things avoid excesses. "Be not righteous overmuch," He says, but recognize that a line of conduct that may be right under one condition may be evil when pushed on too far.

Other books of Elbert's published that year were *Ruskin-Turner* and *The Legacy*. He also turned out reprints of the works of others, including George Bernard Shaw's essay, "On Going to Church," first in an abortive

Just turning forty and tasting success with his Philistine magazine,
Elbert was a poised public figure and strikingly handsome. Photographers
everywhere invited him for a "sitting."

Hubbard's handyman "Ali Baba" poses with friends in front of original Roycroft Print Shop built in 1896 "after the fashion of the old church at Grasmere, England."

(it lasted for three issues) *Roycroft Quarterly* and then in book form. Though he had Shaw's written permission to reproduce the work, he made a few slight changes and incurred the wrath of the testy Irishman. Shaw's knocks were a boost to Elbert and thus broadened his attention-getting technique, which was already paying dividends through the knock and counter-knock bits he published monthly in his "Philistine Sidetalks" column.

That August he wrote to Julia Ditto Young's husband concerning the printing details of a book of hers the Roycroft had in progress. He also worked in a plug for a special edition of the Shaw book and paid a compliment to Bertha:

> August 10, 1896
> 2 P.M.
>
> Dear Mr. Young:
>   I have just come from Garretson's. My, my, my! but that is a pretty book—really better than I expected 'twould be. We will all be proud of it—inside and out.
>   Mr. Boyce showed me your choice of material and I must congratulate you and the Lady Young on your good taste—in fact I could not have done better myself.
>   Mrs. Hubbard has decorated nearly all of the 25 copies of Shaw's little book—the vellums. She has struck a very pretty scheme in sepia landscapes and adding a touch of color to the initials. Please have the Lady come out and see how we do it, before she decorates the "Glynnes" —it may suggest something.
>   Have recorded Mr. Ward's order; also got one order from an outsider—a rank outsider this A.M.
>   My kindest regards to you ever.
>
> *Hubbard*

Notwithstanding Bertha's help-meet efforts, faithfully done midst the duties of raising three boys and baby Katherine, she wasn't a professional artist. She knew that as well as did her husband. With her blessing he set out that very August to woo an artist into the Roycroft fold.

He wrote a long letter on August 14 to W. W. Denslow. In portions of it he demonstrated the carrot-and-stick approach he would frequently employ in the future to lure the supportive talent he wanted at the Roycroft:

> I have one wife, three boys and a daughter. My oldest boy is 13, the daughter 7 months. We keep one hired girl, one cow, a pony and 100 chickens. My wife keeps my accts, opens and answers most of my correspondence and takes care of my money. She is not a literary woman is not so awful damn smart, but you can guess that she is a great help to me. . . .
>   . . . I have a following scattered all over the earth, not large but a few people who say: Record my order for a copy of everything you write or print.

Hubbard's personal bookplate designed by early Roycroft artist Samuel Warner.

A Roycroft artist's studio–living quarters.

Elbert Hubbard and Roycroft sculptor Jerome Connor in "St. Jerome's" studio on the Roycroft campus.

A few of these people are rich and our vellum paper books @ $5.00 have sold first, and I now see that a book with a dash of hand color in it is prized. How much in dollars I do not know. Our little printing shop works only two men and two women. It is a tuppeny affair, but we can print beautiful books.

People buy hand painted china and pay a hundred dollars a piece; will they do so for books? The soft (Holland) paper used in The Song of Songs is not right for decorating, but vellum paper is and genuine vellum is better still. I am going to reprint the enclosed Goldsmith Essay on Japanese Vellum—breaking the text up into chapters, thus leaving large open spaces that can be filled up. This will give the artist a chance. Then I am going to make up a list of our choicest customers and find out how much they will pay for a beautiful book.

There is no competition in this line, for the reason there is no demand. It is a virgin field. Now, having spied out the land can you and I go in and possess it? Do you want to cast your lot and couple your name with Roycroft? Of course if we make a success of it others will follow, but we must keep free of competition by doing better work than the imitators—We must hold our pose as the *Great* and *Only*. . . .

His postscript to the letter made it clear that he wasn't intending to cut Bertha out of the picture. He just wanted to recruit an instructor for his atelier plans.

P.S. In decorating books it is alright to duplicate your designs. An edition of 300, say, would be so scattered that no two would probably ever come together. This would allow you to use some 'prentice help. My wife and one girl are now making impossible flowers on margins. I would want you to take hold with them, showing them how I can't.

Denslow eventually did come and then leave for more fertile fields. He gained lasting fame, not through his work at the Roycroft but for his illustrating of *The Wizard of Oz*. Other artists would come and go over the ensuing years—Samuel Warner, Alex Fournier and others. During their respective stays they would teach others in the art of book decorating. One such was Dard Hunter who apprenticed at the Roycroft and went on to become a leading authority on paper-making.

14

"The Memory of a Great Love Can Never Die"

Following Katherine's birth, grieving Alice had precious little to cheer her life while her Elbert was turning his own shame and sorrow into productive effort. Miriam was her only real joy. Elbert saw to it that she received weekly support and copies of the growing literature output of the Roycroft, and while she told herself these were symbolic of his lingering affection for her, each arrival of these things seemed to be but one more stone in a wall that was abuilding between them.

She slowly regained her health and composure and by the spring of 1897 began thinking about teaching again. Only this time, she resolved, it would be far away. She began searching for jobs and landed one for the fall term in Denver, Colorado. While waiting, she studied Elbert's writings ever more closely for a ray of hope that he was not forever lost to her.

She was proud of him when he spoke out in the April 1897 *Philistine* against the cruelty of branding as "illegitimate" those children born out of wedlock:

According to Eastern history, recently deciphered, there dwelt in Egypt about four thousand years ago a man by the name of Musas, or Moses. He was a member of the King's Court and a man of worth and power. But he occupied a rather anomalous position, being the son of one of the daughters of Pharaoh, his father a Hebrew. Now the Hebrews being in bondage, practically slaves to the Egyptians, no marriages were recognized between them.

But love knows no barriers, and when the daughter of Pharaoh went away to her summer place by the riverside and came back after some months with a fine Israelitish boy, explaining how she had found him floating in a basket, a few people smiled knowingly. The rest very properly considered it none of their business; and when the child was adopted into the household of Pharaoh no protest was made. People who protest in an absolute monarchy are certainly very foolish.

Now it often happens that the crossing of blood produces the best results; it was so here, for Moses grew in strength and stature, and in understanding was far beyond the inbred children of his own age. Indeed it is not seldom that love children possess a very superior mental and moral stamina. And were it necessary I might name a dozen and more of the strongest among all the sons of earth—men who have shaped the world's destiny—who were born outside the pale of the marriage contract.

The expression we use to distinguish such is a wrong one and surely its use was well rebuked by that gentle woman, Frances E. Willard, when she exclaimed with fine scorn, "Illegitimate! Who dare say that any one of God's children is illegitimate!"

Much to Alice's pleasure Elbert got the message across again that year in his Book of Job, another Bible-oriented work.

Then too, she read something special—just for her—into a little thought he penned for the May 1897 *Philistine*.

The desire for expression of the sentiments and emotions is very much akin to sexual desire. Each is reaching out for perpetuation, a bid for immortality, a protest against extinction. The gratification that follows an artistic success is the finest intoxication that comes to a mortal. But like all pleasures it must be shared to be complete. "When I have sung well," said Patti, "and the curtain is rung down, I want Someone to just take me in his arms and tell me it was good—I don't care so much for the applause of the audience!"

When I write a fine thing, and it's all complete, I just want to run and find Someone and kiss her cheek and read the Ms. aloud—don't you know what that is? Well never mind, you need not confess it if you do not care to.

Alice put down the "Phil" after reading this and, in the loneliness of her room cried aloud, "Beloved, I *do* know what it is but why do you taunt me to confess it miles away from your arms?" But, of course, her question wasn't heard or answered by Elbert for he was pledged to avoid her and was trying mightily to keep the pledge, though he now knew full well that fate had decreed Alice his Someone.

On the last day of summer 1897, Alice kissed Miriam goodbye after assuring her she would be home for Thanksgiving or Christmas. "Be a good girl for Aunt Emma!" she admonished, and turned quickly away to hide her tears.

Clutched in her hand all the way to the railroad station, and as she boarded the train for Denver, was a note that Maud Husted had given her earlier that day asking that she not read it until she was on her way.

On the back of the folded note was the inscription "Aufwiedersehn—to be read on the train." Alice settled back in her seat as the engine's first chug reverberated back through the cars and as the Buffalo scene passed all too slowly by her window, she opened the note.

August 31, 1897

My dear Alice,

I want to be with you so much when you leave the city that I cannot be content without at least writing a goodbye if I cannot speak it.

Dear Alice, I cannot make myself realize that you are going so far away, for you do not leave me behind dear. My love is close to you and wherever you are, there I am too.

Two souls separated by a distance as great as that between Denver and Buffalo *may* be closer than two who are in the same city. All true relations are spiritual and if we continually meet in God we are never separated from each other.

We do not know just when we will meet again, dear Alice, nor is it necessary we should dwell on it too much; we are God's children, we are put into the world to try to make the little spot in which He has placed us cleaner, sweeter and better because of our sojourn there and all we need feel anxious about is that we should be faithful to the trust.

Dear, let us pray daily that we may not be disobedient to the heavenly vision. Let us trust that when we meet again and each shall look into the other's eyes we shall see there more purity, more nobility of nature, more devotion to the will of God.

I send with this a little love token, dear, just to mark the day on which hope was high and courage strong. I want to feel that a little bit of me goes with you in a tangible form to your new home in Denver so that whenever you happen to glance at it during the glad days and the sad days (if they should come) it will say to you "Dear Alice, Maud loves you and is saying 'Friend, come up higher!'"

Dear sweet girl, my pure-hearted Alice let us make a sacred compact dear that we will each hold the other to her heart, that is the meaning of friendship, "That we may be nearer to God when nearer to each other."

I leave you in God's hands my friend, may His peace fill your heart and know that my love is with you now and will abide.

Your faithful
Maud

Alice put the letter in her purse and reflected, not tearfully, about how strangely close she and Maud had become as her old classmate had nursed her back to health after her breakdown. Well perhaps it was best now in still another way that she was going away. "Two women shouldn't become so dependent upon each other," she thought. How much more consoling to her would be those words if they had been written by Elbert but it was sweet of Maud to express unqualified thoughts of love and friendship when all from other sources had seemed to dry up and blow away like falling leaves of Hingham after Miriam's birth.

There was little about Denver to remind Alice of home except everything—the loneliness of being 1,000 miles away from her lover and her child.

The snowcapped Rocky Mountains to the west served only to remind her of the great barrier that society to the east had drawn up between her and Elbert.

Denver, incorporated in 1861, had been combined with a larger community, Auraria, by the territory of Jefferson. It became the official capital of Colorado in 1881, the year that Elbert had taken Bertha as his bride. The South Platte River, which lazied through the center of the city, was going someplace while she was for the moment just standing still . . . a lonely elocution teacher at North Side High School.

It was, withal, a beautiful city but it couldn't compare with Hingham, she thought. For Alice, Denver's only saving grace was its progressive public school system, which gave her some solace. Two teaching associates there, Allene Seaman and Beulah Hood, helped her pass the empty nonteaching hours. They became her lifelong friends.

Nearly all the leaves had fallen when Elbert boarded a train for Oregon. He was due in Portland on October 28 to begin a series of lectures there. Between that date and November 15 he gave 15 lectures of which eight had been arranged by five different ministers. It was strange, yet not so strange, because the Song of Songs, Journal of Koheleth and Book of Job had intrigued these men of the cloth and Elbert in turn was intrigued by their interest in him. Elbert Hubbard the lecturer and philosopher was now well linked with Elbert Hubbard, author, editor and publisher. The several in one were on their way!

In 1898, with his son Ralph and his long-time friend Dr. Mitchell, Elbert again traveled to Europe, this time being away from mid-June to mid-September.

Along the way Elbert gained new book customers, new subscribers to the *Philistine,* new contacts with important persons, new thoughts, new lecture engagements, and new confidence.

Widely known through all these media by 1899, a quickly-tossed-off essay for that year's March issue of the *Philistine* catapulted Hubbard to undisputed national prominence and a permanent place in American literature. It was his "A Message to Garcia," a little homily on initiative, centered around the unusual dedication to doing a task demonstrated by a U. S. Army colonel, Andrew S. Rowan, in taking a message from President McKinley to a General Garcia during the Cuban revolt.

Such was the broad impact of "A Message to Garcia" that Tufts College awarded the Harvard dropout an honorary M.A. degree before the year 1899 had drawn to a close. Within another 70 years the essay

A Denslow caricature of New York Central's general passenger agent, George Daniels, and Elbert Hubbard. The "tickets on suspicion" expression was an inside joke referring to Hubbard's then well-known and successful mail-order scheme of mailing Roycroft books, unsolicited, to potential customers "on suspicion" that once they saw them they would buy them. His hunch was right—most did just that.

would reach a reprinting figure of over 90 million copies. It was inspired, he explained, by a little argument "over the teacups" with his son Bert as to who was the real hero of that war, the general or the man who successfully carried the message to him. Bert had claimed it was the messenger and Hubbard, exclaiming "The boy's right!", jumped up from the dinner table and dashed off his essay "hot from the heart" in a matter of minutes.

In that same year he finally got around to finishing his book about John Brown and published it under the title "Time and Chance." By then he didn't need the $1,000 prize that had prompted him to begin it back in 1895. In rereading it in preparation for putting on the finishing touches before publication, his thoughts were taken back to his romance with Alice and a new-but-old need that was again building up within him.

It was in 1900, on the first leg of a lecture tour that was to take him to several cities—Denver included—that Elbert found himself seated at a desk in the home of an Illinois preacher, his host for the night. He held in his hands an advertising poster, sent to him by the president of the Denver civic club that was sponsoring his lecture in that city, along with a note asking him to advise them if any change was to be made in the poster.

The words danced before his eyes: "Elbert Hubbard, noted author, philosopher, lecturer and publisher, will be in Denver on —" The words faded. He stared off toward the fireplace.

In the years since Hingham, never a day had passed that he hadn't thought of Alice. Even now he could almost smell the faint lavender scent of her clothes, almost see the proud chin, the high, delicate cheekbones, the clear, deep eyes with their disarming directness.

He glanced again at the poster. His hand shook as he folded it. inserted it in an envelope and addressed it to Miss Alice L. Moore, 803 Colfax Avenue, Denver, Colorado.,

"Certainly she would want to know I'm to lecture in Denver," he told himself. There was more to his gesture than that, of course, but Elbert Hubbard—the man who understood others so well—wasn't ready yet to face the truth about himself.

As his trip took him closer and closer to Denver, he was beset by doubts. On the one hand, he was worried that Alice would come to the lecture; far worse was the alternative—that she wouldn't.

She came, of course. She sat in the fifth row from the front, several seats in from the aisle. She was wearing a dress in the soft, becoming shade of red he loved so well. As she watched the audience file in and waited for the lecturer to be brought to the stage, she relived in her mind the day her mail had brought her a plain white envelope with an Illinois postmark—an envelope addressed in the handwriting she knew so well. Her heart had pounded as she tore open the envelope and smoothed out the poster. A dozen thoughts raced through her mind, but again and again she came back to the thought she wanted most to believe: *He* wanted her there!

When Elbert reached the stage, he saw her almost instantly. The inevitable occurred. Once again, as in that first Chautauqua Circle meeting over a decade previously, his eyes met "those of a personage" and the two locked once more in a "soul embrace." East Aurora, Springfield, Boston, Searsport and Hingham kaleidoscoped before them, and suddenly, but all too briefly, Denver, too, seemed heavenly.

A careful but dangerous new alliance began. The door was opened for Alice to talk again about picking up where they had left off five years before—the life together with their child and their work.

In those five years the togetherness of Elbert and Bertha had gradually taken on many of the same aspects that had characterized it back when he was a successful soap company executive. He was traveling a lot and she busied herself as before with household duties and social functions. With the influx of artists and other help she had been relieved of the print shop duties but this had also taken away an avenue of work association with Elbert. They had drifted back to polite pecks on the cheeks and the dullness of routine dinners and neighborhood visits when he was at home.

Bertha was relaxed. Alice was refreshed. Elbert was vibrant and vulnerable. The stage was set for a new drama.

Much more was at stake now. Elbert had built a three-story addition to the original print shops in 1896, added a dining room that stretched southward toward his home in 1897, and an eastward wing to that in 1899.

Stones from East Aurora's outlying farms were bought by Hubbard at a dollar a load to build the still standing Roycroft Shops.

Monument to determination. Hubbard's massive print shop rose to replace the little church-like shop he started in.

Notables were coming from all over the country to see the Roycroft and the local hostelry accommodations weren't adequate. The result was that Hubbard had to put many up at his spacious home. This being unsatisfactory from many standpoints, he elected to build his shops across the street and turn the existing buildings into an inn. Hubbard the innkeeper was emerging. Yet, for the persistent love of one woman to whom he was strangely attracted, he was once again risking everything!

The checks he sent to Alice for their daughter's support sometimes got cashed and sometimes didn't. In addition, Elbert, busy with his multitudinous activities, fell in arrears in his payments. Wayland Woodworth was a charitable person but no philanthropist—especially when it came to weighing his lot against what seemed to be the increasing fortunes of a man for whom he had absolutely no respect or sympathy.

Being an attorney, he took, in early 1901, the kind of action most logical to him. He filed suit against Hubbard demanding that he pay up some $3,500 in back child-support payments and continue henceforth on a current basis.

Elbert was caught by surprise because this was one account Bertha hadn't kept and he had neglected—not deliberately but carelessly. That Emma would have let her husband, however distraught, risk her sister's good name, so well protected for so long, added to Elbert's consternation.

For Alice it was the last straw in a long, delicate relationship with her

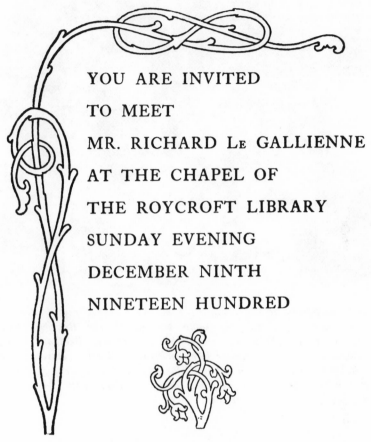

YOU ARE INVITED

TO MEET

MR. RICHARD Le GALLIENNE

AT THE CHAPEL OF

THE ROYCROFT LIBRARY

SUNDAY EVENING

DECEMBER NINTH

NINETEEN HUNDRED

Poet-playwright Richard "Dickie" Le Gallienne spent some time as a Roycrofter and was, like other greats and near-greats of the early 1900s, introduced formally to the citizens of East Aurora and environs by Fra Elbertus.

older sister. She came home from Denver, reclaimed her child, and hurried to Concord, Massachusetts. There, with assistance from Elbert, she rented the old Bartlett home on Lowell Road, a few doors down from the historic Colonial Inn. Elbert paid the monthly rent of $35.00.

There was something symbolic in her staying in the Revolutionary War village of Concord. Elbert and Alice were making their own bid for freedom.

The publicity attendant with the filing of the Woodworth suit was not widespread beyond Buffalo. Bertha, who had been in on the secret since 1895, was naturally embarrassed by the open revelation of it but had

A family gathering at the Hubbard home on Grove Street (later torn down to make room for the salon portion of the Roycraft Inn). Identifiable in the photo are son Ralph (standing); Bertha's mother, Mrs. Crawford (seated, extreme left, back row); Bertha (extreme right, back row) with Katherine on lap and Elbert beside Katherine. Son Sanford is seated immediately in front of his father. Bertha's sister, Myrtilla, is seated at extreme left of front row.

steeled herself against that eventuality. While its coming out in the open distressed her, the fact that she and Elbert had been reconciled and were living a new life that all had witnessed, including an addition to their family, made the situation more bearable. Moreover, her husband's now undisputed fame in itself seemed to have built up a protective barrier for all concerned.

The thing to do now was to try to quiet things down as quickly as possible by squaring accounts with the Woodworths and settling everything before the case would go to trial.

A complication in this approach was not known to Bertha. Alice's feud with her sister, her removal to Concord with her daughter and Elbert's renewed, deeper involvement with the school teacher—these things she didn't know.

On the surface, it seemed that resolving the Woodworth misunderstanding was possible and in progress, for Elbert barely lost a step in the

The Bartlett house in Concord, Mass. as it looked when Alice was living there awaiting the outcome of Bertha's divorce procedings against Elbert. Elbert II took the photo during a visit with his father.

steady cadence of his march toward continued fame as a writer, publisher, philosopher, lecturer, epigrammatist and innkeeper. But with it all there was now a coolness between them, born of their drifting apart to separate lives in the past two years and the more recent bitter rehashing of his earlier behavior which had brought on the current embarrassment.

Alice regained the initiative in the new situation and, again, without Bertha's knowing it. At Concord she was known as Alice Moore, nurse to Hubbard's daughter. Visits to her home by Elbert Hubbard, basically secret as his arrivals and departures were, aroused no serious suspicions in that tourist-plagued village when his presence was occasionally noted.

Indeed in that very year Albert Lane, owner of Concord's Erudite Print Shop and editor-publisher of the *Middlesex Patriot,* undertook, with a remarkable lack of erudition, the first published biography of Hubbard. Titled *Elbert Hubbard and His Work,* the 154-page book, published in 1901, devoted no words to Elbert's personal life; all were to his work, his thoughts, and his writings.

Two selections from Hubbard's writings, chosen by Lane for inclusion in the biography, had more significance than Lane realized.

Marriage is only a way-station. Trains may stop two or twenty minutes for lunch. The place may be an ugly little cross-roads or it may be a beautiful village; possibly it is the end of the division, but egad! dearie, it's not the end of the journey. Very young people think it is, but they find out their mistake. It's a nice place very often, but not the place they thought it was. They bought one thing and when they got home found something else in the package. And nature will not change. That's God's fault, not hers.

Bertha could have read that with more care when Elbert first said it in the *Philistine* and thus better prepared herself for things to come, but she had been either too busy, or too disinterested in his every printed outpouring.

Then there was this selection from Hubbard's writings in Lane's book:

The memory of a great love can never die from out the heart. It affords ballast 'gainst all the storms that blow. And although it ends in unutterable sadness, it imparts an unspeakable peace.

Alice *had* read both of these—and everything her Elbert had written since *The Man.* To her, the unspeakable peace had always been and would always be worth the unutterable sadness. And now, once again, they resumed their almost daily exchange of letters. More careful than he had been when writing to "Mrs. Hubbard" at Hingham, Elbert now addressed his letters to A. L. Moore, Box 6, Concord, Mass.

With Alice now back in the East, Elbert found more and more excuses to make trips to Boston. Inevitably, the short side trips to Concord were included. He spent considerable time at Lane's Erudite Print Shop and this provided fodder for little Lane items in the editorial column of his weekly *Middlesex Patriot.*

In the December 6, 1901, issue, Lane wrote:

Well, well! And wouldn't this make a chapter for a Little Journey? Hubbard of East Aurora—and occasionally of Concord—not content with printing a magazine, making books, welding andirons, antique and chandeliers, weaving grandmother carpets and turning out sixteenth century furniture—not content with doing these things, the mild-eyed Fra has established an up-to-date boarding house and advertises "meals thirty-five cents; board and lodging by the week seven dollars" and this same Hubbard, the confessed prototype of William Morris, advertises that on the boarding house tables are served the fifty-seven varieties of Heinz Pickles. Ye Gods! What a glorious twist!

It was true, of course: Hubbard had expanded his enterprises to include handicrafted items. He had put artisans to work fashioning furniture and decorative items for the inn which he had found necessary to build for his visitors. Many such visitors admired the hand-wrought things so much that Hubbard encouraged the artisans to stay on and produce more to place on sale. Another new venture had been born and was taking hold.

If Bertha had subscribed to the *Concord Enterprise* and the *Middlesex Patriot* for the year 1902, she could have better confirmed her suspicions that Elbert, often away from East Aurora, was somewhere again seeing "that woman."

Concord Enterprise—January 15, 1902

Elbert Hubbard of Roycroft fame was in Concord last week.   ·

Concord Enterprise—April 9, 1902

There is a rumor afloat that a stock company is to be formed to turn the Wright Tavern into a sort of Roycrofters Shop. Albert Lane of the Erudite to take charge, and here would be printed books similar to those issued by Elbert Hubbard. This is still in the embryo.

Middlesex Patriot—April 18, 1902

The report, so generously spread by Mrs. Grundy, that the Philistine and the Erudite are to be issued from Wright Tavern is a pretty choice bit of gossip. But really, there's nothing in it.

At last accounts, East Aurora has been given a place on the map, and a letter from Hubbard bears proof that he is doing middlin' well at the Roycroft Shop, and with troubles enough of his own to keep him busy. As for the Erudite and the little shop here in Concord—well, we have troubles that cannot be laughed away and are not at all anxious to add to them.

Middlesex Patriot—May 2, 1902

Elbert Hubbard of East Aurora spent several days this week with relatives on Lowell Road.

By this time Elbert, sensing that a permanent break with Bertha was only a matter of time—and maybe only a short time—decided that he had better get his eldest son, Bert, now 20 and in the employ of his father, acquainted with Alice and Miriam. He took the lad with him on what was to be just one of several visits that year to the Bartlett house in Concord.

The beautiful little girl plainly took an immediate liking to her big "Brud" and he to her. She loved to sit on his lap and to romp with him when the four of them visited the North Bridge, the Lexington-Concord battlegrounds, Emerson's home and Walden Pond. He took her picture beside a brook near Walden with his 5" x 7" Corona box camera. A bond between them that was to last all their lives had its beginnings that summer. A respect for intelligent, thoughtful Alice began developing then too—not the kind of love Bert had for his mother but more of an understanding of the aura about her that had charmed his father.

Definitely, Bertha could have learned about Bert's visits and other

matters had she been a subscriber to the two Concord-area papers.
Middlesex Patriot—June 20, 1902

Elbert Hubbard and his son, Elbert Hubbard, Jr., of East Aurora, N. Y. have been spending a few days in Concord.

Concord Enterprise—July 2, 1902

A large delegation of Concord people attended a recital of Mrs. Walter S. Leland's pupils in Association Hall Wednesday evening. The pianists were assisted by Jenny L. Hatch, soprano. The pupils from Concord who took part in the pleasing program were: Ruth Raymond, Kittie Mahan, Lilla M. Wheeler, Hilda A. Raymond, *Miriam Hubbard,* John A. Urquhart, Evlyn H. Emmott, Ned Caiger and Elsie C. Lawden.

15

"We Have Come by the Thorn Road"

Alice moved freely about the Village of Concord. It was the land of Thoreau and Emerson. Such names sent her thoughts back to 1890 when she had written from Springfield to her Emersonian friend, Elbert. So many things had happened since.

A neighbor on Lowell Road was Alfred W. Hosmer, son of a local merchant, descendent of a Revolutionary War hero, and recognized authority on Thoreau. Chatting with such interesting persons, reading at the Concord Library, writing to Elbert and caring for Miriam kept her well and happily occupied between Elbert's visits.

The seasons seemed to come and go all too quickly though, and little had been resolved with the Woodworths. Both Elbert and Alice sensed that something would soon have to happen. It did, but not from the direction they had anticipated.

Bertha had found some of their Concord love letters and decided that the time had come to legally end her marriage with Elbert. She confronted him with the evidence and he was defenseless. She informed him that she would file for divorce and move out of their home as soon as possible.

Elbert, to avoid any further quarreling, left their Grove Street home and took up temporary residence a block away with his aging parents.

He wrote to Alice:

I have moved down to Mother Hubbard's cottage and have the spare room off the parlor. "My boy has come home " said the Dear

Mother and wiped her eyes on her apron. Dear Good Mother, it is all sort of confusing to her—but she has the faith that all will be well.

Elbert knew better. All would *not* be well. Bertha meant everything she said. Divorce papers were filed on December 8 and a Summons and Complaint was served on Elbert just as he was leaving for a lecture engagement in Wisconsin.

He read it as he rode the commuter train to Buffalo to make night-train connections to Milwaukee. He tucked it away in his breast pocket and wrote a note to Alice.

4:15 P.M.
December 9, 1902

My Own:
I am on a train bound for Buffalo where I take the Michigan Central at 7:25.

Just before I left East Aurora a constable handed me a Summons and Complaint. It calls for "Absolute Divorce" and names you as corespondent.

The charges are very brief and several, the "offences" being committed in Concord. New York State law calls for only one "reason," you know.

I will mail the document to Arthur C. Wade at Jamestown from Buffalo. There will be no defense and the only argument will be the matter of alimony. If she is reasonable that will all be arranged quickly—within a month.

You will not be called as a witness nor have any papers served on you. It might be well to caution Sweetie not to answer any questions as to our sleeping arrangements—I leave all that up to you. Reporters may call—you will say nothing.

I am tired, Beloved, but Rest is only a little way. We have come by the Thorn Road—what a journey! It is worth the price—Rest is near.

I get so hungry for you that when we meet, knowing parting is tomorrow, we clutch a little—we visit fast.

Possibly when I see you next, we will meet never to part again. Rest is near! Thank the Good God!

On receipt of this, telegraph me at Milwaukee, Wis. care of the Phistes Hotel, the single word "Browning" and sign it Alice Moore and I will know all is well.

(Show the enclosed clipping to Mrs. Hosmer.)

The Buffalo newspapers that day carried front page stories detailing the allegations set forth in the suit papers. The public was eagerly awaiting the fuller story because the *Buffalo Courier* had already broken the news of the pending action on the Sunday previous.

The wire services picked up the story and it seemed most unlikely that rest was near for Elbert.

Reporters tracked down Alice at Concord and she was noncommittal. Elbert, ordinarily anxious to meet the press wherever he was, found himself studiously avoiding reporters as he kept his lecture engagements.

It was a time for sides-taking. His mother and father stood by him. His sisters did not. Oddly enough, Bertha's mother was not among those who stood against him. Most of his employees, now well-known across the country as the Roycrofters, remained loyal to him.

Elbert was prepared for more bitter comments about himself from the press and public as a result of the divorce publicity. However, one thing that the newspapers had already learned was that Hubbard had a fairly powerful retaliatory medium of his own in his monthly *Philistine* magazine, which by now had a national circulation of 90,000.

In the July 1902 issue, a few months after the Woodworth lawsuit, he devoted two full pages to what various other publications were saying about him. He titled the collection of criticisms "Sundry slight Acerbitations of certain Good Men and Virtuous temporarily Disgruntled with Themselves":

Nixon Waterman in Good Cheer (Boston): One who is at once the most saintly and the most devilish man I ever saw.
Indianapolis News: The idol of silly sentimental women.
New York Nation: He says he is not a college graduate, a fact that need not have been stated.
Albany Argus: A freakish combination of impudence and art.
The Straight-Edge: We called at the Shop and found him lallygagging with two female visitors—he had no time for us. We consider him a fraud.
Munsey's: A disappointment to his friends.
New Orleans Picayune: In his youth they thought he might be a great man—alas"
Kansas City Journal: Supremely selfish.
Buffalo Times: An enemy of religion and good order.
Cincinnati Examiner: Ungrammatical and untaught.
Rochester Herald: The Fra just falls short of being a great man.
Hartford Courant: The P. T. Barnum of art.
New York Sun: Eminently crude and outrageously vulgar.
The Free-Life: The East Aurora scheme for the betterment of mankind is a sham—only the rich can afford a Roycroft book.
Elkhart Review: The PHILISTINE is dangerous to the young.
Boston Transcript: Disgustingly frank.
New York Tribune: The Roycraft books are only imitations of what has been done well.
Buffalo Express: Bizarre and barren. Why not bind in tin and copper rivet the cover?
William Marion Reedy, St. Louis Mirror: Is he a degenerate?
Des Moines Leader: It is said that he drinks.
Chicago Journal: His egotism is insufferable.
Chicago Tribune: His motto is, Love one another and knock.
Atchison Globe: We hear he has been arrested for non-support.
Omaha Bee: He is an avowed free-lover.
Toronto Globe: The whole scheme seems to be founded on hypnotizing

talented men and women into the belief that they are having a good time.
Kansas City Independent: We are glad to know that our prophecies concerning this all 'round rogue are being fulfilled.
Opie Read in Chicago American: The John Alex. Dowie[1] of literature.
Louisville Courier-Journal: The admittance was one dollar, the lecture two hours long, and the subject was himself.
Peoria Star: The chief aim of his life seems to be deprive the local barber of all joy in his work.
Harold McGrath in Syracuse Standard: The only man we know who has the supreme crust to charge a dollar for hearing him advertise his own goods.
Hornellsville Times: His success is owing to the fact that there are many suckers being born Every Little While.
Christian Advocate (Chicago) : Preaching doctrines dangerous to the young, and threatening the stability of the home.
The Presbyterian (New York) : Under the pretense of bettering society he is really placing dynamite under it.
Jackson (*Mich.*) *Patriot:* The Roycroft vogue, happily has now come to an end.

Comments such as these had served only to enrage Elbert's followers and many had taken up his defense by writing to the editors of the denouncing publications. Many of his subscribers were themselves unhappy in their marriages and were not to be denied a bold champion of their secret wars against their Victorian imprisonment.

Elbert sensed that it would be so again as he faced a new onslaught. His own mail as editor of the *Philistine* helped him to accurately gauge the mood of his particular public and the public at large. The divorce scandal, played up by the press, actually gained him new followers and new subscribers!

One male Buffalonian, calling himself "a new Philistine," wrote on December 7, 1902:

Fra Elbertus:
Sympathy and strength in the hour of domestic tie-breaking. It is said that the whole world loved Lord Byron and his work except his unfortunate wife. History is repeating itself again.

Incompatibility of temperament! Incompatibility of temperament! Incompatibility of temperament! It is the greatest of all reasons for matrimonial severance. Because it is nature's reason. The wren cannot be happy with the nightengale, neither can the eagle be happy with the duck.

Fraternally,
(—————————————), a new Philistine

1. John Alexander Dowie (1847–1907) was a Scotland-born American faith healer who built a wooden tabernacle in Chicago in 1890 and attracted a large following for a time.

Beginning with the January 1903 *Philistine,* Hubbard launched his defenses in an indirect way for both the Woodworth suit and divorce case, even though it now seemed likely that they wouldn't come up in court before spring. He lashed out at a stupid lawyer who bore marked resemblance to Wayland Woodworth; praised, by name and case example, his own attorney, Arthur C. Wade; lauded the courts; explained incompatibility; called for sympathy for folks who had gone astray; denounced newspapers who thrived on scandal by pandering to the sick minds of readers who savored the unsavory, etc.

Midst all such dissertations he dropped easy-to-remember epigrams which would stick if the longer messages wouldn't. In due course these and many other epigrams were printed with decorative borders in both poster and envelope-stuffer size. They became popular with Hubbard fans and Roycroft visitors and added dollars to the coffers of the enterprise. Subsequently he gathered them into a book, *1,001 Epigrams.*

Some which served his immediate need to properly influence his audience were:

Don't try to eliminate the old fashioned virtues—many have tried it, with indifferent success.

* * *

No disappointment is quite so bitter as the disappointment that comes when you are disappointed with yourself.

* * *

To understand Self is to rise above all sorrow, fear and pain.

* * *

Would you make better men—set them an example.

* * *

It is absurd to try to prove things: even truth can be proved—sometimes.

* * *

When a minister takes a vacation, the congregation usually enjoys the vacation more than the minister.

* * *

*Hubbard's epigrams and mottos of a nonmotivational type were equally
in demand by the general public and visitors to the Roycroft "colony."
Many of them related to his personal life though few of his fans realized
it at the time. Here are some examples.*

The love
your lib-
erate in
your work
is the only
love you
keep......

Fra Elbertus

·TRY THESE:

A KIND · · · ·

· · ·THOUGHT

A KIND · · · ·

· · · · WORD

A KIND · · · ·

· · · · DEED

—ELBERT HUBBARD

Never explain:
Your Friends do
not need it and
Your Enemies Will
Not Believe You Anyway
—Elbert Hubbard

There is no Freedom
on Earth or in Any
Star for those who
deny Freedom to
Others —Elbert Hubbard

Man's boldness &
Woman's caution
make an excellent
business arrangement
—Elbert Hubbard

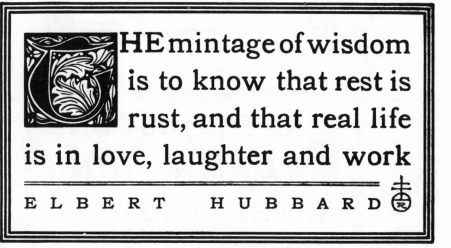

THE mintage of wisdom
is to know that rest is
rust, and that real life
is in love, laughter and work

ELBERT HUBBARD

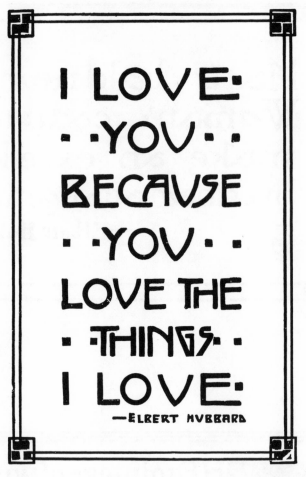

I LOVE·
· ·YOU· ·
BECAUSE
· ·YOU· ·
LOVE THE
· ·THINGS· ·
I LOVE·
—ELBERT HUBBARD

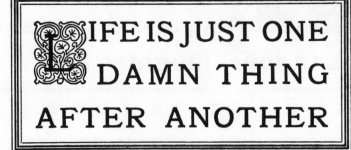

LIFE IS JUST ONE
DAMN THING
AFTER ANOTHER

Hubbard was thinking out loud about everything that tormented him—sin, repentance, denunciation by self-righteous critics, the now-smug piety of preachers who had previously sought his company, etc. While unburdening himself and showing humility he gained new sympathizers and caused some of his critics to reevaluate themselves. Readers who didn't know of his troubles took the epigrams at face value and liked them.

The Woodworth suit came up on the trial calendar in May 1903. It was settled before going to trial. A poor record-keeper, Hubbard still felt that Woodworth had the same failing—and even hinted he might have had a deliberate tendency in that direction—but nevertheless he agreed to pay $3,000 in back child-support monies to Woodworth.

Close on the heels of the satisfactory settlement of this action, the divorce trial got under way on June 25.

Elbert was not contesting the grounds, but the matter of alimony and his ability to pay were contested. It lasted only a few days, but long enough for Bertha's attorney, Norris Morey, to shoot barbs at Hubbard on the witness stand. Morey had depositions from Samuel T. Crosby and Mrs. Millet C. Stringer of Hingham, plus those of Chief of Police Craig and landlord Edward J. Bartlett of Concord, nailing down the adultery charges which Hubbard wasn't contesting. Hubbard's attorney, Arthur C. Wade, pointed out that the Hingham events did not relate to the current action because they were incidents prior to the Concord infidelity charged in the original divorce complaint. He nevertheless agreed to their admission so that they could get onto the matter of alimony and Bertha's request for the custody of Katherine and Ralph. The two older boys, Bert and Sanford, were working for their father and staying with him. Both were with him in court. Ralph was with his mother there but Katherine, then only six, was not present.

It was established in the course of the trial, which centered mostly around Hubbard's ability to pay, that he had poured most of his earnings back into the business. Lyle Hawthorne, secretary of the now-incorporated Roycrofters, was examined on the stand by both lawyers. Wade asked him, "Is it not a fact that the firm has not made any considerable profit in the last year?"

Hawthorne replied, "Yes."

Justice Kenefick, after hearing the pleadings of both sides, concluded the trial after two days and reserved his decision as to the amount of alimony. Hubbard's attorney had agreed to the custody arrangements sought by Bertha's attorney.

Surprisingly enough, the adverse notoriety stemming from the trial did not impede the progress of Elbert Hubbard and his Roycrofters. Their annual convention, which by this time included hundreds of "Roycrofters-at-Large," who were Hubbard fans and *Philistine* subscribers, was held as usual in the village grove on July 4. The speakers were Hon. John Temple Graves, Atlanta, Ga.; Rev. Madison C. Peters, Baltimore, Md.; Rev. George D. Herron, New York, N. Y.; Rev. John E. Roberts, Kansas

City, Mo.; Col. Andrew W. Rowan, Topeka, Kans.; Hon. T. V. Powderly, Washington, D. C.; Eli Perkins, New York, N. Y.; George Wharton James, Pasadena, Cal.; Byron W. King, Pittsburgh, Pa. and George Murphy, Grand Rapids, Mich.

Several months later, on October 9, 1903, an interlocutory judgment was handed down in Bertha's favor, granting her $1,500 a year plus $500 a year for each of the two children in her custody until they became of age.

Now free of the strain that had haunted him ever since he first became involved with Alice, Hubbard began to write more and more about the pressing issues of the day, developing an insight and style that widened his reputation as a writer and influencer of events, views and trends.

In the December 1903 *Philistine* he predicted:

> The people will yet own and control the railroads just as we do the post offices . . . but the change cannot come by voting out the strong men who have brought railroading up to its present high degree of excellence. . . . We will make terms with these strong men and retain them in power.
>
> . . . and the change will come as quietly and imperceptibly as a change in schedule. It will be evolution, not revolution.
>
> Yes, I am a Socialist—a Fabian Socialist. I do not flout everything offered because it is not exactly what I would like. I take what I can get and thank Heaven.

On January 15, 1904, Hubbard was in Washington, D. C., to deliver lecture and was staying at the Cairo Hotel. His son Bert checked his ther's itinerary for he had important news for him. From the East urora Western Union office, Bert sent this wire:

> WADE SAYS FINAL JUDGEMENT ENTERED AND SERVED JANUARY ELEVENTH. LETTER.
>
> ELBERT HUBBARD, SECOND

Elbert relayed the good news without delay in a wire to Alice at Concord.

Victory had come! Alice hugged Miriam—now named Miriam Elberta Hubbard instead of Miriam Crosby Hubbard—but didn't dare allow herself the dream of legal marriage. They had talked of it and Elbert, just a few weeks before, had transferred Roycroft stock to her, but would marriage really happen? Well, at least while previously there had been valid obstacles, there couldn't be any now. She had never lacked resolve and the final barrier to their long-awaited togetherness had now been removed. Oddly, the thing she wanted most now was the kind of marriage that she and Elbert had told themselves wasn't necessary if the "Divine Presence" had already sanctioned a union.

She didn't have to wait long for an answer to the questions she had put to herself. Elbert, winding up his lecture engagements in Washington, headed for Philadelphia where he was to speak at the Clover Club on the 21st. He sent for Alice and, on Tuesday, January 19, 1904, the *Buffalo Courier* told the wedding story. The paper also speculated on the future while not being prone to forget the past:

HUBBARD MARRIED TO
MISS ALICE MOORE

(Special Wire To The Courier)

East Aurora, Jan. 18—News reached here today of the marriage of Miss Alice Moore and Elbert Hubbard at Philadelphia Sunday afternoon. The wedding was quiet, only six persons being present. The ceremony was performed by the Hon. Thomas B. Harned, literary executor of Walt Whitman, and took place at the Hotel Walton. The announcement of the wedding caused little surprise here, as it was generally understood that the event would occur during January. A dispatch to the Courier two weeks ago foretold the wedding.

Mr. Hubbard left here ten days ago for a lecture trip, which included talks at Baltimore, Washington and Philadelphia. The last lecture of the series occurs at Philadelphia tomorrow night, after which, it is expected, Mr. and Mrs. Hubbard will return to this village.

The story then recapped the "skeleton in the Hubbard household" stories of the Woodworth and divorce trials, summing up this way:

MAY BE COLDLY RECEIVED

It is presumed that Mr. and Mrs. Hubbard will soon come to this village. For the present it is understood they will reside in one of Hubbard's houses on Oakwood Avenue, but in the spring they will take possession of a log house that is being built in the rear of the Roycroft property on Grove Street. . . .

. . . What sort of a reception local society will give the second Mrs. Hubbard is rather of an enigma. However, it seems likely to be of a frigid order. It is understood that the child, Miriam, over which the first court action occurred will live with Mr. and Mrs. Hubbard here.

Elbert's talk before the Clover Club on the 21st did not receive the warm response that had been accorded his talks in Washington and Baltimore but he didn't sense it was due to the chill that the *Courier* was predicting would await him and Alice in East Aurora.

One thing he was sure of, *this* audience would get a going over in his *Philistine* before long.

Within a week, Alice, Elbert and Miriam settled into temporary quarters, as predicted, in a home he owned on Oakwood Avenue, just around the corner from the expanding Roycroft enterprises. As if to goad their critics, they named it "Hyacinths" and hung that name above the door.

The townspeople were, for the most part, cool as expected. It mattered little to Hubbard because by now the greats and near-greats of the nation were frequent visitors to the Roycroft. That's where the action was and folks interested in seeing and hearing something of the world outside the village, without touring the nation, were obliged to cross the welcome threshold of the Roycroft. The coolness bothered Alice only from the standpoint of the transferred cruelty to their innocent daughter.

As for the Roycrofters themselves, their choice was only slightly different from that open to any of the villagers. Hubbard was also the major employer. He expected loyalty. That was the keynote of his essays on employee–employer relations and they all understood the message.

To broaden the obligation, he soon put Alice in charge of the office because he had to be away so much of the time on his lecture tours. No one was openly unfriendly to Alice. A few, who had worked with Bertha in the early days and had loved her, soon resigned. Those who remained soon came to respect Alice for she went out of her way to extend the hand of friendship.

Hubbard, meanwhile, pursued his Philistine pennings about happenings outside of East Aurora.

Admiral Richmond P. Hobson of the U.S. Navy was thumping for a bigger fleet and an appropriation of "two billion, five hundred million" to accomplish that end. In the February 1904 Philistine, Hubbard devoted much of his "Heart To Heart" talk to denouncing the idea as a prelude to war. Some excerpts:

> War is waste. Where men waste, men and women must work to make good this waste.
> To prepare for war is to have war. We get what we prepare for, and we get nothing else.
> The danger to this Country is from within—it lies in idleness, ignorance, superstition and the false education of individuals like Hobson, so that they are experts in the inutile. Hobson does no useful thing, and yet demands honors in inverse ratio to the square of his inefficiency. This is the warrior idea, and traces a pedigree straight back to Caius Marius, Sulla, Cato, Pompey and Crassus.
> This country raises for our public schools, two hundred million dollars a year. And the appropriation for war and war appliances were, for the year just past, over four hundred million dollars.
> Hobson's desired appropriation would double the pay of every school teacher in America for ten years, and place manual training apparatus in every school house from Cape Nome to Key West.
> Now suppose we quit talking about war and set ourselves to this problem of educating our boys and girls.

After the New York Central popularized Elbert's "A Message to Garcia"
as a reading-rack item, other firms bought quantities for their employee
communications programs and looked to the author for more little gems
of philosophy for employee motivation. The head Roycrofter gladly obliged
with hundreds of "quickies." Here are some of the most popular ones.

MOST inaccuracies come from not really listening to what is said, or not really seeing what you put down.

Give your eye and ear a square deal 🌷 🌷 🌷

Elbert Hubbard
Employe's Help-Service

RESPONSIBILITIES gravitate
to the person who can shoulder them, *and* Power flows to the
man who knows how.—*Elbert Hubbard*

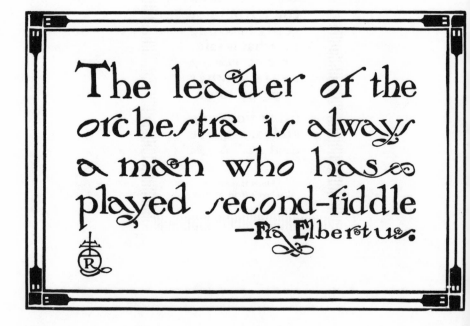

The leader of the orchestra is always a man who has played second-fiddle
—Fra Elbertus

FOLKS WHO NEVER DO
ANY MORE THAN THEY
GET PAID FOR, NEVER
GET PAID FOR ANY MORE
THAN THEY DO—Hubbard

THE less you require looking after, the more able you are to stand alone and complete your tasks, the greater your reward ✻ Then, if you can not only do your work, but direct intelligently and effectively the efforts of others, your reward is in exact ratio, and the more people you direct, and the higher the intelligence you can rightly lend, the more valuable is your life.—*Elbert Hubbard*

HORSE SENSE

IF you work for a man. in heaven's name work for him. ⁋ If he pays wages that supply you your bread and butter, work for him, speak well of him, think well of him, stand by him, and stand by the institution he represents. I think if I worked for a man, I would work for him. I would not work for him a part of his time, but all of his time. I would give an undivided service or none. ⁋ If put to a pinch, an ounce of loyalty is worth a pound of cleverness. ⁋ If you must vilify, condemn and eternally disparage, why, resign your position, and when you are outside, damn to your heart's content. But, I pray you, so long as you are a part of an institution, do not condemn it. Not that you will injure the institution—not that —but when you disparage the concern of which you are a part, you disparage yourself. And don't forget —"I forgot" won't do in business

The Busy Man's Creed

I BELIEVE in the stuff I am handing out, in the firm I am working for; and in my ability to get results. I believe that honest stuff can be passed out to honest men by honest methods. I believe in working, not weeping; in boosting, not knocking; and in the pleasure of my job. I believe that a man gets what he goes after, that one deed done today is worth two deeds tomorrow, and that no man is down and out until he has lost faith in himself. I believe in today and the work I am doing, in tomorrow and the work I hope to do, and in the sure reward which the future holds. I believe in courtesy, in kindness, in generosity, in good cheer, in friendship and in honest competition. I believe there is something doing, somewhere, for every man ready to do it. I believe I'm ready—RIGHT NOW!— *Elbert Hubbard*

⚜ ⚜ ⚜ ⚜ ⚜ ⚜ ⚜ ⚜ ⚜ ⚜ ⚜ ⚜

NO greater blessing than the artistic conscience can come to any 🙐 worker in art, be he sculptor, writer, singer or painter. Hold fast to it, and it shall be your compass in time when the sun is darkened. To please the public is little, but to satisfy your Other Self, that self which watches your every thought and deed, is much. No artistic success worth having is possible unless you satisfy that Other Self.

E L B E R T   H U B B A R D

In April 1904 he "Philistoned" those Clover Club members who made his January lecture visit to Philadelphia miserable by chiding him for his long hair and by making snide "Old Mother Hubbard" references:

I was told that several leading members of the Clover Club had arisen from very lowly walks of life—in fact, that they were once veritable guttersnipes. And I could well believe it.

For a time I kept thinking I was at that dear Hamlin's Stock Farm: we were getting all the refinements of the bull-pen, and these Pigs in Clover carried with them the etiquette of the sty.

"Get your hair cut!" Certainly, that is why I don't. I would miss the ribaldry to which, for a score of years, mine ears have become accustomed.

. . . Then there was the play upon my name—it invited the Clover Club Touchstone to tap his snuff box and say things.

There is nothing like the mellow tinge on chestnuts—and clover.

As a whole they look like men who have been cured of the mumps by the liberal use of sheep-nannie tea, the whole caboodle are candidates for melancholia, and bedlam will yet bag them all.

To the trough!

All in all, Elbert Hubbard had been strengthened by the trials that his weakness had brought down upon him. His principal weakness—the inability to stay away from Alice—was, paradoxically, what had finally brought him strength. He didn't like to sneak but for the love of Alice he had to. He didn't like to lie but to avoid bringing the wrath of Mrs. Grundy down upon himself, Alice, Bertha and their families, he had often done so, even when, at times, the truth would have served better. He didn't like to hurt but for Alice he did—and even hurt her.

He had learned some bitter lessons and had, with Alice, paid a bitter soul price that could never be fully offset no matter what financial success might lie ahead. But at least now, with Alice at his side, he could concentrate on his strengths and perhaps impart some helpful philosophy to his followers.

He had time to think about all this during peaceful 1904 and, in one of many little Philistine messages that year, he put it this way:

An East Aurora clergyman stopped me on the street last New Year's Day and asked me this question, "Dear Brother, do you feel that you are better, wiser and nearer God to-day than you were a year ago?"

The man meant well, even though the question implied a rather indelicate assumption.

I side-stepped the issue by a common-place, wished the good man a happy New Year, and passed on.

Busied with other things, I forgot my clerical neighbor, until the next afternoon when I was riding horseback down from the lumber camp. The early winter night was settling down, and the sleet had turned to rain. I had missed my way and missed my dinner. In attempting a cut 'cross lots I had jumped my horse into a gully eight feet deep, that was snowed level full. The horse went down end over end. I jumped from the saddle to keep from scoring a final touch-down in the mix-up; the horse scrambled out and made for home at the rate of one fifty-nine.

Then by a strange inconsistency the question swept over me, "Are you better, wiser and nearer God than you were a year ago?"

And I said "No." The sense of failure and defeat was upon me— my enemies had had their way. I was shelterless, hungry, cold—deserted.

And I started to trudge thru the sleet and snow for home.

As I walked, I sort of warmed up, and things grew brighter. Finally the lights of the village glimmered in the distance; and I laughed aloud to think that an hour before discouragement and chagrin had settled down on me like a pall.

When I laughed I began to think better of myself.

I congratulated myself on the fact that a four-mile walk was nothing but a privilege. The horse wasn't hurt, as was clearly proven by the way she had put distance between us. I had a comfortable home ahead, and supper and rest were awaiting me.

Then it came to me that whether we have made head or not is merely a point of view—it is largely a matter of physical condition. Take your spiritual inventory before dinner and you will find small assets—after dinner you are rich.

Without a doubt there were those among Hubbard's 90,000 subscribers who found his life's lessons style of philosophy helpful to them in their own trials.

Even Bertha, who loved and lost, felt some easing of her pain in knowing that Elbert seemed to have found himself, for she still loved him. Strong in her own way, she had acknowledged defeat when she filed for divorce and was now accepting it more gracefully than had either Elbert or Alice during their temporary setbacks over the years. Her life now was devoted to Ralph and Katherine and she followed Elbert's career ever after from the sidelines and through the headlines, eventually with dispassionate eye.

16

"We See Our Highest Ideals Reflected"

In one of his little homilies of his divorce period, Elbert wrote:

No man should be pitied, excepting the one whose future lies behind and whose past is constantly in front of him.

Now his "past," which in the eyes of his fellow-villagers and much of the national press meant Alice, was neither behind him nor in front of him. She was legally at his side. And peace, to him, was the prospect of putting his restless energy to work at ideas and projects that the complexity of his personal life had thus far forced him to shelve.

Another of his observations during this transition period was:

What we microbes think of God does not make much difference to God—we can only mirror ourselves. We see our highest ideals reflected and call them "God." As we change our ideals, we change our God. God is getting better all the time—higher, nobler, wiser, gentler, kinder. We are parts and particles of God—God's in His heaven—which is right here—all's right with the world.

Although Elbert wrote these thoughts in an article about the Mormons in the *Philistine,* it was at the same time a personal cleansing. And it was admission of his microscopic significance in the eyes of God as well as a pledge to Him that the particle he, Elbert, constituted would henceforth be higher, nobler, wiser, gentler and kinder.

There followed a fast-paced decade in which only his confirmed critics could fail to see the sincerity of his efforts and the importance of Alice to the whole man.

In 1908 Hubbard came forth with a new magazine, *The Fra*, which he called "a journal of affirmation." It was, in format (9″ x 14″) and context much different from his pocket-sized *Philistine*, that "periodical of protest" which continued to grow in popularity right along with its new, more sophisticated companion magazine.

The Fra added a new dimension to Hubbard's talents. It was large enough to accommodate illustrated advertisements and national advertisers flocked to its pages. They represented the "Who's Who" of American business of the era—businesses that would live on. Among them were Wrigley's Chewing Gum Co., H. J. Heinz Co., Waltham Watch Co., W. K. Kellogg, Armour Co., Equitable Life, Burroughs Adding Machine Co., Burpee's Seeds, B. F. Goodrich, Oliver Plow, Knox Hat Co., Studebaker, Chalmers, Ford—and in due course, virtually all of the emerging automobile manufacturers.

Hubbard, the author, epigrammatist, publisher, inn-keeper and lecturer, also became a leading advertising copywriter of his day. He originated the signed advertisement—"an advertisement by Elbert Hubbard"—and his clients vied for his especially written, folksy blurbs about their products or services.

A contemporary advertising man, George Batten, a founder of Batten, Barton, Durstine & Osborn, eventually said of him, "For anyone to deny the cleverness of Hubbard is like saying that flying machines can't fly. Hubbard has always been smart. He makes and sells everything from literature to andirons."

Soon everything that Hubbard undertook served to indicate the need and desirability of broadening his base.

The personal approach to writing ads called for visiting his clients' home offices. He met the captains of business and industry, many of whom had long been using his initiative-building "Message to Garcia" as an employee-reading-rack booklet. They wanted more such motivational pieces. He gladly obliged and thus became a pioneer in that field too. Hubbard used the occasion of his visits to discuss with the business leaders their personal backgrounds and then added a new dimension to his "Little Journeys" pamphlets. He wrote hundreds of business "Little Journeys" which were bought by the subject firms or businessmen and women in quantities of tens of thousands. He wrote about all of them from Standard Oil Co. to Lydia Pinkham.

As he widened his activities he broadened his reputation and expanded his publishing and printing operations at East Aurora.

One of the first projects that Alice undertook while her busy husband was on the go was the enlargement of the Roycroft Inn to accommodate the ever-increasing numbers of Elbert Hubbard followers and clients who seemed to be almost magically drawn to the village he spoke of as being "more a state of mind than a place."

Before long, the Inn became famous as the "in" place where aspiring writers, artists, political figures, businessmen and others could see and be seen by the greats and near-greats of the American scene. At various times such diverse personages as Henry Ford, Booker T. Washington, Clarence Darrow, Richard Le Gallienne, Carrie Jacobs Bond, Dard Hunter, Carl Sandburg, Robert Frost, Sadakichi Hartmann, Sydney Kaufmann, Earl Carroll, and Clara Barton made the trek to East Aurora, as did a host of others.

The Roycroft enterprises expanded beyond a printing and publishing business to a crafts complex, à la William Morris. It was a sort of atelier where hand-crafted furniture, copper, brass and silver wares, and wrought-iron decorative pieces were turned out in surprisingly great quantities by unskilled artisans learning crafts under the tutelage of skilled artisans. The same was true of the expanded fine books business where young men and women learned the printing trade, how to bind and illumine beautiful books, tool leather, etc.

Hubbard brought to middle- and lower-class Americans an interest that hadn't existed before for them—that of owning fine books. The dream he had explored with Denslow came true a thousandfold! In the process, many of these same Americans got to looking between the covers of the prestige pieces they had bought to grace their library shelves and suddenly acquired an interest in literature.

In the years to come, many persons who rose from humble beginnings to the pinnacles of success would ultimately credit a book "bought on suspicion" from Hubbard as the move that started or helped them on their way. Not the least of these was Conrad Hilton of hotel fame who, in his autobiography *Be My Guest* told of the important part Hubbard's "Little Journeys" played in his career-building.

There were countless others who received more direct encouragement from Hubbard. Carrie Jacobs Bond, whose sentimental songs "The End of a Perfect Day" and "Just A-Wearying For You" were being hummed everywhere in the first decade of the 20th century, was given the encouragement and train fare by Hubbard to go to New York to audition her music. Later, the Bond Shop—her own music-publishing house in Chicago —was admittedly inspired by Hubbard's Roycroft Shop and in her autobiography she credited Hubbard with starting her on the road to fame and fortune.

But there were, in addition, the hundreds who gained employment at the Roycroft "colony." They, while not reaching the heights in fame or fortune, idolized Hubbard for the chance he gave them to improve their lot in life far beyond their wildest dreams. If they couldn't be a Carrie Jacobs Bond, they could see her up close when she visited the Roycroft, be released from work to hear an impromptu recital by her on the Roycroft campus and get her autograph. If they couldn't be a Henry Ford, they could brush elbows with the man who put America on wheels. If they couldn't put together their talents well enough to aspire to the legitimate stage, they could participate in weekly Roycroft recitals with their peers and hear Hubbard applauding louder than the others.

The "Fabian Socialist" looked more and more like a paternalistic employer and if a name had been given to his type of enterprise it would more logically have been "Hubbard Capitalism." It was, in fact. a kind of socio-capitalism that he led many of the captains of industry toward—not consciously, but effectively—for he became, through his *Fra, Philistine* and other media, not the paid apologist that many believed, but rather their paid conscience. He stood up for them when he felt they were right but publicly chastised them when he felt they were wrong—even at the risk of losing their advertising business. He was an anti-muckraker who used muckraker techniques to clear the air so that all sides could be seen.

Typical of his use of this technique was a 1910 *Fra* article about Ida Tarbell after she had published a book attacking the Standard Oil Company:

> To understand her book, it is not enough to read it—you must have a glimpse of the author. Ida Tarbell has 23 pictures of John D. Rockefeller in her book but none of herself. Her own history is written between the lines and her picture is on the fly leaves.
>
> She shot from cover and shot to kill. Such literary bushwackers should be answered shot for shot. Sniping the commercial caravan may be legitimate, but to my mind the Tarbell-Steffens-Russel-Roosevelt-Sinclair method of inky warfare is quite as unethical as the alleged tentacled-octopi policy which they attack.

In the same article, however, Hubbard, like the public relations practitioner that he was before the term had been invented, confessed for the oil industry its past sins while calling for recognition of its long-since more enlightened role. And, because he called his shots as he saw them, he was one of the few outsiders to penetrate John D. Rockefeller's inner circle and try his hand at golf with the old gentleman at his Cleveland estate. That wasn't by any means a long-cherished milestone in Hubbard's life but indicative of his growing prominence at the time. He was equally at home with Steinmetz, the eccentric electrical engineer, "wizard of General Electric," Freddy Welsh, the boxing champion, or his East Aurora hired man, "Ali Baba."

Magazines such as *Cosmopolitan, The Independent, Munsey, Hearst,* etc., which had sent many rejection slips to Hubbard in the past, sought pieces from him now and he obliged. He also entered into a contract with Hearst newspapers to do a daily column.

His prominence as a lecturer grew and he became one of the most popular and best-paid single attractions on the Orpheum Circuit under the sagacious managerial guidance of Major Pond. Each facet of his many-sided career called attention to the others and all kept growing.

*When Henry Ford visited the Roycroft. This June 1, 1913, photo shows
(l. to r.) Hubbard, Ford, Mrs. Ford, Edsel Ford, Mrs. Buck, Alice,
Miriam and Mr. Buck.*

CONCERT
Sunday Evening, April 7th
ROYCROFT SHOP

*CARRIE JACOBS-BOND will sing
and the admission will be free to all
Good Roycrofters and their friends*

*In her autobiography song writer Carrie Jacobs Bond credited Hubbard
with starting her on her way to fame. This announcement demonstrates
one of the ways he did it. Her rendition of her famous song, "The End
of a Perfect Day," left audiences misty-eyed.*

When Hubbard visited John D. Rockefeller at his Cleveland, Ohio, estate. (l. to r.) Hubbard, Rev. Dr. Bustard, and "John D."

The hecticity of the life led by Elbert and Alice from 1904 through 1915 was spelled out in letters and telegrams to her from him as he criss-crossed the nation on research, business or lecture trips. In total, they added up to a big, eleven-year love letter, punctuated with myriad date-lines from Manitoba and Boston to Atlanta and San Francisco.

He took Miriam with him on a short business trip through Pennsylvania in December of 1907. From the Leister House in Huntingdon, Pa., on December 17, he sent this brief note to Alice, addressing the envelope to "Rev. Alice Hubbard, East Aurora, N.Y.":

Select $100 worth of furs for yourself and never say I never gave you nothing!

He enclosed with it a letter to Alice from their 13-year-old daughter:

Mother,

We saw the iron mills at Emporium and we saw the fire dash up from a kind of iron cage. We went over there and saw the furnaces where they melt the iron. They have two machines with immense wheels apiece, 500 horsepower each, just to blow air into the furnaces.

There were places where they put the pig iron and we were too late to see it put in.

Where I was [it was] wonderful. We stopped in Loch Haven in a hotel that would make your hair turn green, blue and yellow. When we woke up (we had to be called) the man was breaking the door in. I expected to see his fist come through any minute. It's beautiful here and oh but that lunch was good!!! We ate all but part of the cookies and a package of sandwitches [sic]. Tell Mother Grant at that beautiful and magnificent hotel we had for breakfast: 1 dry hot apple apiece, a greasy balony (?) sausage, some potatoes (greasy) some coffee *and* some pancakes made with some grease in them. Also a bit of rubber to give them a spicy chewy consistency.

We are almost at Tyrone so I'll leave the rest to your imagination.

　　　　　　　　　　　　　Baby (Miss Hubbard and
　　　　　　　　　　　　　　　　　her father)

Alice was greatly amused by Elbert's envelope salutation and also by Miriam's note which she knew full well Elbert had helped her write. The furs? She would think about that for there was a payroll to meet and she was a careful manager. The love behind the thought was all she cared about and now it was exclusively hers.

Their love did not fade after marriage as many onlookers had predicted. It grew, for it had been well nourished for so many years outside the bonds of matrimony and the food had been more of a work than sexual nature. Elbert had tried to spell out the proportions in a book he published in 1906 called *Love, Life and Work.*

They were busy with work now but they didn't abandon the physical

Pretty and pensive, Miriam spent her formative years midst the nation's greats and near-greats who came to the Roycroft to visit her popular parents Alice and Elbert Hubbard.

aspects of the union. In letters or telegrams they revived and frequently used their old love symbol of 1, 2, 3, 4.

Also unchanged was their keen interest in the world about them which had always invaded their love letters from the very beginning.

Roycroft artist Gaspard did this sketch of Alice in her early days as Mrs. Hubbard and manager of her husband's workforce.

Elbert to Alice:

Enroute to Pittsburgh
April 22, 1908

Blessedly:

Have just left Altoona. Spoke to big audience with big feed afterward. Gable is a Royal fellow.—he sent you yesterday a piece of Rookwood. You can write to him direct and acknowledge it. William F. Gable, Altoona, Pa.

Am a bit of a rock with loss of sleep and much handshaking but *will* catch up this afternoon.

1 2 3 4

Gable was owner of Altoona's leading department store and a great booster of Hubbard.

Alice saved all of Elbert's wires. She cherished them as she did his love letters and they became a sort of loose-leaf diary, a spot check of which at any time measured the tempo of his activities.

1909

POSTAL TELEGRAPH

New York, N.Y.   1-18-09

DELIGHTFUL INTERVIEW WITH ARCHBOLD HOME TOMORROW NIGHT. [Archbold was a Standard Oil Co. executive.]

WESTERN UNION

Denver, Colo.   9-12-09

O THAT DEAR OLD DENVER. HOMEWARD BOUND SEE YOU SATURDAY MORNING.

1910

POSTAL TELEGRAPH

Hamilton, Maine   1-22-10

HOME TOMORROW EVENING.

The following year was an extremely busy on-the-road year for Elbert. Two February letters to Alice preceded many wires and they explained to Alice how vaudeville—"vode" he called it—provided a great advertising medium for him, her and their Roycroft enterprises.

Alice, really a pioneer in the women's liberation movement, had gained much recognition with her book, *Woman's Work,* in 1908 and had developed a lecture of her own titled "The New Woman." Elbert was using his reputation as a lecturer to help launch her.

"Fra Elbertus" strikes a lecture pose to model a summer suit for a clothing manufacturer's ad in his FRA magazine.

The Roycroft Fraternity

East Aurora, Erie County, New York State

a 72/31

FRIENDS:—You ~~may~~ *must* send me Elbert Hubbard's Complete Works, express paid, ~~on inspection~~, at ~~Ten~~ *Two Hundred* Dollars per volume, as fast as issued. It is understood that I have the privilege of canceling this order at any time, *if go broke* at my option.

Date *Friday, July 30* 1909

SO HERE THEN is a photographic reproduction of Thos. W. Lawson's order for a set of the Complete Writings of Elbert Hubbard. ¶ Being interpreted, the order reads as follows:

The Roycroft Fraternity,
East Aurora, Erie County,
New York State.

Friends:—

You must send me Elbert Hubbard's Complete Works, express paid, at Two Hundred Dollars per volume, as fast as issued ¶ It is understood that I have the privilege of canceling this order at any time I go broke, at my option.

Thomas W. Lawson,
Boston.

Date, Friday, July 30th, 1909.

¶ Seven of the books have been issued and sent to Mr. Lawson. For these he has paid us Fourteen Hundred Dollars and expressed his great satisfaction with the purchase. There are yet thirty-three volumes to be issued, and these will come along, say, at the rate of four or five a year.

¶ Mr. Lawson's set of books will cost him Eight Thousand Dollars, but when the last tome is in Tom's hands the value of the books will be double what he paid for them.

¶ Mr. Lawson is a very wise man, as well as a lover of pinks, pictures and poetry.

Within a few years after Elbert's divorce from Bertha and marriage to Alice he saw indisputable signs that his followers were forgiving and new ones were frantically buying everything he offered from finely bound collections of his writings to the handmade furniture and copper and leather wares of his Roycroft craftsmen. Boston banker Thomas W. Lawson was one of the higher paying customers but Elbert had something for all in any income bracket. Alice was his strong right arm in his new era of peak success.

Hotel St. Francis
San Francisco
February 24, 1911

Blessed:

Better get these tickets[1] printed and send me here care "The Orpheum Theatre" at once.

The whole town is celebrating the Washington success and they recognize you and me as factors. I've reminded them that this is merely an opportunity.

1 2 3 4

The next day another letter gave her instructions as to where to store valuable books on the Roycroft campus and gave her some things to think about as to whether he should continue his vaudeville schedule or get back to a tighter writing schedule, taking only occasional lecture engagements.

Hotel St. Francis
San Francisco
Feb. 25, 1911

Bless:

In spite of precedents, the Chapel basement is the safest place you have for books, so you had better fill it up and trust in God and George Germain.

When Health & Wealth is gone we will print no more. But The Man of Sorrows and White Hyacinths we will reprint and carry in stock for 99 years. For them there is a steady demand.

Love, Life and Work was a great title and that we might want to reprint with additions.

When I get back I am going to work with Jimmy and focus on advertising. Am declining all lecture engagements although I see I could make a lecture date in each of these vode towns and get a big crowd. Vode is a great advertising scheme. We'll talk about it when we meet—talk! Well, I rather think we will talk—I have bushels to tell you.[2]

1 2 3 4

---

1. Accompanying the note were the ticket instructions: 500 tickets. Admit one. Lecture by Alice Hubbard, Colonial Ball Room, St. Francis Hotel Friday evening March 17, 1911. Subject "The New Woman" One Dollar

2. Hubbard had published his book about Christ—*The Man of Sorrows*—in 1906, *White Hyacinths* in 1907, *Health & Wealth* in 1908.

N evening with MARSHALL P. WILDER

in the Roycroft Salon

Monday, Aug. 9

AT EIGHT O'CLOCK

PROGRAM

1. Violin—Sonata No. 3 . . . . Handel
   PROFESSOR CHENEY

2. Marshall P. Wilder . . . . . .

3. Magic Fire Scene (Die Walkuere) Wagner-Brassin
   EDITH CORNELL HUNTER

4. Violin—Romanze . . . . Beethoven
   PROFESSOR CHENEY

5. Marshall P. Wilder . . . . . .

6. Violin—Selected . . . . . .
   PROFESSOR CHENEY

7. Marshall P. Wilder . . . . . .

8. Waltz—Op. 34, No. 1 . . . Moskowski
   EDITH CORNELL HUNTER

Roycrofters and East Aurorans were regularly treated to free lectures and cultural entertainment, courtesy of Fra Elbertus, during the heydey of the Roycroft movement. Marshall P. Wilder was a leading humorist and author of a ten-volume work titled The Wit and Humor of America *(1909).*

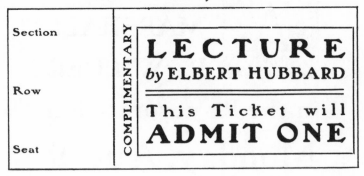

If you hired Hubbard for a lecture appearance he made certain that you also got a supply of complimentary "complimentary" tickets to give to the press and local dignitaries. His Roycroft Print shop knocked them out by the hundreds. They also printed the postcard announcements of Hubbard's forthcoming visit to wherever he was going to appear. Mailed to Fra and Philistine subscribers in a given city and to known Hubbard fans or customers there, it insured a good turnout for his sponsors.

Elbert Hubbar

will give his lecture

" Getting Together

Auspices Jovian League of Warren, Ohio,

at the

OPERA HOUSE
WARREN, OHIO

FRIDAY EVENIN

April 23, 1915

at Eight o'Clock

PRICES OF ADMISSION: Fifty and Seventy-f
Cents

Love by wire continued as before:

1911

WESTERN UNION

Alice Hubbard c/o   Oakland, Cal.
P.C. S.Fe. Train No. 3   Mar. 13, 1911
WILL MEET YOU UNLESS TRAIN IS TWO HOURS OR MORE LATE IN
WHICH CASE GO DIRECT TO ST. FRANCIS AND MAKE YOURSELVES
COMFORTABLE WHERE I WILL SEE YOU THE NEXT MORNING AT NINE
O'CLOCK. EVERYTHING LOVELY HERE SUNSHINE FLOWERS AND A
LOVING WELCOME.

WESTERN UNION

Alice Hubbard   Omaha, Neb.
East Aurora   April 6, 1911
EXACTLY ON TIME WILL BE OUT ON THE FIRST TRAIN FRIDAY MORN-
ING ONE TWO THREE FOUR PLUS.

POSTAL TELEGRAPH

                     Toledo, Ohio
                     June 19, 1911
NEVER TURNED DOWN ONCE SOLD SEVEN HUNDRED PAGES HOME IN
MORNING.

POSTAL TELEGRAPH

                     Pittsburgh, Pa.
                     Oct. 13, 1911
VOTES FOR WOMEN IN CALIFORNIA SURE.

East Aurora, N. Y. _____**191**__

ELBERT HUBBARD, BANKER
(50-534)

Pay to the
  Order of_____ **$**_____

_____ **Dollars**

No._____   _____

---

*Hubbard operated a bank on the Roycroft Campus mostly to encourage
his employees to be thrifty. He did, however, offer the services of his
bank to the readers of his* Fra *magazine and used the expression "Bank by
Mail" long before it became a popular bank slogan.*

As Bees in Honey Drown

POSTAL TELEGRAPH

New York
Feb. 8, 1912

HOME IN MORNING BIG BUSINESS.

On April 14, 1912 the S.S. *Titanic* struck an iceberg. Hubbard was asked by the Hearst newspapers to write a piece about the tragedy and do it in the first person, as though he had been aboard and had witnessed the behavior of the passengers. He was to focus particularly upon the notables aboard the ill-fated liner, Mr. and Mrs. John Jacob Astor, Mr. and Mrs. Isador Straus, William B. Stead, Benjamin Guggenheim and others.

The sea had long held much fascination for Hubbard, particularly with respect to its secrets and its awesome fury and so Hubbard went at his task with a deep sense of involvement.

He began, "It is a night of a thousand stars. The date, Sunday April 14, 1912. The time, 11:20 P.M. The place, off Cape Race—that cemetery of the sea . . ."

It was a graphic, stirring and sentimental saga—just the kind for which Hearst papers were famous.

Its conclusion seemed to have in it some of the same melancholia and resignation that had marked Elbert's mood when he had written to Alice when he first sailed to Europe back in 1894:

Happily, the world has passed forever from a time when it feels a sorrow for the dead. The dead are at rest, their work is ended, they have drunk of the waters of Lethe, and these are rocked in the cradle of the deep. We kiss our hands to them and cry, 'Hail and farewell— until we meet again!'

But for the living who wait for a footstep that will never come, and all those who listen for a voice that will never more be heard, our hearts go out in tenderness, love and sympathy.

These dead have not lived and died in vain. They have brought us all a little nearer together—we think better of our kind.

One thing sure, there are just two respectable ways to die. One is of old age, and the other is by accident.

All disease is indecent.

Suicide is atrocious. But to pass out as did Mr. and Mrs. Isador Straus is glorious. Few have such a privilege. Happy lovers, both. In life they were never separated, and in death they are not divided.

Hubbard, in his imaginary witnessing of the tragedy at sea, had Mrs. Straus refusing to leave her husband as women and children were offered places in the lifeboats. Her husband had quietly and gently tried to persuade her to go but she was adamant, saying, "All these years we have traveled together and shall we part now? No our fate is one."

Alice thought Elbert's piece was beautiful and she wept as she read it.

```
            AFFIDAVIT.
            ──────────

State of New York :
                   : SS
County of Erie     :

Personally appeared before me this day the following

persons, to me known:

      Elbert Hubbard, Editor Philistine Magazine

      Alice Hubbard, General Manager Roycroft Shops

      James Wallen, Advertising Manager for The Roycrofters

      A.V.Ingham, Superintendent of Printing

All and each of whom made solemn affidavit, as follows:

The edition of the Philistine Magazine for the

month of October, 1911, the first form of which

is now on the press, will be two hundred thous-

and copies, all of which are now subscribed for,

sold, and ordered.


Sworn to before me, this

fifteenth day of August, 1911.

Village of East Aurora.


                        Notary Public.

                        Commission expires March 30 1913
```

By 1911 the circulation of the Philistine *had risen to 200,000. Alice's prominent role in influencing the rising tide of her husband's success was clearly evident in this advertising circular–circulation affidavit.*

A beautiful Miriam Hubbard graced the September 1911 front cover of Hubbard's second magazine, The Fra. *The magazine was 9" x 14".*

So did the hundreds of thousands of subscribers to Hearst newspapers throughout the country and so did Hubbard's subscribers to *The Fra* in which it was reprinted.

There was no letup in the pace at East Aurora nor away from it. Highlight telegrams saved by Alice continued to testify to the latter:

POSTAL TELEGRAPH

Chicago, Illinois   6-15-12

MEET ME CENTRAL STATION THURSDAY AFTERNOON THREE O'CLOCK BRING AS MANY OF THE FRIENDS AS AUTO WILL CARRY ALSO WHAT IS THE MATTER WITH SUPPER.

POSTAL TELEGRAPH

Chicago, Illinois   6-19-12

I HAVE ONLY ONE TICKET BUT IT IS YOURS AS I HAVE SEEN ENOUGH OF THIS DOG FIGHT TO LAST ME FOR FOUR YEARS YOU BETTER LEAVE ON EIGHT-THIRTY TRAIN MICHIGAN CENTRAL THURSDAY EVENING. IF I DO NOT MEET YOU AT STATION COME DIRECT TO BLACKSTONE.

(Pro-Taft Hubbard was covering the Republican Convention where ex-President Theodore Roosevelt was trying to thwart incumbent President Taft's bid for a second term. There was a bitter intra-party fight but Taft won the nomination. Roosevelt bolted and became a third-party candidate. The Republican split gave Democrat Woodrow Wilson the Presidency. Hubbard lampooned the convention in his September issue of *The Fra*.)

POSTAL TELEGRAPH

Chicago, Illinois   8-20-12

GOT THREE BIG WRITE UPS COL. JACK JOHNSON WILL PROBABLY SPEND A FEW DAYS WITH YOU NEXT WEEK. HOME FRIDAY MORNING.

POSTAL TELEGRAPH

Kansas City, Mo.   8-21-12

BREAKING MOOSE TO DRIVE TANDEM HOME SATURDAY AM.

POSTAL TELEGRAPH

Kansas City, Mo.   10-11-12

LETTER FROM OLIVER SEEMS TO SHOW THAT NATIONAL COMMITTEE WILL GET BUSY HOPE SO HELP THEM ALL YOU CAN FOR A CONSIDERATION EVERYTHING LOVELY.

(The October issue of *The Fra* carried an eight-page special section, written by Hubbard, boosting William Howard Taft.)

Lines of adversity finally showing in this 1912 photo of Alice could not diminish the signs of poise and determination that had always shone through to give her husband the strength he needed.

1913

POSTAL TELEGRAPH
Chicago, Illinois   1-29-13
LOTS OF BUSINESS HERE AND I AM RIGHT AFTER IT.

POSTAL TELEGRAPH
Madison, Wis.   3-17-13
BEAUTIFUL LITTLE THEATRE VERY APPRECIATIVE AUDIENCE SPLENDID
HOTEL AM TO DINE WITH PRIEXIE TOMORROW.

POSTAL TELEGRAPH
Chicago, Illinois   3-24-13
THANKS FOR LETTER SPLENDID RECEPTION AND EVERYTHING LOVELY
PLEASE HAVE WEAVER SHIP SMALLEST SOW IN THE EMERSON BARN
POULTRY HOUSE PEN TO THE GREAT RAYMOND STUDEBAKER THEATRE
CHICAGO. IF POSSIBLE GET PIG OFF ON THE FIVE TWENTY MONDAY
VIA AMERICAN EXPRESS. ONE TWO THREE FOUR.

POSTAL TELEGRAPH

Winnipeg, Manitoba   5-5-13

SPLENDID AUDIENCE AND EVERYTHING LOVELY.

POSTAL TELEGRAPH

San Francisco, Cal.   5-16-13

BEAUTIFUL SAN FRANCISCO WITH VERY MANY CHARMING PEOPLE GOOD AUDIENCE AND EVERYTHING LOVELY.

POSTAL TELEGRAPH

Los Angeles, Cal.   5-19-13

SEND COPY OF JUNE PHILISTINE TO JOHN H. PATTERSON AND SOLICIT ORDER FOR QUANTITY ALL WELL SPLENDID AUDIENCE HOMEWARD BOUND.

(Hubbard had first met Patterson, founder of National Cash Register Co., in Dayton, Ohio in April of 1912—another business Little Journey subject that was paying off well for both men.)

POSTAL TELEGRAPH

Phoenix, Arizona   5-21-13

ALL RIGHT. PUT PICTURE OF WINSLOW ON FRA COVER. GET BRANDEIS

Single girls in the employ of the Roycroft Shops lived at Emerson Hall a few blocks away from the crafts complex. They took their meals there away from the busy dining room of the Roycroft Inn.

Printing Roycroft motto cards and advertising mailing pieces.

"Roycroft girls" at work in the collating room of the original printshop.

ARTICLE IN PHILISTINE TEXT BUT LET ME READ PROOF. EVERYTHING LOVELY HERE. AM WITH OUR DEAR FRIENDS MR. AND MRS. GARTH CATE WHO SEND THEIR LOVE TO EVERYBODY.

POSTAL TELEGRAPH
Oklahoma City, Okla.   5-26-13
ALMOST HOME HAVE AUTO MEET ME CENTRAL STATION BUFFALO FRIDAY MORNING AT TEN FORTY ALL WELL.

POSTAL TELEGRAPH
Detroit, Michigan   9-12-13
HAVE AUTO MEET ME MICHIGAN CENTRAL STATION BUFFALO TEN TONIGHT.

POSTAL TELEGRAPH
Boston, Mass.   10-31-13
OH THAT DEAR OLD BOSTON.

In November Alice was away for a change and Elbert was at home. He wired to her at the Parker House in Boston where she was in the company of famed woman lawyer Marilla Ricker of Washington, D.C.

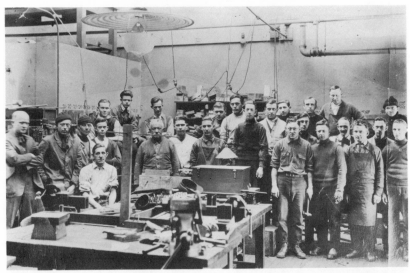

Copper craftsmen gather for department photo in early 1900s.

Hand Illumining made Roycroft books something special for customers then and for collectors today. It was interesting work for the young ladies of East Aurora with an artistic bent. This young lady, Alta Fattey, caught the eye of Elbert Hubbard II, who wooed her and won her hand in marriage.

With a baseball team and a band Hubbard was far ahead of most employers of his day in the field of employee relations.

Roycroft employees "doubled in brass" as members of the Roycroft Band. They played for Roycroft gatherings and community events.

POSTAL TELEGRAPH

East Aurora, N.Y.   11-16-13

WRESTLING WITH CROUSE MADE ME MISS CARRYING YOUR INDE-STRUCTO TO STATION GOT THOUSAND DOLLAR ORDER BUT HAVE TO PREPARE TEST AND THIS WITH OTHER WORK MAKES GOING TO BOSTON NOW INEXPEDIENT GOOD LUCK WE WILL GO LATER.

1914

POSTAL TELEGRAPH

Chicago, Illinois   4-19-14

SECURED THREE BIG ORDERS BEST CAN COME HOME TUESDAY MORNING ONE TWO THREE FOUR.

POSTAL TELEGRAPH

Ogden, Utah   9-10-14

ARRIVE CHICAGO SATURDAY MORNING IF ANYBODY THERE TO SEE WRITE CARE HOTEL SHERMAN.

POSTAL TELEGRAPH

Chicago, Illinois   9-12-14

HAVE BERT WRIGHT BUFFALO STATION TOMORROW SUNDAY MORNING SEVEN O'CLOCK.

POSTAL TELEGRAPH

Boston, Mass.   10-31-14

THAT DEAR OLD BOSTON HOME IN MORNING.

It seemed fantastic to Elbert Hubbard's employees—his Roycrofters—that a man who traveled so much would have any energy left upon returning home but he had it to spare.

He wouldn't fail to deliver a little talk for them at the Roycroft chapel on Sunday nights when he was home, even if he had just arrived back home that morning. He would tell them of the cities he visited, the people he met, the sights he saw or maybe try out a new road lecture on them—one he had penned on the train or dictated that afternoon. His secretary didn't mind Sunday work nor did any of the Roycrofters if it was needed to help their leader. Many of them were prideful of that dedication until their dying day.

Four persons who rarely missed Elbert's little Sunday night talks were Alice, son Bert, and the aging Dr. and Mrs. Hubbard. To Elbert's delight, his severest critic and front-row heckler was his father who would frequently shout aloud, " 'Tain't so! 'Tain't so!" causing all to chuckle and Elbert to remember that a son is always a son, no matter how famous he might become.

17

"The Crazy Kaiser Will Not Win"

In the January 1915 issue of *The Fra* both Elbert and Alice addressed themselves to the war in Europe, which had not yet reached the proportions that would give it the name of a World War, and ultimately World War I.

Elbert, not anticipating the direct involvement of the United States, spoke of the "waste and woe of war across the seas" but saw the U.S. in the eventual role of helping the stricken masses of Europe once the war ended. "It will be for us largely to feed and clothe a starving and shivering Europe," he wrote, and "Many of the things we have depended upon Europe for, we will now make for ourselves." On balance, he saw the eventual outcome of the war as "a grain of gain" for the United States, lamentable as it all was.

Speaking of the character-building outcome he wrote, "But the great gain from this war is in the heroic attitude of mind which forgets to complain and declines to whimper. The weather has ceased to be a topic for conversation. We have discovered that all weather is good, and stormy weather is glorious. Things are comparative."

He had been through a personal war and since his legal marriage to Alice in 1904, had adopted a frame of mind that made him forget to complain and decline to whimper.

His helpmeet in developing a new frame of mind was, herself, not able to take such a detached view of the war.

She wrote, "One of the mysteries of war is the undoubted fact that soldiers are not nearly as good haters as civilians. The truth is you cannot kill a man without realizing that he is your brother. The British subaltern who kicked the unsuspecting German patrol rather than shoot him in cold blood was more than a humorist, more than a sportsman—he was a human being."

And speaking of mother love in time of war she wrote:

Men cannot divine the deeps of agony endured by the mothers of Europe. They cannot overpass the great barrier which separates the heart of the father from the heart of the mother. The love of a father for his son is different in kind as well as in degree from the love of a mother for her son. The poverty of the language forces us to use the same word for the two affections, but there ought to be a word to express the wonderful passion of motherhood.

We speak of mother-wit, but seldom of mother-love, and yet mother love is the highest form of all love. It is in its supreme form utterly selfless. Wherefor when a country asks a mother to give her son to its service it asks for something that is dearer than life itself. There are few mothers who would not prefer to give their own life rather than the life of the son they bore. Greater love has no man than the love of the mother who gives her son's life to her country.

In the February *Fra,* Hubbard wrote about "The New Year—1915":

Roycroft girls in the book bindery. Happy in their work and proud of their craftsmanship, their productivity was amazing.

East Aurora's postoffice gained First Class status thanks to the Roycrofters'
heavy volume of magazine, booklet and crafts output.

> This is a genuine New Year. It is the newest New Year that the
> world has ever seen. Americans are at peace with one another as we
> have never been before.
> We have gotten rid of many of our whims, prejudices, superstitions.
> In degree, we have eliminated hate and fear and doubt, and the truth
> stands out limned against the sky.

Without realizing it, he was echoing the wishful thinking that Woodrow
Wilson had been expressing without due regard for the sure but more
subtle signs of an unerring United States policy course toward the involvement with troops, ships and planes.

Thus it was the usual busy life for Elbert and Alice in the first several
months of the New Year. He was still yielding to the lure of the lecture
circuit which he had considered abandoning.

As he moved about the country he heard more and more talk of inevitable United States involvement in the European war in which the Germans
seemed to be gaining the upper hand.

In the October 1914 issue of the *Philistine* he had opened inky warfare
against the Kaiser in an article titled, "Who Lifted the Lid Off Hell."

Now he re-issued it in pamphlet form. In it, he emphasized that the German people were cultured people who needed to see how the Kaiser was leading them astray:

> The Emperor does not represent the true Germany. He symbols the lust of power, the thirst for blood.
> He is a maniacal Night-Watchman—drunk on power— who thinks he owns the factory.
> The crazy Kaiser will not win. The wisdom of the world backs the Allies, and St. Helena waits. It must be so.

As spring approached Elbert told Alice that he was thinking of going abroad to gather some firsthand facts about the war. She reminded him of the promises he had made to her in his love letters sent back from Europe in 1894. If he was going, she wanted to go along. He demurred, speaking of the risk, however slight, of sailing the seas when German U-boats were seemingly everywhere and skippered by nervous captains. She wasn't buying, and so he set about to make arrangements for the two of them to sail on the Cunard Liner S.S. *Lusitania* from New York on May 2.

Elbert was committed to giving a lecture at the Ben Ali Theater in Lexington, Kentucky on April 29. His appearance was sponsored by the Lexington Board of Commerce and he selected the subject "Getting Together." The lecture dealt with cooperation and the bright prospects for business that seemed to lie ahead in 1915.

It was a weary Elbert Hubbard who hurried back from Lexington to pick up Alice and head for New York to board the *Lusitania*. He was also a bit worried about Alice's safety for the Germans had boldly placed an ad in the New York papers on April 22 warning travelers that vessels flying the flag of Great Britain or any of her allies were liable to destruction when in the war zone.

For the first time son Bert and other Roycrofters heard their leader discuss what they should do if he didn't get back. At the time they didn't dwell much upon his out-of-character show of pessimism for he seemed to only inadvertently insert the "if" in his instructions as to what to do while he was away.

On May 7, 1915, at eight minutes past 9:00 A.M. "dear old Boston" time, it happened. Off the Head of Old Kinsale along the Irish Coast, a German U-boat torpedoed the S.S. *Lusitania*. Explosions rocked the big liner and she began to list.

Charles E. Lauriat, Jr. of Boston was on deck near Elbert and Alice. He turned to them and suggested they go to their stateroom for their lifejackets. They all had time, he figured, even though his stateroom was on the starboard side of deck B and theirs was on the port side.

They did not heed his suggestion and in his book survivor Lauriat recalled, "Mr. Hubbard stayed by the rail affectionately holding his arm

One of the last photos of Alice and Elbert together. To the end Alice
stood in awe of the man she adored.

around his wife's waist and both seemed unable to act."

He did not see them again. The sea closed in around the ship and those who had not abandoned her—even some who did—and it was done.

Epilogue

The news of the sinking of the S.S. *Lusitania* by the Germans shocked the world and since only 35 out of 159 Americans on board survived, Americans seethed with anger. It signalled this country's direct involvement in the war.

Roycrofters waited in vain for word that Elbert and Alice might be among the survivors. Thinking back to the mood of the night the couple left East Aurora, they all had a sense of foreboding which was not long in being confirmed. Alice and Elbert would never again be with them except in the memories that had already begun to race through their minds.

Although such prominent Americans as millionaire Alfred Vanderbilt, Charles Frohman of theatrical fame, novelist Justus Forman, explorer J. Foster Stackhouse and others lost their lives in the tragedy, Elbert Hubbard was the one about whom virtually every newspaper in the United States wrote editorials. They conjectured as to what his loss meant to the nation. Nearly all expressed a feeling of great loss and in many cases they were the same papers which in his hour of marital crisis published the "ascerbitations" which Hubbard had repeated in the *Philistine.*

On May 16, the *Macon* (Georgia) *Telegraph,* in a long editorial titled, "The Passing of the Fra" said, in part:

> In these calmer hours when we are able to take stock of our national loss through the murder of innocents on the Lusitania, there is no doubt that the passing of Elbert Hubbard will be regretted and bring more sorrow to the American people than any of the noted men who went down on the big liner. . . . He was fearless in his personal life, for he married a Magdalene and made her a Madonna—and gloried in it. He saw the good as well as the evil in the great and the evil as well as the good in the lowly. It has often been said that he prostituted his craft and genius to pelf, that he could be bought, but while he openly admitted that he accepted money for much that he wrote in The Fra,

the writings themselves were obvious in that respect. He did not exploit, nor gloss over those things which were bad and had no merit. If a firm was good it sought Hubbard to exploit it in that human, breathing way he could, but if it were not it never dreamed of seeking his services. For he was not to be stultified by money.

In the last number of the Philistine he remarked that when it came time to die he would "like to die like a Belgian." He did. And so be it—God rest his soul.

The *Jefferson City* (Mo.) *News* editorialized this way:

Death is the great dignifier of men and of lives, but it seems hard, even in the hour of his death, to write seriously of Elbert Hubbard— printer, publisher, philosopher, press agent—and arch-Philistine. He made East Aurora famous; he made phrases that stuck in the mind; he made little journeys to pretty much everywhere, and wrote about famous men with a sort of extemporized intimacy which gave to the not-too-exacting reader the feeling of real acquaintanceship. He discovered the remunerative secret of gluing a piece of limp leather to the leaves of a book and persuading the indulgent public that it was bound. If P. T. Barnum had altogether reconstructed William Morris and picked him out with touches of Sam Slick and Walt Whitman, a second Elbert Hubbard might have been the result. The Sage of East Aurora was master of a wholly illusory art of making his readers think they were thinking—but when you count up the members of serious-minded men in black coats or academic gowns who have done the same thing just as futilely, with infinitely less of the audacious and the entertaining, who would deal hardly with him for that? The world of promotion and promoters has lost a jaunty and an engaging figure.

The *Des Moines* (Iowa) *Capital* said, in part:

Absence of any further word would confirm the report that Elbert Hubbard went down with the Lusitania, himself a victim of that Prussian militarism which he so mercilessly denounced. It is difficult to believe that he is really lost; we have the feeling that it would be just like him to come up somewhere even yet with one of his characteristic witticisms.

As with most men who gain the reputation of being humorists, it was often difficult for the American public to take Hubbard quite seriously. We were never sure how seriously such a man takes himself.

Elbert Hubbard was a unique personality. Dreamer, farmer, author, publicist, successful manufacturer, advertising manager, smasher of conventions, vaudeville top-liner, philosopher, clever literary clown, quaint combination of Rabelais and Poor Richard, always original and withal lovable for his very all-too-humanness, there was much about him which was essentially American.

Hubbard's best-known writing is the "Message to Garcia," which has doubtless been more widely printed and circulated than any other document written in this country in this generation. Starting his little

A NATIONAL LOSS.

There seems no longer reason to hope that Elbert Hubbard, philosopher, writer and business man, was saved from the Lusitania disaster. Undoubtedly he is dead, and with the statement the Fra becomes a thing of the past, the Philistine is ended, and the Roycrafters are immeasurably bereft.

There was no more forceful writer in America than Hubbard. His vocabulary was abundant and his choice of words original and peculiarly striking. His diction enjoyed a subtle nicety and exactness oddly blended with carefree abandon. And while he was deft with the tools of his trade there was more to him than that. He was far better than merely clever. He had learned to look below the surface of things and see the hidden motives, the first causes, the primal foundations. He was a consistent optimist and shed sunshine in his writings and with his presence.

And in Hubbard the business world lost a valuable helper. Successful in a business way himself, he wanted others to succeed. He wanted the world to learn the importance of business and the folly of unbusinesslike processes and policies. He understood that poor business is the cause of much unhappiness and he tried to teach good business.

The sage of East Aurora will be sadly missed by a legion of his readers.

Editorial titled, "A National Loss" from the May 12, 1915 Joplin, Mo. Globe. Virtually every newspaper in the U. S., big and small, editorialized on his tragic death in the sinking of the S.S. Lusitania on May 7, 1915. Most were along these lines.

printshop in determination to publish his writings, which had been rejected by leading journalists, Hubbard has had an unmistakable influence upon the journalism of this country in breaking up certain stereotyped forms of expression.

The *Jackson* (Miss.) *News* on May 12, 1915, devoted a 10-inch double-column editorial to Hubbard and fence-rode its lament to the very end. It said in part:

> The most picturesque person who perished on the Lusitania was Elbert Hubbard. Beyond any question of a doubt, he was the most unusual figure in American literature.
> It cannot be said that the world of letters has sustained a great loss in the death of Fra Elbertus, as he was popularly known. His philosophy did not appeal to any orthodox mind, his personal code was not above reproach, and he contributed little to literature that will be lasting—perhaps his famous "Message to Garcia" will be about the only effort of his pen that will be remembered in the years to come.
> However, it is not our purpose to quarrel with or criticize the strange figure that now lies at the bottom of the sea. . . .
> . . . . A queer figure, indeed, was Elbert Hubbard, and there are many who will mourn his death.

Even in death, Hubbard dared others to throw the first stone and those inclined to accept the challenge did so gingerly, half-heartedly. It was as if they feared he might somehow yet manage to have the last word. In a way, the ineptness that this prevailing fear forced upon them did give him the last word—and from his critics' own pens.

There were services held throughout the country in tribute to Elbert and Alice Hubbard. The village of East Aurora, where the *Buffalo Courier* had rightly predicted there would be a cool reception when Elbert brought Alice back as his wife in 1904, had in the meantime grown warm. When memorial services were held for the couple after it was certain that they were forever lost, mourning citizens in dark clothing followed the mayor down Grove Street past the Roycroft Inn for services on the Roycroft campus and tears were hot and plentiful.

Miriam, stunned, came home from college for the family services where Elbert's parents, all of his children, his sisters, employees, close friends, neighbors, and Bertha, the wife of his youth, had gathered.

And dear Bertha was heard to say, "I have conquered the bitterness but not the pain, for I loved him."

Some weeks later Bert Hubbard, upon whom fell the major responsibility of continuing the work of the Roycrofters, found a piece of manuscript in his father's desk. It was titled "The Sea":

> The Sea knows all things, for at night when the winds are asleep the stars confide to him their secrets. In his breast are stored away all the elements that go to make up the round world. Beneath his depths lie buried the sunken kingdoms of fable and legend, whose monarchs have long been lost in oblivion. He appropriates and makes his own all that is—dissolving the rocks that seek to stop his passage—forming, transforming, rearranging, never ceasing, tireless. Tireless ever, for he gets

IN MEMORIAM

Commemorative

of

Elbert and Alice Hubbard

Lost with the ill-fated " Lusitania," off the
Old Head of Kinsale, Ireland,
on May 7th, 1915

A SERVICE

of appreciation and regard by the
people of the Village.

Held
at East Aurora, N. Y.
May 23d, 1915,
three o'clock.

*The program (cover and inside) for the memorial services at East Aurora.
Many similar services were held by "Roycrofters-at-Large" throughout
the United States in the weeks following. Newspapers from coast to coast
solemnly editorialized on the great loss that Hubbard's untimely passing
brought to the nation. Some appeared in the same papers that had ex-
coriated him and Alice a decade before, when their love affair was revealed.*

his rest in motion. With acute ear he listens along every coast and lies
in wait for the spirit of the offshore wind. All rivers run to meet him,
carrying tidings from afar, and ever the phosphorent dust from other
spheres glimmers on his surface.

It is not to be wondered that men have worshipped the ocean, for
in his depths they have seen mirrored the image of Eternity—of Infinity.
Here they have seen the symbol of God's great plan of oneness with
His creatures, for the sea is the union of all infinite particles, and it
takes the whole to make the one.

Men have fallen on their faces to worship the sea. Women have
thrown him their children to appease his wrath. Savagely yet tenderly
has he received the priceless treasure and hidden it away where none

On May 23, 1915, after it was certain that Elbert and Alice could not have survived the sinking of the S. S. Lustitania, the Roycrofters and citizenry of East Aurora turned out en masse for a commemorative service at the Roycroft campus on Grove Street. A touching aspect of the solemn procession was the sight of the famous pair's riderless horses, saddles turned backward, being led by Roycroft department heads. (see center of photograph.)

could recall. He has heard the dying groans of untold thousands, and drowned their cries for help with his own ceaseless roar; but still his ear has not failed to catch the whispers of confession that have come from souls about to appear before the Maker. And yet how beautiful and kind he is in his apparent relentless cruelty, for he keeps only the transient part, and gently separates the immortal and wafts the spirit back to God who gave it.

And what does the sea do with all these secrets, mysteries and treasures? Go shrive thyself, and with soul all in tune to the harmonies of the Universe listen to the waves and they shall tell thee the secrets of life!

Appendix: The Roycroft Institution after Hubbard's Death— The Shadow of One Man.

The "Emersonian friends," Elbert and Alice, had died in love's embrace. Ralph Waldo Emerson, whose influence upon their lives had been great and mostly good, once said, "Every institution is the lengthening shadow of one man." This was particularly true of the Roycroft enterprises, created and nurtured by the one and only Elbert Hubbard. He had set a generation agog and a legacy agoing. It fell to "Bertie," Elbert Hubbard, II, to take the helm.

When it was ascertained beyond all doubt that Elbert and Alice had perished, and after the memorial services had been held, Bert sat down at his Roycroft desk above which there hung a portrait of his father. He penned the preface to a book titled, *In Memoriam,* a selection of condolence letters from among thousands received. He said, in part, "Elbert Hubbard looks down upon me as I write . . . he smiles at me as ever . . . I know he has gone on his last little journey, and that somewhere he is traveling the way. His inspiration will forever hold me to my task."

Bert was worldly wise, articulate and an able writer himself. He could have taken his inheritance and struck out on his own, instead of trying to perpetuate an institution that had been so uniquely centered around one most unusual man. But in life there had never been a generation gap problem for this father and son and they were still communing.

Bert clearly saw the two-fold task ahead. One duty would be to henceforth guide the flourishing Roycroft enterprises, which by now were the livelihood of nearly 500 villagers. The other was to perpetuate the public

memory and the writings of his illustrious father. The former was by far
the greater task for Elbert Hubbard had already stamped his name rather
indelibly in the history of American literature.

Certain basic decisions had to be made. First off, Bert made it abundantly clear to the public that he knew there was only one Elbert Hubbard
and that his name, Elbert Hubbard, II, was in this larger sense a misnomer.

As an initial step, the *Philistine* was phased out with a "Valedictory
Number" in July 1915. It was put together by Bert and his fellow Roycrofters in a mood of great loss.

The keynote message read:

July [1915] is the last number of the Philistine. The Philistine was
Hubbard himself, his voice, his thought, his heart. His life for twenty-one
years poured into it. His personality made it—and now that he is gone,
it seems to us sacrilegious to continue it.

Shrewd businessmen will tell you that there exists a field for the
Philistine, that a Periodical of Protest will not want for an audience
in America. There is real work to be done.

Given an editor with an eye for injustice—a conscience that instinc-
tively knows a sham, a dislike for dead conventions, and what boots it
that his "style" is not Hubbard's? Moreover, the very name of the
Philistine carries prestige; success hovers around the corner! Magazines
of all sorts with editors who have neither courage nor convictions secure
circulation—in quantities. Dollars are to be had!

All this may be true—and certainly East Aurora lacks neither equip-
ment nor ability to make the experiment! But there remains so little
that The Roycrofters, men and women, may give to the memory of
Hubbard—the World has given so much! To us it seems the one great
Gift to give, within our power, is the Philistine itself!

The Philistine has been Hubbard's armor, his shield, his sword for
long years. He has left us for a Little Journey, we know not where.
He may need his Philistine—and so with tears on it, we give it to him.

Over there, it may help him get acquainted, to make friends! By it
they shall know him!

And, in this final issue of the "Phil" Bert spelled out what *would*
continue:

I know of no memorial that would please Elbert Hubbard half so
well as to broaden out the Roycroft Idea.

I am a Roycrofter. I know the Roycroft Shops, their possibilities,
their market—their friends. I am now President of The Roycrofters,
Incorporated—and I come to you with the suggestion that if Elbert or
Alice Hubbard meant anything to you, stand with me now.

We will continue to make handmade furniture, hand-hammered
copper and modeled leather. We shall still triumph in the arts of printing and bookmaking.

The Roycroft Inn will continue to swing wide its welcoming door,
and the kind greeting is always here for you.

N. S. E.

The Philistine

A Periodical of Protest

NEUTRALITY: The attempt of a prejudiced mind to convince itself that it is not prejudiced.

Vol. 41
No. 2

Printed Every Little While for the Society of the Philistines and Published by Them Monthly. Subscription, One Dollar Yearly ✠ ✠ ✠ ✠ ✠ Single Copies, Ten Cents

J U L Y , 1 9 1 5

VALEDICTORY

Last issue of Hubbard's popular Philistine *Magazine. Its size was 4½" x 6"—a "pocket-size" publication.*

The Fra will not miss an issue, and you who have enjoyed it in the past will continue to enjoy it.

The Philistine belonged to Elbert Hubbard. He wrote it himself for just twenty years and one month. No one else could have done it as he did. No one else can now do it as he did.

And so the Roycrofters moved forward on charted, yet choppy seas.

The actual Roycrofters and the Roycrofters-at-large, those tens of thousands of Hubbard followers throughout the nation, did stand with Bert as he had asked.

The annual Roycroft Conventions continued and though they now took

Elbert's parents, Dr. Silas Hubbard and Juliana Read Hubbard in 1917, two years after their famous son died at sea.

on more of a memorial theme, Bert had but to ask and the "name" personalities of the nation would grace the speakers' platform. Felix Shay, who had handled the advertising for *The Fra* under Elbert Hubbard, came back, at Bert's request, as editor.

But World War I became this country's war soon after the sinking of the S.S. *Lusitania*. On April 6, 1917 the United States declared war on Germany.

The first blow to the Roycrofters—dealt by a people preoccupied with an unwanted war—was a reduced readership for *The Fra,* an expensive, two-color magazine. Editor Shay described the magazine as Hubbard's "successful attempt to formulate a national forum in print." More than that he said, "it was a delight to the eye of the one who appreciated the artistic, and to the eye of the one who depreciated propaganda."

The forum, though, had gone international and expenses sky high. *The Fra* gave way in September 1917 to the *Roycroft* magazine. It was a return to the pocket-size publication and, with a brown "butcher paper" cover, was reminiscent of the abandoned *Philistine*. Bert was editor-in-chief and Felix the editor and, while it had much good copy in it, it was neither a *Philistine* nor a *Fra* and soon took on the aspects of an external houseorgan for the Roycrofters, a role and flavor that predominated it and its eventual successor, *The Roycrofter,* in the years to come.

Still, for over another decade, hundreds of visitors a day were shown through the Roycroft Shops, attracted mostly by Bert's astute staging of the Roycroft Conventions and his national promotion of Roycroft wares through Roycroft departments in virtually all the major department stores in the United States.

Then too, Bert's reprints of his father's popular "Little Journeys," plus compiled writings under the titles *Selected Writings, Notebook, Scrapbook, Philosophy,* etc., marketed by Wm. H. Wise & Co. and drop-shipped from East Aurora also helped keep the Roycrofters afloat.

But the end was in sight as the 1920s roared along. Elbert Hubbard had written, impressed and prospered in an era when Americans mostly stayed at home, read much and treasured fine libraries lined with handsomely bound books. This same man did much to coax Americans out-of-doors and onto wheels—to take their own Little Journeys whether they were rich or poor. His friend, Henry Ford, did much to make Americans as mobile as Hubbard had enticed them to be.

After the war Bert witnessed the quick succession of the eras of the automobile and the radio which blended into one big era of fun and financial frenzy. Seriously eroded was the interest of Americans in fine books and philosophical magazines. Then came the mass production of leather and copper wares to make serious competitive inroads on the markets for the hand-made wares of the Roycrofters.

The stock market crash of 1929 dealt The Roycrofters, Inc.—and many businesses—a staggering blow. By 1938 the bankrupt company was counted out by a referee.

Roycroft-made items were sold throughout the United States. These re-produced pages from a Roycroft catalog show the turn-of-the-century prices. Collectors' items today, they sell for two to four times their original price.

ESSAY ON SILENCE

Elbert Hubbard was a past master in the Cadmean art. He took the twenty-six letters of the alphabet and the seven punctuation-marks, and manipulated them like a juggler does his glass balls. Elbert Hubbard used more words than Shakespeare. By many of the literati he was acknowledged as the greatest writer—vocabulary and range of ideas considered—that America has produced. The things he said made some folks glad—and others mad. Elbert Hubbard rejoiced in his friends and smiled at his critics. Only once did he unloosen the vials of his wrath and get back at the carpers. The *Essay on Silence* is the result : the textbook of the neutral. Beautifully bound in Semi-Flexible Leather.   Price, 30 Cents.

GUEST-BOOK

The ornaments of a home are the friends who frequent it. The Roycroft Guest-Book provides a permanent record of the visits of your friends, and possesses a rare intrinsic value, by reason of the autographed contributions penned in its pages. The Roycroft *Guest-Book* is a source of joy in its reminiscences of those who have graced our home with their presence.
Deckle-edge, watermarked paper, bound in finest Ooze-Sheep, turned edges.   Price, $3.00.

Limp Leather, $2.00

THREE GREAT WOMEN
By Elbert Hubbard

Being three of Elbert Hubbard's graphic Little Journeys — Harriet Martineau, Elizabeth Barrett Browning and Madame Guyon — wherein the author tells us much of the philosophy and work of these three great women, linning their lives and times with his magical pen—that pen which cast a purple shadow !
A beautifully printed book, on English Boxmoor Paper; illustrated with photogravures, and bound uniquely and craftily in Art Goatskin. Price, $1.00.

OLD JOHN BURROUGHS
By Elbert Hubbard

Nature taught Elbert Hubbard many things. He was a brother to the trees and every living thing. And this Little Journey to the Poet-Naturalist of Slab Sides is instructive and delightsome.
Printed on Holland handmade paper and bound in Limp Leather, with frontispiece from an original drawing.   Price, $1.00.

AN AMERICAN BIBLE
Edited by Alice Hubbard

A book without mystery, myth, miracle or metaphysics—a commonsense book for red-blooded people who do their own thinking. *An American Bible* is the gospel according to America's own—Ben Franklin, Thomas Jefferson, Tom Paine, Abe Lincoln, Walt Whitman, Bob Ingersoll, Emerson and Elbert Hubbard. It teaches you how to live—you can die without assistance. Bound in Semi-Flexible Leather.
          Price, $2.00.

THE BOOK OF BUSINESS
By Elbert Hubbard

Elbert Hubbard believed in the divinity of business. This book stands for health, happiness, reciprocity, mutuality and co-operation—the ingredients of all successful enterprise. It was written for the captains of industry and the workmen alike, with an appeal and an inspiration to the hearts that love, the brains that think, and the hands that work.
Printed from classic type on watermarked paper and bound in Semi-Flexible Leather.   Price, $1.00.

BALLADS OF A BOOKWORM
By Irving Browne

Being a rhythmic record of thoughts, fancies and adventures a-collecting—by Irving Browne. A quaint and curious collection of verse, bound together by a thread of subtle sarcasm and half-hidden satire that is delightful. Printed on handmade paper with all initials hand-drawn in water-colors and title-page richly illumined. Solidly bound in boards.
A rare and beautiful book bargain.   Price, $1.00.

ROYCROFT MODELED LEATHER

The Masters of Old modeled the leather from the top side, and sometimes the work was beautiful, and sometimes the tool slipped. The Roycroft Master plans to the smallest detail and makes his design before the leather is cut. ❡ Formerly, the artist had to cut in the outline of the design ; now we do not injure the surface of the beautiful leather. We get our results by raising the ornament from the back. Not alone will the exquisite designs and the execution of the same satisfy you—the marvelous coloring, too subtle to describe, will call forth your admiration.

FRITZ KRANZ
MASTER LEATHER-WORKER

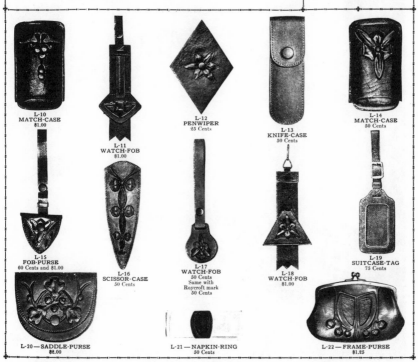

L-10
MATCH-CASE
$1.00

L-11
WATCH-FOB
$1.00

L-12
PENWIPER
25 Cents

L-13
KNIFE-CASE
50 Cents

L-14
MATCH-CASE
50 Cents

L-15
FOB-PURSE
60 Cents and $1.00

L-16
SCISSOR-CASE
50 Cents

L-17
WATCH-FOB
50 Cents
Same with
Roycroft mark
50 Cents

L-18
WATCH-FOB
$1.00

L-19
SUITCASE-TAG
75 Cents

L-20 — SADDLE-PURSE
$2.00

L-21 — NAPKIN-RING
50 Cents

L-22 — FRAME-PURSE
$1.25

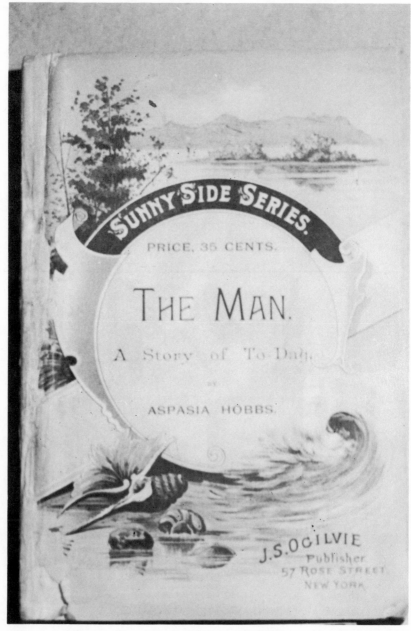

Alice and Elbert secretly collaborated in the writing of The Man, *a 160-page novel put out in 1891 by J. S. Ogilvie, Publisher, New York. Elbert used the pen name "Aspasia Hobbs."*

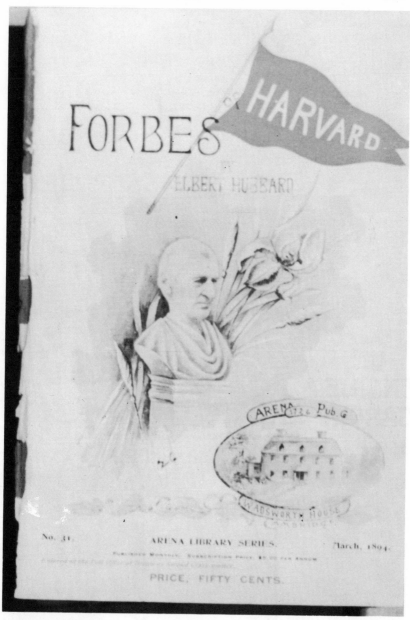

Hubbard's Forbes of Harvard, *a 328-page paperback novel was published by Arena Publishing Company, Boston. The closing words, "Married— on Christmas Day, at the residence of Mrs. Tyler," had greater significance than readers imagined.*

A portion of Hubbard's original manuscript for A Message to Garcia, *the motivational essay dashed off quickly and printed in the March 1899 issue of his* Philistine. Magazine. *It caught on instantly, was reprinted in pamphlet form in many languages. It is still alive and has been reprinted an estimated eighty million times.*

But Bert kept the other part of his dual promise of 1915. Until his dying day, November 7, 1970, at the age of 88, he was working on ways to perpetuate the fame of his father and his success in so doing was considerable. Through all of his life Bert found it a loving challenge to corral and define his father's total person. It was an unfinished task for as Hubbard had warned, "Fences were made for those who cannot fly."

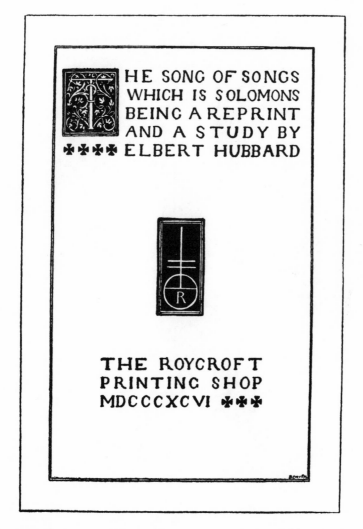

First advertising broadside of The Roycroft Press. The art for the title page of the Roycroft's first book was a hand-lettered effort of devoted Bertha Hubbard.

Index